Reviews and Commentary
About the Author and the Book

WARNING: This is *not* just another run-of-the-mill guide for parents and teachers of teens. As the title suggests, it's the "Real Deal," the secret questions that adolescents discuss among themselves, often excluding those of us who are supposed to help them reach maturity. This book doesn't pull punches; it's sometimes politically incorrect and controversial... but it is also grounded in real life, meticulously documented by thousands of interviews with teenagers across America who want tough questions answered truthfully by their families and mentors. Read at your own risk. It may make you squirm, it may force you to re-evaluate your own past... but it opens doors to more open and honest communication with the teenagers in your life.

"Here is a down-to-earth, sensible prescription for parents of teens. No one has spoken to and, more importantly, *listened to* more teens and pre-teens than Yehuda Fine. His lifetime of caring shines through the pages of *The Real Deal*, and it is a beacon for parents (and any adult who works with our youth). Parents and teens need not live in parallel universes. *The Real Deal* prescribes guidelines, point by point, that make conversing with youngsters as normal as breathing — and almost as easy. Yehuda Fine's book offers parents a hope-filled recipe for connecting with their youngsters."

— Dr. Pat Montgomery, Founder and Director *Emeritus* of the Clonlara School Home Based Accredited Education Program

"We shouldn't see these kids as oddballs, but as kids who are desperately crying out for help," Rabbi Yehuda Fine says. He is a family therapist in Evergreen this week to present a keynote address on school violence..."
— Janet Simmons, "Tragedy at Columbine," *Rocky Mountain News*

"Rabbi Fine has been delving into the psyches of adolescents for decades and now with his second book he has written a parental guide on relationships with parents and their teenagers. He has helped shape the counseling technique used in my practice of adolescent medicine."

— James G. Scelfo MD, FAAFP,
Medical Director, Disney Marathon and the Citrus Bowl;
Medical Consultant, NBC affiliate WESH Channel 2, Orlando

"Yehuda Fine is an interpreter, a conduit, a bridge builder. He perhaps better than anyone knows how to repair the downed lines of communication between adolescents and adults. America: dial him in before those worlds drift too far apart."

— Chris Mercogliano,
Director of the Albany Free School and author of *Making It Up As We Go Along* and *Teaching the Restless*

"Finally a book for parents of 'tweens' and teens that conveys a clear, concise message for American families. Not only a great read, but a book every parent will find extremely helpful. This is *the* parenting book and is a one of kind endeavor, for no one has spoken to more teens and parents than Rabbi Yehuda Fine."
— Dr. Efrem Nulman
Senior University Dean of Students
Yeshiva University, New York

"Rabbi Yehuda Fine is more than a national treasure, he's a necessity, and sadly, something of an anomaly: A frontline spiritual warrior for the rights and survival of America's youth, whether they are struggling at home or adrift and written-off in the back alleys of our cities and towns. But what gives added credence to this powerful book is that Yehuda Fine is also a father of a brood of fantastic kids of his own. He walks the walk, he talks the talk and he works tirelessly and boldly in a shadowy world that precious few have the courage to penetrate and most would like to ignore."

— Alex Winter
Writer/Director and Actor,
Bill & Ted's Excellent Adventure, Lost Boys, Freaked, Fever

"Rabbi Yehuda Fine's hand may be the hand that saves your family. I should know: Yehuda reached out for me when I was a sixteen-year-old high school drop-out, and helped me discover the beauty of my own hungry mind and thirsty spirit...*The Real Deal* is a reminder that we do not need to have all the answers; what we need is the willingness to ask questions, and to truly listen to the response."

— Mirabai Starr, author of critically acclaimed new translations of the Spanish mystics. She is also a professor of Philosophy and Religious Studies at the University of New Mexico and a certified grief counselor.

THE REAL DEAL

THE REAL DEAL:

For Parents Only — The Top 75 Secret Questions Teens Want Answered Today

Yehuda Fine

Copyright © 2006 by Yehuda Fine

All rights reserved under Title 17, U.S. Code, International and Pan-American Copyright Conventions. No part of this work, whether in printed or digital form, may be reproduced or transmitted in any form or by any means, electronic or mechanical, including (but not limited to) photocopying, scanning, recording, live performance or broadcast, or duplication by any information storage or retrieval system without prior written permission from the author(s) and publisher(s).

Cover designed by Mary Kramer (www.MilkweedGraphics.com) as a work for hire, Copyright © 2006 by Unlimited Publishing LLC ("UP"). The cover and/or interior designs may incorporate one or more fonts specifically licensed by and customized for the exclusive use of UP, which may not be used elsewhere.

This book is publicly offered contingent on the reader's prior understanding that any financial, health, legal, medical, psychological or other professional advice of any kind should always be independently confirmed with more than one qualified source. The author(s) and publisher(s) accept no responsibility of any kind for conclusions reached by readers of this book. If you do not agree with these terms, you may return this book in good condition for a full refund.

Library of Congress Control Number:
2006934491

ISBN:
Paperback 1-58832-137-1
Hardback 1-58832-145-2

Unlimited Publishing LLC
Bloomington, Indiana
http://www.UnlimitedPublishing.com

Acknowledgements

To all parents who want to connect more deeply with their children.

Major kudos go to Fred Bay of the The Josephine Bay Paul and C. Michael Paul Foundation for seeing the importance of this book, and for allowing me to secure the services of the best editor in my world — Betty Christiansen.

For my fallen brother, Rabbi Oren: You dreamed the dream even though that dream brought you down... but I will never forget and I continue on.

Those who stuck with me through thick and thin as I wrote my second book are second to none in my life: Thank you Mom, Sis, Nolly, Miriam, Joanne, Ef, Joan Cohen, Edie, Mark, Rosa, David, Julie, Olivia, Esther, Alex, and and Chris.

To Danny O. Snow of Unlimited Publishing LLC and his co-workers who grabbed this important project and ran with it: Thank you.

Thanks to the thousands of parents, and tens of thousands of teens, who unabashedly shared their secret questions with me: Without all of you, there would be no book.

To every school, church, or other institution that sponsored my live events, and to every newspaper, magazine, radio or television station that covered them: Thanks for helping to get the message out.

And to my readers: I owe you much, and hope I meet your expectations.

Preface:
The 75 Questions

Communication Problems:
School, Friends, and Peer Pressure

1. "What am I going to do with my life? How am I going to figure this out?"

2. "Why are my parents always focused on grades and never on the person I really am? They always are mad at me if I don't measure up."

3. "Where do I fit in? What group should I hang out with, and how do I know if this is the right crowd for me?"

4. "I want to have my friends over more, but my folks always put limits on it. They think I have too much work to do or whatever. We just like to hang out, talk, and play video games. What's wrong with that? I live here, too."

5. "Some of my friends have fake IDs. They all like to go to clubs and party. They're not dopers and don't get drunk, but they love to dance. I have gone with them a couple of times, and no one cares if I am underage or ever asks me for an ID. Is there really a problem with that? Everyone does it."

6. "I exaggerate way too much. Lately, I'm having trouble keeping track of my lies. I want to quit, but I don't know where to begin."

7. "I lied to my best friend. Really messed up. How can I try to get things right again?"

Sex, Sexuality, and Relationships

8. "A lot of my friends talk about sex. It kind of embarrasses me. I mean, I know all the health class stuff, but not so much about the other stuff. So I don't know what I should say when this topic comes up. I would like

to talk to my parents about it, but that seems weird, too, and could be really embarrassing."

9. "What are the benefits of having premarital sex versus waiting until I get married? I'd like to talk to my mom about this, but she has already been married twice, so I don't think she knows what to say about sex and waiting."

10. "Why is sex considered the most important part of a relationship?"

11. "When is a good time to have sex? My friends say I'll know when I'm ready, but that doesn't help at all."

12. "Is it wrong to want sex right now, as a teenager?"

13. "How do I know if I am truly in love?"

14. "Why are guys who have sex looked upon as being 'cool' and girls who have sex called 'sluts' or 'whores'?"

15. "What is wrong with wanting sex when you are wasted?"

16. "What is wrong with oral sex? I mean, we are not having intercourse."

17. "I was at a party, and I saw one of my friends go upstairs to have sex when I knew she didn't really want to. What can I tell her next time? She could have gotten raped or something up there."

18. "I'm pretty sure I'm gay. I need someone to talk to about this. How can I tell my parents?"

19. "How do I tell my friends I'm gay? How will they react?"

20. "I am getting ready to break up with my girlfriend. I am afraid she is going to freak out. What should I do to make sure she leaves me alone and doesn't hassle me or get all weird and clingy?"

21. "I broke off my relationship, and no way do I want to get back together again. But I still feel bad that it ended. Why do I feel this way?"

22. "My ex-boyfriend won't leave me alone. He calls all the time. Shows up in the middle of night. Follows me when I am out with my friends. I've told him I just want to be friends, but he is beginning to scare me. What should I do? How can I get him to stop?"

23. "I am trying to get a date for the junior prom. I asked two girls and they turned me down. What should I do?"

Family Problems: Secrets, Fighting, and Divorce

24. "Why do my parents never admit that they have problems? Why does it seem that they are keeping secrets from me?"

25. "I really try to avoid talking to my mom and dad. They're just way too serious. If I try to talk to them about anything important, they either get hysterical or lecture me."

26. "My mom says one thing and punishes me for another thing. My dad gets home and changes the punishment. Sometimes it's worse, or sometimes nothing happens. This drives me nuts. It makes me mad at my parents. What is going on with them? They never seem together when it comes to me."

27. "I want to add a couple more piercings to my ears. My mom says no. This really makes me angry. I mean, I am not piercing my tongue or anything. I love earrings and think I will look really good with some more. Why is she fighting me?"

28. "My parents always tell me I am out of control. Things have gotten really bad at home. I hit my mom last week. I really blew it. I think my parents are going to ship me off to some boarding school or something. Why don't they just leave me alone?"

29. "I am having trouble at home with my mom and dad. They are always fighting. Then they fight with me over their fights. I don't listen to them anymore. What should I do?"

30. "I hate my mom and dad. I want to run away from home. What should I do?"

31. "My parents are divorced, and my dad always talks bad about my mom. Every time he calls me, he goes off. I've tried to tell him that I don't like it, but no matter what I say he does not seem to get the point. What should I do?"

32. "My parents keep fighting all the time. They're divorced. They keep trying to use me to get at each other. It makes me sick. Is there something I can do?"

33. "My parents just got divorced. I know a lot of my friends live with only one parent, but I still really feel depressed about it. I go to my dad's house, and every time I'm there, he has to say something mean about my mom. My mom is no better. I tell them to cut it out and leave me out of it. Why do they keep doing this? I'll be a senior next year and just plan to go away to college and come back as little as possible."

34. "My parents are divorced, and I live with my mom and stepdad. My dad lives in another state. He never calls me. If I call him and leave a message, he doesn't call back. Do you have any suggestions about what I should do?"

35. "My mom got remarried. I am seventeen and can't wait to get out of the house — it's a mess all over again. I mean the fighting and the screaming, this time with the new husband. What is going on here? I tell my mom that this is bothering me. All she says is, 'Girl, we will work it out.' Is she blind or what?"

36. "My parents are divorced. My mom and dad are constantly fighting. Then they end up fighting with me. I get so pissed off at them that I fight way more with them than they even fight with each other. I want to the fighting to stop, but they won't get off my back. What should I do?"

Violence and Abusive Relationships

37. "Why do parents abuse their kids?"

38. "My best friend told me that she was raped by her father. She also has had a lot of boyfriends who have used her for sex. She told me that she hates herself. She feels that somehow she is to blame and doesn't know what to do. What should I tell her?"

39. "My best friend was abused by her stepfather. Her mom threw him out of the house, but she still feels like she is dirty. How can I help her let go of these bad feelings and feel better about herself?"

40. "I am in serious trouble at home. My father gets scary drunk. Every few months, he beats on my mom and threatens me. I am old enough to get out of the house, but what about my mom and my little sister? There is no stopping my dad, so don't tell me to talk to him."

41. "My mother is an alcoholic. I always have to watch out for her. It's hard 'cause I also have to take care of my little brother a lot of the time. What should I do?"

42. "My boyfriend every so often gets drunk. When he is drinking, he gets mean. He hasn't hit me, but he has come close. He has smashed stuff, hit the wall, and threatened me. After it is all over, he tells me he is sorry and that he didn't mean to do it. He says it was the drinking. I love him and want to help him, but sometimes he really scares me. What should I tell him?"

43. "I am pretty certain I was raped. What do I do and what do I tell my parents?"

44. "I've kept this a secret. But now I think I ought to tell my parents I was sexually assaulted."

45. "My best friend told me a secret. She was raped at summer camp. What should I do to help her?"

46. "If you are drunk and someone has sex with you, is that rape?"

47. "All of us are afraid of date rape and date rape drugs. We know 'roofies' and other drugs are around, and some guys use them on girls. So how can we keep partying, have fun, and stay safe?"

Drugs and Alcohol

48. "What's wrong with doping or drinking at a party?"

49. "There's a big party I really want to go to this weekend. My parents are freaked out that there will be drugs and beer there. What should I tell them that will make them calm down?"

50. "How come we have these D.A.R.E. programs at our school? We do get some information, but it's also a joke. Does the school really think this works?"

51. "Didn't you use drugs in college?"

52. "I am pretty sure my parents tried drugs in college. I am also quite sure they lied to me about it. Should I even bring it up?"

53. "All my friends get drunk all the time. They get really wasted — pass out and puke all over the place. They think it's funny. What can I say to them?"

54. "Is there something wrong with having a drink or two in the morning before school? My friends and I drive to school and pass a bottle around in the parking lot before hitting class. School is a total bore, and at least I get through the day without any trouble. I am not flunking or anything."

55. "I smoke dope once in a while. I gotta tell you, I don't see anything wrong with it."

56. "Weed is my best friend. I smoke every day and I see nothing wrong with it. Why does everyone hassle me about it? I am doing okay."

57. "My doping has really gotten out of control. My friends and I are wasted way too much of the time. They might not admit it, but I know I am in trouble. I need to get some help. What should I do?"

58. "Some of my friends use ecstasy regularly. If they are going to a dance club, they always use it. I haven't tried it, but everyone tells me it is safe as long as you don't get a bad batch. I gotta tell you, they love it. It makes them feel great. Is it really a problem if I take it?"

Depression, Suicide, and Self-Harm

59. "I feel really sad all the time, but how can I talk to my parents about it? I don't even understand it."

60. "Does it mean anything if you don't care whether you live or die?"

61. "Why is life so difficult?"

62. "How can I tell if my friend is serious when he talks about suicide?"

63. "My friend is really depressed but wants me to keep it a secret and not do anything. What should I do?"

64. "I broke up with my girlfriend. Now she says she can't live without me. She even said she might kill herself. I feel bad and scared. She keeps calling me all the time and following me around. What am I supposed to do?"

65. "One of my good friends cuts herself. It really scares me. She tells me it makes her feel good. That makes me more scared. Her parents know about it, and she sees some counselor, but why does she do it?"

66. "People tell me I am wrong because I think I am not thin enough. Is there anything so wrong about wanting to get down another size? What is wrong with being super thin?"

Spirituality and Social Consciousness:
The Quest for Ethics and Values

67. "Since the terrorist attacks on September 11, 2001, a lot of my friends are really angry. They say stuff like, 'Let's kick every Muslim out of our country,' or 'We ought to go over and kill those guys,' and all kinds of other things. I want to talk to them about tolerance, but I feel weird about it. We have Muslim students at my school, and some of them are freaked out. I am just as angry as my friends and want to go after terrorists, but I see tolerance as important, too. What should I say or do?"

68. "Is religion important? Does it make a difference in anyone's life?"

69. "Why is it that, so many times, when there is every chance for something bad not to happen, it does anyway? Is there something you can do to prevent such things, despite that fact?"

70. "I have so many questions about life. Who am I? Why don't I know who I am?"

71. "Why do so many kids put down other kids? What can I do about it?"

72. "Why is life so hard? Why is it easier for some people and not for others?"

73. "Does someone's beliefs really make a difference in their life? Can someone really make a difference in the world?"

74. "If God cares so much about the world, why is there so much suffering?"

75. "I see so much going on in this world — so much pain, so much fear. I even see it among my friends and in my school. I want to do something, but I feel so small. What can I do that will make a difference?"

Table of Contents

INTRODUCTION — 1

CHAPTER 1:

MEET YOUR TEEN — 13

CHAPTER 2:

COMMUNICATION PROBLEMS — 29

CHAPTER 3:

SEX, SEXUALITY AND RELATIONSHIPS — 51

CHAPTER 4:

FAMILY PROBLEMS — 91

CHAPTER 5:

VIOLENCE AND ABUSIVE RELATIONSHIPS — 121

CHAPTER 6:

DRUGS AND ALCOHOL — 161

CHAPTER 7:

DEPRESSION, SUICIDE, AND SELF-HARM   **197**

CHAPTER 8:

SPIRITUALITY AND SOCIAL CONSCIOUSNESS   **221**

AFTERWORD:

THE GREATEST GIFT   **249**

Introduction

I shot upright in bed, jolted awake by the nightmare that finds me no matter where I am. Panicked, I opened my eyes to a dark, unfamiliar room. As the ghosts of sleep faded away, I began to remember where I was: in another hotel in a strange city, the latest stop on a speaking tour of high schools in America. Covered in sweat, I tried to toss off my dream.

Although it has been nearly ten years since Danny died on the street, my subconscious refuses to let him go. Danny was a New York City street kid I had reached out to for over a year. He'd been on his way home from a local youth center when he stopped at an all-night grocery to pick up some milk. Inside, a robbery was taking place, and he didn't see what was coming. He took two bullets in the chest and died at the entrance to the store.

My dream is always the same. I scream at him to get down; the bullets hit; I bolt upright in bed. Sitting there, I always feel like I've been stabbed in the heart. I imagine him lying there, dying; the cement is cold against his face.

Danny was a good kid who, along with many others like him, never got the chance to live out his dreams. These kids come to my dreams on a rotating schedule, reminding me never to let the memory of them fade from this world. For more than a decade I reached out to these kids in the world of the New York City night — particularly in Times Square, which is still a cesspool of hustlers, drug dealers, triple-X theaters, and the magnetic draw for lost kids: runaways, throwaways, homeless, and addicts. My job, as a rabbi, therapist, and finder of missing kids, was to seek them out and befriend them, give them someone they could trust, find them shelter, and lend them some hope. Sometimes these kids made it off the streets and made miracles of healing and transformation. Many met worse fates. They died or simply disappeared. Still, they visit me in my dreams.

The truth is, I'm honored by their hauntings. If it were not for all the street kids I've known, I never would have had the opportunity to reach out to thousands of teens across America. In a terrible way, their loss has brought forth life. Carrying their memory allows me to link their lost hopes and dreams with the lives of kids today.

I now spend less time on the streets, but these days I carry my message of hope to kids in high schools across the country. While their situations may be less dire — or at least appear to be — their concerns are just as serious, their futures just as uncertain, and sometimes they are filled with just as much pain. I come to talk with them, to listen, and to bring them some hope. Then, I talk to their parents.

On this particular morning, after my early and abrupt awakening, I am preparing once again to do just that. As I pour some coffee, I think about the 200-some kids I am about to speak with. In the last few years, I have spoken to more than 24,000 high school students, in small towns and major urban centers, of every race and religion, from gang members to the privileged, in every nook and cranny of the country. They listen to me not because I am a rabbi and family therapist, but because of the time I spent down in the dark world of the street, and because of the memories I carry with me of Danny, Claudia, Rick, Margie, and so many more. Once I share these memories, once the kids begin to see me as someone who understands the worst of what they're facing today, they do a miraculous thing: They open up and tell me exactly what is going down in their lives. I ask them to write out and share, anonymously, their most serious questions, their deepest secrets, the things they can't ask their parents but wish they could. Amazingly, they do, with heartbreaking honesty. Yet the hardest part in all of this is getting their parents — and the community — to listen fully to what they have to say, and respond to what they need. As a father who's raised three teens of his own, I know that adolescents are not very many adults' cups of tea. Still, I keep trying to build bridges between teens and the adults who love them — and need to hear them. After all, these kids are our next generation. And they're just starting out.

After my coffee, I work my way through morning prayers. When I reach the silent prayer, I pull down all the names and faces of the kids I have lost. I remember their smiles, their voices, their little dances on the street, their laughter, their good memories, their hopes and dreams. I invite them to come with me. I tell them where I am going and ask them to help me speak to this new set of kids. I tell them that it is because of their dark and violent stories that we now can prevent other kids from going over the edge and losing their dreams. And I always remind them that I love them, care for them, and know that no matter what the world did to them, nothing — and I mean nothing — can ever touch the purity of their souls.

I came off the New York streets to move upstream — a little closer to the source — and catch as many kids as I could *before* they had the chance to fall. I came upstream to help kids make real sense of their very real issues. I came upstream to empower parents with honest information about what their kids needed and wanted. Without that information, families and family unity easily break down.

My action plan is very simple. All those years out on the street have allowed me to come in and say to these kids: "Hey, you tell me flat-out what your issues are in life. All of your secrets. Just lay them out. Let's talk about them. You tell me what you see, and I will tell you what I have seen. Then I will take all of your questions to your parents. I'll explain to them what is going on and what you need from them. Let's see how that goes. Let's see what happens."

24,000 kids later, I can tell you what happens. The kids take their issues seriously. In some communities, the kids even drag their parents out the door at night to listen to me. The parents listen because, for most of them, this is the first time they've gotten a real chance to hear their children's secrets and issues. There is no room for a debate about what their children need or want — it is here, written in their kids' own words. There's no more ambiguity or guessing about family needs. It is all in front of us, written anonymously by thousands of kids on the index cards I have handed out.

Talking to Teens

Talking to teenagers is not exactly a popular mission in communities or, for that matter, in many families. I guess no parent likes to know that normal high school kids still do the same things they did when they were teenagers: They still get laid, listen to weird music, drink booze, smoke dope, drive too fast, spend too much time on the phone (or, today, online), and don't like to visit their relatives. These facts are hard for parents to hear. Worse yet, they take them as a sign of personal failure. The truth is that kids' problems, though seemingly acute, are often quite normal. They may need feedback, but don't necessarily signal an emergency.

For me, talking to these kids is always a joy because of the positive responses I am blessed to encounter over and over again. Kids today thirst for the opportunity to talk to an adult about how they, or those sitting next to them, have sex, get drunk, try drugs, think they might be depressed, or have been abused. The key, for adults, is getting them to open up. And when they do, a bridge of trust is built between these teens and the adults in their lives.

My job is to get the teens to share their most pressing questions and concerns about life — to be that key that opens them up. When they are finished, I gather up their secrets and fears — anonymously written on those index cards — and I bring them to their parents during a meeting that takes place later that evening. Armed with their children's questions, my aim is to help parents gain insight and wisdom in dealing with their issues and, most importantly, to learn to define trouble.

You see, trouble does not come in the form of experimenting with things like drugs, alcohol, or sex. Trouble comes when use of these things becomes chronic in a kid's life. All the students I talk with know the difference, and they know who among them is in trouble. They know who is addicted to drugs and alcohol, who is depressed, who is abused, and who is suicidal. My mission is to set up a system that has its net out for kids in trouble. My mission is to teach parents not only how to spot trouble, but how to stay in touch with their kids and possibly prevent it.

In the Schools

Neatly summarized like this, my plan appears deceptively simple, too good to be true. Reality always hits when I find myself, as I am this morning, faced with a couple of hundred teenagers in a high school auditorium. In the minutes before they settle down, their collective voices echo around the room, they fidget and squirm in their seats, they smirk and eye me skeptically. I simply let my mind float back to all my dreams and the kids on the street. I pull up their images and see their faces. Remembering each of them gives me strength. In my mind's eye, I invite them, too, to my talk. Thinking of all the kids who have come and gone focuses my attention. I know, having talked to so many high school students, that before I can earn their trust, before they'll share with me their secrets, I must have their attention, too.

I begin by telling them stories from the street. I tell real on-the-edge-of-your-seat stories; tough, sometimes graphic stories about the lives of street children I knew and loved that make them gasp or even cry. I know I have less than five minutes to get their attention, five minutes to convey that I am not the kind of rabbi they thought, nor the therapist they may think I am. I am from the street, and I also grew up in their world. I have to connect, and I nearly always do, because these stories speak of drugs, abuse, gay issues, suicide, brutality, rape, alcoholism, and addiction — the very secrets they keep and the concerns on their mind.

Then, it's their turn to be honest. I ask them to answer some questions by raising their hands.

"How many of you have a friend who has a drug or alcohol problem?" I ask. "How many of you know someone who's depressed... has thought about suicide... is regularly having sex?

"How many of you worry about violence since 9/11?

"How many of you want to get married eventually? How many think you'll have a fulfilling marriage? How many think you might get divorced?

"How many of you think you can turn to your parents for support in a crisis? How many of you wish you could talk more openly with your parents?"

No matter where I travel in America, the results of this informal survey are nearly the same:

- 100% have a friend who has a drug or alcohol problem.
- 100% have a friend who has been depressed.
- 100% know someone who is regularly having sex.
- 100% encounter insults and/or bullying on a daily basis in school.
- 90% or more have a friend who has thought about suicide.
- 90% are worried about violence, particularly since 9/11.
- 75% want to get married eventually.
- But only 20% think they will have a fulfilling marriage.
- More than 50% think they might get divorced.
- And most striking of all: Only 15% think they can turn to their parents for support in a crisis, but 85% wish they could talk more openly about all these issues with their parents.

Although it might appear to the contrary, I find these results very encouraging. They tell us that teens are keenly aware of the most important emotional issues they face. They also indicate that adolescents today are sensitive to their friends' struggles and want to be engaged. One other thing is very clear: Teenagers want adult input. And while parents and other adults who interact with teens often encounter off-putting instability and mood swings, the teen years are exactly the time when the support and stability of a strong family and community are needed most.

The reason we find it so difficult to connect with our teens is simply because we haven't taken the time to ask them what they want to know about the cutting-edge issues in their lives. Before we can effectively talk with teens about their tough issues, we need to know what they are thinking, not what *we think* they are thinking.

So, after I administer my show-of-hands survey, I hand out the index cards. Then, I ask the kids to anonymously write down their most pressing issue or question for me to respond to. The atmosphere is electric as I read them out loud:

"What's the difference between experimenting with drugs and having a drug problem?"

"Does having oral sex mean I'm not a virgin?"

"How should I go about dealing with my friend's alcohol problem?"

"I want to try and get help for my friend who is being abused at home, but I'm afraid she'll hate me if I say anything."

"Is it safe for me to talk to a teacher or guidance counselor about my problems or my friend's problems, or will they just throw us out of school?"

The questions go on and on. Suddenly everyone knows there are people in the room, maybe even their closest friends, who are facing very tough issues. I answer as many questions as time permits, always keeping in mind that these are the questions of our next generation of community leaders, business leaders, teachers, mothers, and fathers.

When our time is up, after about two hours, there is always a disappointed groan from the students with pleas for me to answer a few more questions. But it's time to leave and get ready to meet with their parents. Before the crowd breaks up, I remind them to tell their parents to come and meet with me tonight, and give them my e-mail address.

The Parents Arrive

I follow up my teen seminar with a long lunch with the faculty and administration. Right after that, I meet with the guidance counselors and then my hosts. My goal is to go over as much with them as I can — give the community professionals a sense of the deep and secret issues of their students, answer their questions, and gather more information. After a rest at my hotel, I arrive at the venue for the parent meeting at least an hour before my talk begins. I need to center myself, relax with a cup of coffee, and most important, talk to any parent who arrives early — the more quality time I spend with the people who brought me to their city, the better.

I confess that I feel a lot of pressure. Sure, I have done this scores of times before, but today I am in *their* town. This is *their* event. They expect not only a good turnout, but a high-impact experience. It is what I want to happen, too, and I am determined to give my hosts — and the parents who attend — just as much as I gave those street kids on those long dark nights. No way am I going to let them down.

As parents trickle in and take their seats, I greet each one. To me, every parent is precious. I make certain to welcome even the ones who sneak in and try to sit anonymously in the back of the room. I get their names, talk about baseball, ask what brought them and what they hope will happen, and crack jokes. It doesn't take long for all of them to feel that this night is going to be different. We may be in a meeting room or a restaurant banquet hall, but before long, it feels like we are gathering in someone's living room.

The room takes on a buzz. "Who is this guy?" the parents whisper. "What did he say to you?" "Did you know he's a baseball fanatic?" "I see why my kid likes him." Among the voices, I inevitably hear someone say, "I'm here because my kid told me I *had to* come." As my host steps up to introduce me, I look around and make eye contact. I smile. I really do feel like I know these parents. I also know they are very nervous. They wouldn't have come out on a weeknight if they weren't worried about their kids.

After I am introduced, I step up and say, with a big smile: "I am here to talk to you about your kids. I guarantee after one hour with me, you are going to be able to tackle any issue your kid could possibly bring to you."

Naturally, I see skeptical looks exchanged in the audience. But unlike other speakers who have come to lecture them on parenting, I have a unique edge: I come armed with their kids' most private questions. This fact immediately gets everyone's attention, and skepticism is set aside. No one can deny the relevancy of the subject matter. We get right down to work.

First, I go over the survey. They are stunned. I then read several of their kids' questions. There are always gasps, followed by silence. I have their full attention. It is an attention based on their kids' reality, not what they thought it was or hoped it would be. The medium is the message.

The parents may express apprehension, but overall, they seem to understand that this is leading up to something powerful, useful, and good. I promise them from the outset that they are not going to have to learn a new system of parenting or memorize any rules. I am here to bring out the best of what they know. I am not here to monkey with their values or their family system. Every family is different. The principles I discuss apply and work for all.

My main point is that the goal is to make contact, not to solve problems. I let every parent know that we are all on the same ship. We all want to make a difference in our kids' lives. We all are searching for answers. We all want to find ways to talk about our kids' issues. I don't gloss over the problems that stare nearly every parent in the face. They do not want them sugar-coated. They want the truth.

But sadly, I also know that, back at home, most families are not sitting down at the dinner table or any table to discuss their concerns. In a recent issue of the *Woodstock Times,* it was noted that teens average about eight minutes of conversation with their mothers and three minutes with their fathers each day. Our children are left on dangerous ground. Day after day, we pick up the newspaper and read that more trouble is happening to more kids somewhere. In the worst cases, we parents are stunned to hear that other kids knew something "bad" was going to happen, and yet no adult was notified until it was too late.

Children, without emotional support, either turn their pain onto themselves — resulting in addiction, depression, and self-harm — or they turn it outward into anger and violence. Adolescence is when children most need support, stability, and encouragement. It's a myth that teenagers don't want to be close to their parents. In fact, for teens to grow, they need their parents as a safe haven from the world. But today, many parents feel vulnerable, too helpless in their inability to connect with their children. They feel they lack the tools to cope.

How do parents make contact? All the education in the world on drugs, guns, and violence will have little effect unless each child can have a significant relationship with an adult in his or her life. Is that possible? Obviously, the answer is yes, and it's way, way easier than most pundits could ever expect. My job is to open the door to simple, direct solutions that do make contact.

It is at this point that I remind my group of parents that I am going to keep my promise. I point out again some of the 100% answers to my survey of their kids. I reread some of the toughest questions. I ask them to think about just how they would answer any one of these questions if their teen came to them and asked. Sometimes I take a little break and have them, in shorthand, write an answer, just for themselves. Then I launch them into what I call the Parenting Principles. The context changes as I explain over and over again that the goal is to *make contact*, not *solve problems*. Teens want their parents not to fix everything, but to give them the strength, tools, referrals, love, and support to work through their difficulties without feeling guilty or condemned or, worse yet, feeling they must keep everything a secret.

To help parents do this, I hand out the "short list" of my Parenting Principles, and we read them together.

The Parenting Principles

- You don't have to be an expert, you just have to care and share.
- Talk to your children about everything — that's how they will develop values and direction in life. No topic — sex, alcohol, depression, violence — is off limits. If your child brings it up, it is important. Otherwise, your child will get the information from the local drug dealer, peers, or television.
- Children want to be involved in family matters and family problems. So involve them.
- Never ignore the big topics — 9/11, sex, drugs, relationships, hurricanes and other natural disasters, depression, even suicide. Children want to know what you think.
- Never be afraid to admit you were wrong and to apologize. It demonstrates how mistakes can bring out love.
- Ask questions, avoid lectures, and listen to what your kid is saying.

This develops good communication and underlines that you value your relationship with your child.
- Praise your kids for who they are and what they do. Be specific and don't forget the little things.
- Tell your kids you love them, and why.
- Hug your kid every day. Don't be fooled into thinking they don't cherish a warm embrace, or that words are a substitute for contact.
- Share your own struggles with your children. Let them know there is much to be learned from facing problems and growing spiritually.
- Ask your kids what was fun and difficult in school today. Ask for their opinions about their classes, teachers, friends. This signals that you are involved in their daily lives.
- Go with your children to movies, ballgames, etc. Your kids *do* want to spend time with you.
- Have fun and goof around with your children. Being a parent is more than being a serious adult.
- Share what has touched your life. Talk about what you believe in — God, love, compassion, truth, kindness, honesty — and your uncertainties about these topics.

The parents and I read these principles together. As I explain them, I illustrate with their kids' own questions. When we are finished, the parents see that no matter what questions their teens raise, they now have a way to approach them and talk to them.

But next, they wonder, "How do I begin?"

I tell them this: "You begin when you go home tonight. You begin the next time you see your kid. You change the context. You use some of these principles. Besides, as you will see, you already know all of these principles. I am simply here to remind you of that."

Now, it is true that in spite of all the hard work you do to build a relationship with your child, trouble can come anyway. Teens — even the most carefully raised ones — do make big mistakes. But parents don't have to be haunted by the knowledge that they were not there for their child. By opening up to their issues, by listening objectively to what they have to say, and by being honest with them about the struggles that we face even as adults, we can make a dramatic difference in the lives of the teenagers we love. In fact, we hold the most important key to helping them reach adulthood safely and confidently. And what is that key? I can summarize it in two points:

1) As simple as it may sound — and it is very simple — every parent needs to consistently ask their teen questions.

2) No matter what answer they get back or what issue comes up, parents can respond. Not with a pat answer, but with a honest statement of concern coupled with the assurance that, even if the question makes them embarrassed, makes them nervous, or makes them sweat — no matter what — they are there to talk, help, and assist. The goal for parents is not to find *the* answer, but to engage their kids with love, caring, and honesty.

Simply put, the more discussion, the more dilemmas addressed, and the more troubles struggled with, the stronger the values teens will have as they move into adulthood. The family is the growing ground where teens are nutured, are strengthened, and become wise about the world. No classroom can teach that, the streets cannot give that, and certainly their peers are not experts in the trials, traumas, and confusion of life. The family is the place where the engine is tuned, rebuilt, remodeled, and test-driven. It is the safe haven in which each teen can figure out his or her own unique nuts and bolts in life. Parental involvement simply means giving their kids the tools and always making the tools available. Do that, and your child will have the skills of life needed to face adversity, rise from failure, and deal with success.

Chapter 1:
Meet Your Teen

"An Extraordinary Generation"

Kids today are amazing — their generation is extraordinarily alive. Everywhere I speak, I run into incredible young people. They possess an irrepressible energy for life, they are deeply thoughtful, they ask hard questions and contemplate what it means to be alive. These kids are idealistic, but in a different way than we, their parents, were in the 'sixties and 'seventies. They're fiercely committed to their friends' welfare, much more so than kids were in my generation. If I could bring you into one of my seminars and have you listen in, you'd hear these young people saying things like this:

"When I heard you read the questions from my class, I was surprised at how deep some of the students' problems were. The questions about drug problems, suicide, and family problems made me realize that many people who look fine on the outside are really troubled on the inside. We know now for sure it is important to talk and try to get help. Here's something I think we all agree on: The more you are concerned about your friends, the better a friend you are."

"I have endured my own burden of pain, a family history of depression. That did not make me feel too content about myself. But this morning, I stood back and looked at everything I have accomplished so far, and everything I have to be thankful for, and it makes me smile. I will always do the most important thing that anyone could ever ask of me — I will listen."

"I really enjoyed how you acknowledged me and the other students like adults. Most adults don't really think of us kids as being very mature and smart about these things. It was very comforting to me."

"In the last ninety minutes, you set a rule in my heart to make me keep going and helping people. You have helped me help others."

There is a passage in the Talmud that says that the divine presence rests within eight feet of an individual. That's where the holiness is to be found. The Talmud also teaches that it only takes a few people gathered together to draw down the divine presence. It doesn't say ten thousand people, just one person reaching out to a couple of others. That is the primary concern of our extraordinarily promising next generation.

Yet teenagers today are at risk. Behind the headlines of Columbine and other school shootings, there is a quiet desperation that pervades our children's lives. In the past two years, in my talks with more than 24,000 high school students, I have discovered that many teens in this generation are cut off from the adult world — there is no one to guide them into the new land they are about to enter. Add to that the fact that kids today are more at risk to drugs, violence, and alcohol, and you have all the ingredients for lives unfulfilled. Without adults to talk to about the issues that concern them, too many kids are in danger of facing a lifetime filled with unhappiness.

Many adults ignore teens in our society. Ignorance of teens' struggles leaves them to fend for themselves in their most desperate hours. There is no comfort in knowing that when kids are raped, abused, depressed, contemplating suicide, or self-medicating with drugs or alcohol, they hold fast to their pain and bury it deep. Sadly, these kids become secret-keepers who, long ago, learned they could never turn to the adult world for help.

Even the vast majority of teens who do not suffer from hidden trauma are certain about one thing: When it comes to dealing with important issues, few adults are available to talk with them in any meaningful way. Few things are more tragic than a child in trouble who truly believes there is no one to turn to for help.

The Challenging World of Teens Today

At the start of each of my high school seminars, I informally survey high school students as I speak to them. I do this not only to uncover the main issues affecting teens, but also (and perhaps most interesting to parents) to discover who *is* talking to them about their important issues. In other words, who is helping to shape the values and decision-making in their lives? In many cases, it's their peers or the media — not necessarily informed or reliable sources.

I have picked a wide range of questions to ask, and regardless of the type of setting I ask them in — inner-city schools, suburban schools, upscale private schools, parochial schools, alternative schools, gatherings of home-schooled teens, and a wide variety of high-school-age youth groups — the answers I receive are surprisingly consistent. Let me repeat a few of the statistics from the previous chapter:

- 100% have a friend who has a drug or alcohol problem.
- 90% or more have a friend who has thought about suicide.
- 100% have friends who are sexually active.
- Less than 15% have ever had an adult discuss these issues with them (with the exception of drugs and alcohol).
- Only 15% think they can turn to their parents for support in a crisis.
- But 85% wish they could discuss all these issues in depth with their parents.

Many people reading these statistics will become alarmed. Any parents who aren't talking to their teens definitely should be. But on the positive side, these numbers tell us precisely how aware teens are of the most important issues they face. Clearly, today's teens are not blind to what they need nor callously insensitive to the major decisions they face on a daily basis. And most important, teens clearly want to be engaged by the adults in their lives (that's you). What can be better than that?

The teen years are a time when the support and stability of a strong family and community are needed most. Although successfully engaging your teenager may seem like a difficult task, the simple truth is that he needs you to make the effort. The antidote to the tough issues teenagers face is for you to stay the course and never give up. Never underestimate the power of consistently being present in your child's life. Being present means you

- Care about him — his feelings, thoughts, and actions
- Ask her about her life
- Be available unconditionally through the good and the bad times

Modern life has taken its toll on the nuclear family. Soon, 35 percent of all adults will have been raised or will be living in step-situations — as stepparents, parents who remarried, or adults with stepchildren (National Survey of Families and Households (NSFH, 2001). The disappearance of close extended families, tightly knit neighborhoods, and communities has also made raising children more difficult. However, study after study emphasizes that every child needs at least one parent fully engaged in his or her life. In other words, your involvement will make a difference.

Teenage trouble often stems from parental neglect, often unintentional. Positive growth takes root in families that talk together. Without more insightful guidance from the adults in their lives, children run the risk of growing up without many of the emotional skills and values necessary for attaining success in their personal lives — resilience and decision-making skills, for example, and values such as honesty, loyalty, and fairness.

When determining where children will receive this guidance, it's easy to hope institutions like schools, churches and synagogues will fill the void. But in truth, the primary focus must always be on the family, whatever its shape. Schools, community organizations, and religious institutions cannot possibly supply all the answers. It is we, the parents, who must make the commitment to put forth the energy to listen and talk to our teens every day. We can begin by stepping out of our reality for a moment and spending some time in our teenagers' shoes.

This may sound like a grueling task. Who of us would ever want to go back to being a teenager, let alone one who has grown up in a difficult, dangerous world that we have only experienced as adults? Yet until we make an attempt to understand their world — not the one we remember when we were their age — we can't begin to understand their unique concerns.

A Different World Than Ours

As children today enter adolescence, parents who dare to step into their world often encounter instability, highly charged emotions, and mood swings. Parenting through this miasma of constantly shifting emotions, thoughts, and styles is not easy for anyone. Trying to muster empathy is even more difficult, especially when our teenagers — as is typical of them — are perfectly willing to challenge everything "to the max" on a daily basis. It's no wonder so many parents fear to tread in this territory, preferring to leave their teens to "do their own thing." Yet the most effective way to be present for your teens is to know, understand, and respond to their questions about their world. And to find out about their world, you must inquire.

Let me give you a preview: In addition to the tribulations of adolescence, teenagers today live in a world full of burdens that didn't exist twenty years ago. It is a world where

- Toxic drugs and alcohol are readily available
- Violence and sexually transmitted diseases stalk the back corridors of family and school life
- Adolescent fancy — a natural curiosity about taboos such as sex, alcohol, and drugs — can quickly turn into a fatal encounter with reality

In addition, parents today must understand their children's culture in order to understand not only their children's emerging values, but also how those values help them negotiate everything in their daily lives. Many adults are quick to blame this culture, but I do not believe our problems are the result of the media, metal and rap music, or violent video games. Certainly a lot of high-impact input is not a positive thing, but it is not the main culprit, either. While I am not recommending any of the above, if families continually make culture the target, they will miss their children's compelling issues. Teenagers don't get into trouble because they go to rock concerts or watch the wrong TV shows. They can, though, get into trouble from a lack of parental love and concern, or from their parents' inability to express that love and concern.

That is not to say that we shouldn't monitor our teens' activities. But the key is always to discuss and ask questions about the issues at hand. And what are these issues? As I have learned in my seminars, they come in the form of questions like these:

- "How can I tell if my friend is serious when she talks about suicide?"
- "Did you get drunk in high school or college?"
- "Why is sex considered the most important part of a relationship?"
- "I'm pretty sure I'm gay. Should I tell my parents?"
- "I hate my mom and dad and want to run away from home. What should I do?"
- "Is religion important? Does it make a difference in anyone's life?"
- "My best friend told me a secret that she was raped. How can I help her?"
- "What's wrong with doping and drinking at a party?"
- "I feel really sad all the time. How can I tell my parents when I don't even understand?"
- "What's wrong with using a fake ID? Everyone does it."

- "How do I know if I'm truly in love?"
- "What age is the right time to start having sex?"

These are everyday questions for teens, and this book will show you how to answer them. As you read through it, you will discover that responding to your teen's questions can be a highly rewarding challenge. But let me place an emphasis on the word *challenge*. And do not make the mistake of thinking that middle-of-the-road high school students — like your own teen, perhaps — are not at risk and do not have profound questions. They do, as we have already clearly seen.

Teens also place a high value on truth, and the way to engage them in honest discussion is to be equally truthful. That can be an incredibly difficult thing for us parents to do, particularly if, up to this point, we have seen our roles as inexhaustible sources of wisdom, as disciplinarians, as sterling role models, or as definitive authorities on certain topics. Now is the time not to instruct but to listen, not to lecture but to confide, not to lead our children through life, but to take a step back and walk by their side. A bit of advice to remember, though: If you resist dealing with your teen's questions, things will get worse. If you accept them — as difficult and perplexing as they may seem — things will get better. I like to say that the truth does set you free, but not until it is finished with you.

It is up to us parents to make sure that every question our teens ask is our family's concern. Discussions must center on our children's daily life, not the lives portrayed by the world at large. Heartfelt talk must be about the issues that most concern our children and our families. Here is the way to touch those hearts.

The Challenge

Your teenager needs and wants to talk with you. This fact has a certain urgency that resonates on many different levels, ones that extend far beyond your family's home. The "next generation" — the parents, teachers, workers, and leaders just ten to twenty years from now — is composed of today's high school students. How teens resolve their conflicts in the present will literally shape our nation's future.

In light of this fact, what parent doesn't pause and wonder, "Will my child be able to make good choices when faced with decisions regarding drugs, sex, and other conflicts of values?"

The good news found in this book is that values and ethics *can* be transmitted — through real talk between parents and children. As you are about to discover, every parent can reach his or her child emotionally. How our teens meet and resolve their ethical dilemmas depends on their connection with us, their parents. Your passion and concern can touch your teenager's life.

Connecting with your teen's emotional mind is the key to laying the foundation of family values. The way to do this is not through lecturing or educating — there's a reason that doesn't work. Research has shown that teenagers resolve big issues not through logic or analytical reasoning, but with their hearts (Laurran Neergaard, "Emotions Are Rationale for Some Moral Dilemmas," *ScienceNOW*, Sept. 16, 2001). Thus, the key to connecting with your teen is through *your* heart. What a relief for us parents — all those feelings, no matter how perplexing or extreme, really do matter.

The balance of my time spent with parents focuses on tackling the questions and issues that their children have raised. They come to understand how essential it is that we engage our kids in ethical discussions about what it means to get high or have sex, or about the ethics of pressuring someone else to do such things. We discuss the fact that kids need us to talk about actual consequences and about how to recognize when they are getting in over their heads. We have to encourage our children to help their friends. We have to tell them whom they can talk to if they see that a friend is in trouble — or if they are themselves.

Who, If Not You?

Adolescence is no picnic for teenagers or parents. As parents, we have to stay focused as best we can through these years. We must remember that we are preparing our children to navigate and, we hope, prosper in the adult world. And we must keep the following question foremost in our minds: *Who is going to teach my teenager how to handle crises, relationships, failures, and mistakes, if not me?*

Skillful parenting on a day-to-day basis has more to do with substance than style. Children learn the most about dealing with life's challenges from their parents — and from their parents' behaviors more than their words. If you don't provide the backdrop of ethics and values for your children, who will? Peers, movies, and television? The street culture, or even drug dealers?

To reiterate, only 15 percent of the teens I surveyed said they would turn to their parents in their time of need. Although teens often deny their need for their parents' support, the simple fact is that meaningful adult contact and interaction is essential as your children make the transition into adulthood. It is a myth that teens need or want less contact with their parents. My survey showed that 85 percent of teens wish they could discuss issues in depth with their parents and other adults, yet don't believe they can.

Older adolescents, age fifteen to eighteen, also have a certain measure of self-reflection. They begin to consider and question their beliefs, actions, and words — and yours as well. It is precisely at this age when the conversation between you and your teen becomes crucial. Our input — asking questions and giving responses — is the key they need to develop the ability to make effective choices and decisions. Additionally, we must strive to transmit our values by truly practicing what we preach. Teenagers, as every parent knows, can see through any discrepancy. Your teen sees every time you stumble into a double standard. The best advice I can give to avoid that pitfall is to keep working on your imperfections — beginning with admitting that you have made mistakes, or that you don't know all the "right" answers. It's not the size of the step that matters, but that you take it. Do that and your teen will notice that you, too, can change.

The Myth of Leaving Home

Many parents mistakenly assume that by the time their kids are in their later teens, it is time to have a "hands-off" approach with them. As a parent, you are ready to go off-duty. After all, you have put in sixteen or seventeen years on the job. You feel entitled to take a break, or better yet, go into early retirement. As a friend of mine once said, "After sixteen years of parenting, I think I deserve something better than a normal sixteen-year-old."

Most parents have a sense of what they consider the ideal teenager, but they have little patience for deviations from that. I often tell parents that teens at times do get drunk, have sex, vanish behind locked doors, mouth off, break curfew, watch too much TV, and listen to migraine-making music. While all of these behaviors require comment from parents, it is important to keep in mind that all of these behaviors, as long as they do not become chronic problems, are nothing more than your child's early quest and rite of passage into adulthood. Mistakes and blunders are incidents and should be considered nothing more than onetime events. Incidents do need to be discussed, but then put to rest. Chronic events, on the other hand — your teenager getting drunk *every* weekend, or having to be bailed out of jail repeatedly — are an entirely different matter. The question to ask is always, "How often does this happen?" If you discover that you are dealing with a chronic problem, then you need to seek out solutions and perhaps professional help. It's time to take the matter to a family therapist, clergyperson, or guidance counselor.

When you find yourself struggling to connect with your teenager, it should come as no surprise that you dream of him leaving the household. In truth, leaving home does not happen in one big burst. In a healthy home environment, it happens step by step. Each foray your child makes away from home also brings with it a need to check back to home base to garner feedback and perspective. There ought to be no sudden break with the family. Nor is adolescence the time for hands-off parenting. Home needs to be a safe, nurturing haven of love and support for your teenager while he explores the world.

Furthermore, when the inevitable dust settles and your teenager emerges as a competent adult, it is comforting to know that, through it all, you stood strongly behind her with love, caring, and an abiding interest in everything she was going through. You were there in time of need.

A Word About Being the Parent of a Teen

Being a parent of a teenager is not an easy task. At times, all parents question how well they know their own child. Sometimes it seems the child at the breakfast table in the morning has transformed into someone else at the end of the school day. There always seems to be a new mood, a new style, new music, and above all a new emotional intensity that ricochets around the household. Even in families with no major problems, parenting a teenager is a challenge. Relax. The good news is that your anxiety is normal. Nearly every parent of a teen has similar thoughts and frustrations.

But challenges can also be positive experiences. In fact, parenting teens can be one of the most rewarding and satisfying times in family life. It can be a time to deeply cement your bond with your child. To accomplish this, it is essential to tackle your teen's questions and issues directly. Our children have so many questions and decisions to make in life. They need our input and advice. The key words here are *input* and *advice*. Obviously, teens don't want lectures — as we've seen here, and no doubt experienced firsthand, lecturing doesn't work.

Don't Be a Perfect Parent

Parents often ask me, "What is the one thing I should avoid doing as a parent?" I often answer that the worst mistake a parent can make is trying to be a "perfect parent."

I consider the "perfect parent trap" to be one of the worst sins in parenting. In truth, the best way to raise resilient children is by being an *imperfect* parent. A perfect parent cannot teach his teenager to face adversity. A perfect parent cannot teach her children to learn from their mistakes.

A perfect parent, by definition, tries always to appear never to do anything wrong. Perfect parents demonstrate that they are living life as one big cover-up. Besides the rigidity and tension that comes from trying to appear perfect, it is also exhausting, disingenuous, and certainly not helpful to your teen. The truth is that your child will grow stronger when you admit your failures. Not doing that creates an impenetrable wall between you and your child. You are unconsciously signaling to your child that in her most desperate hour, she had better not go to Mom or Dad for help. Perfect parenting gives teens the message that they cannot approach you because they haven't measured up to your standards. Children growing up in families where they can't possibly admit their failures are vulnerable and isolated. Perfect parenting, therefore, puts your teenagers at risk.

Why? Because *perfection creates rejection*. If you raise the bar beyond your teenager's reach by creating a false, perfect view of the rules and regulations of family life, you are giving confused messages. Who better than teenagers to understand, as they go through all the complexities and frustrations of adolescence, that perfection is impossible, that it simply can't be attained? As a result of pressing perfection on them, then, your children will know only one rule clearly:

Don't go to Mom or Dad if you are in trouble. They will not understand, and they will not support you!

What makes matters even worse is that teenagers see through the false standards their parents preach. They fear letting their parents down by not handling their own problems "perfectly." Not only is this a recipe for low self-esteem, but it also forces your children to move their emotional life underground, below the radar screen of the family. All of this, if compounded, provides the jet fuel for creating a dysfunctional family life.

Be an Imperfect Parent

In adolescence, your children are on the cusp of the transition into adulthood. They are having the beginnings of adult experiences and challenges in their lives. If parents don't demonstrate the value of truth and honesty, which means exposing your mistakes, vulnerabilities, and imperfections, how are teenagers going to learn how to manage success, failure, and adversity?

Being an imperfect parent means being forthcoming about your mistakes. While it may be painful to let your child witness your vulnerability, ultimately it strengthens their ability and resolve to grapple with their own problems and dilemmas. Sharing your admissions, regrets, and hard lessons learned — as well as your successes — prepares them to meet their own challenges in life. Your example — of being a perfectly imperfect human being in a far-from-perfect world — teaches them how to face consequences and challenges. Most importantly, they are able to recognize how your ethics and standards didn't magically arise from nowhere.

The Parenting principles:
How to Reach Your Teen Every Day

The Parenting Principles, which I introduced to you briefly in the introduction of this book, consist of hard-hitting suggestions for you to follow on a day-to-day basis. These principles, which are astonishingly simple, have proven to be powerful communication touchstones between parents and teens. Many parents have written me after a seminar saying that they keep a copy of the principles in their wallet or purse, or post them on the bathroom mirror or refrigerator. Knowing and acting on these straightforward suggestions is an essential backdrop for being able to effectively tackle the job of parenting a teenager today. Putting the Parenting Principles into practice will open the door to meaningful and thought-provoking discussion, something I know parents and teens alike yearn for.

I have broken these principles down into five simple categories. After hearing about them, parents often remark, "Gosh, is it really that simple? I know all this already, but I never thought it was that important." And that is the beauty of these principles. You do know them already. And they are that simple.

Teenagers are not searching for advanced research on a particular life topic. They are searching for a baseline opinion and meaning that is relevant in their life. You can provide that for your child. You don't have to change who you are. But you do have to *bring forth* who you are into your teenager's life.

Understanding and using these principles opens the door to dealing with any issue and answering any question your teenager might have. That doesn't mean, though, that you will provide the ultimate answer to every question or issue. What it *does* mean is that your teenager will know what you believe and that you are concerned. Your teen will know you are interested in his life and that he can come to you when things are extremely trying — even when he is in trouble.

The principles are the recipe for full engagement in your teen's life. They set the daily stage for your involvement. They open the door through which you can transmit your family's values, and they provide a way to stick by these values and secure the necessary help if things go haywire. All any parent can truly hope to do is give their children an abiding sense of who they are, who the family they come from is, what that family stands for, and how that family sticks together through thick and thin.

I promise that, if you follow these principles, the quality of your relationship with your teenager will improve dramatically, and your responses to any topic will be more valued by your teen than ever before. It may sound too good to be true, but I am about to show you precisely how to accomplish this.

Don't worry. You are not going to have to learn a new system of parenting. You don't have to develop new rituals. You don't have to memorize a new set of communication skills. All you have to do is remind yourself of what you already know to be true, and then act upon it. The advice given here is simple and direct. It works. Thousands of parents across the nation already employ my suggestions on a daily basis, and you can begin putting them into effect today.

But please remember, principles and good advice won't solve all problems. Life is filled with challenges, and there are no panaceas. But by using these principles as the backdrop to communicating with your teenager, you will open up new possibilities. You will regularly have the opportunity to directly engage your teen about his struggles and offer some measure of guidance. By employing these principles, you will be able to be there for your child if and when she is faced with a crisis. Dealing with difficult topics does not have to be a continual source of anxiety. Although the rite of passage through adolescence may be stormy, it can also be the time when deep family bonds are cemented for a lifetime.

Here, I have organized the Parenting Principles into five categories, listed in a way that will make it easy for you to quickly read each one and grasp the point mentioned. I've also elaborated on them, enriching them with examples where appropriate. None of the advice given here will surprise you, but it will deeply affirm that, all along, you *did* have an astute grasp of the obvious.

Dealing with Difficult Matters

- You don't have to be an expert in anything. You simply have to share and care. Knowing that you do not have to be an expert means you can discuss any topic with your teen. He wants your opinion, not your expertise.
- Never be afraid to admit you were wrong and to apologize. It demonstrates how mistakes can bring out love.
- Ask questions, avoid lectures, and listen to what your teen is saying. This develops good communication and underlines that you value your relationship with her.
- Share what has touched your life. Talk about what you believe in — God, love, compassion, truth, kindness, honesty — and your uncertainties about these topics.
- Share your own struggles with your teen. Let him know there is meaning to be found in facing problems.

Daily Input

- Put prime time into your family life. Your most important job is spending time with your kids. Think of all the effort you put into your career — imagine what would happen if you invested that time and effort with your children?
- Make no excuses about not being in close communication with your child. Don't buy off your teen off as a way to avoid dealing with her. And don't use the excuse of poverty or overwork as a way to justify not spending time with your teenager. Your child will learn that you are too busy or too tired to care.
- Encourage your teen to take healthy risks, not dangerous ones. Sports, travel, special events, hobbies, clubs, and the like should be encouraged. They are never out of style.
- Go out with your teen to movies, dinners, shows, ballgames, concerts, picnics, etc. It's not true that teens do not want to spend time with their parents. These can be ideal times for deep conversations and a lifetime of meaningful memories.
- Listen to your teen's music. Play his video games or at least sit and watch him play. Watch her favorite TV shows with her. Not only does this promote discussion, but it will also give you a direct view into your teen's emotional life. The danger in listening to outrageous music or violent video games is not in the music or the graphics, but in how your teen emotionally reacts to them. While I am not recommending what kind of music or video games to allow in your home, if you are at all worried about the effect of media on your teen, this will help put it into perspective. As a parent, you will no longer be on the outside looking in.

Conscious Communication and Participation

- Every day, ask your teen about his school day, classes, teachers, and friends. Ask her who got into trouble; ask about fights, suspensions, detentions, name-calling, threats, bullying, and cliques. Ask what was the best thing that happened at school. Demonstrate to your teen that his daily routine is important to you. Your involvement helps your teen to know it is important to ask others precisely how they are doing. Furthermore, it directly signals how much you care about every aspect of your child's life.

- Never ignore the big topics: sex, drugs, relationships, depression, suicide, etc. Your children want to know what you think.
- Talk to your children about everything — that's how they are going to develop values and direction in life. No topic is off-limits. If your child brings it up, it is important. Otherwise, your child will get their information from the local drug dealer, her peers, or television.
- It's okay to have fun and goof around with your teen. Being a parent is more than being a serious adult.

Reminders for Building Self-Esteem

- Praise your teen for who he is and what he does. Be specific, and don't forget the little things.
- Hug your kid every day. Don't be fooled into thinking teenagers don't cherish a warm embrace.
- Tell your teen you love her, and why. Be specific about her good traits and actions.
- Teens want to hear daily about family matters and family problems. They want to be involved, so involve them.

Involving Yourself and Others

- Don't let your mistakes as a parent make you stop trying. Children learn mightily from how you deal with life.
- Admit your feelings of discomfort in discussing the "hot topics" (sex, drugs, etc.). Talk about them anyway. Sharing your vulnerabilities builds your teen's character. It helps him learn to make wise decisions.
- When in serious trouble with your teenager, be prepared to get competent professional help. When you are drowning, call for a lifeguard.
- Being an effective parent depends strongly on having a working relationship with your spouse or ex-spouse. It is of immense benefit to work together. It will make your teenager feel secure, loved, and protected. Those feelings build self-confidence and strength in your teen, allowing her to take risks and pursue her dreams.
- Who are your teenager's friends? What is the context of their relationship? What do they do together? What do they talk about? You are not going to know unless you interact with them. Make

your home a place for them to hang out. Have them over for dinner or at least feed them. Make sleepovers commonplace. Have an open-door policy for your teen's friends. Talk to them. Roll out the welcome mat. Stay in touch with your teen's world.

Putting Principles into Practice

There it is: everything you need to know about communicating with and raising healthy, capable teens. Of course, no matter how good a set of guidelines looks on paper, it's rarely much help without some real, hands-on guidance for putting it into practice. The rest of this book, beginning with chapter 2, will provide that for you.

In the following chapters, I've taken the very real questions that come up most frequently in my seminars — there are seventy-five of them — and grouped them into seven categories: communication problems, sex and relationships, family problems, violence and abusive relationships, drugs and alcohol, suicide and depression, and spirituality and social consciousness. Each chapter will explore a topic, raise the questions related to it, and walk you, the parent, through discussing them with your teen. While certain questions command straightforward, specific advice — for example, what to do if your teen thinks she has been raped, or if you suspect he is using drugs, or if a friend is threatening suicide — don't be surprised if you hear the same, simple themes over and over again: Calm down. Listen. Ask questions. Share your own stories. Hold a hand. Laugh.

As you read each question and the discussion that follows, take the opportunity — now, even before you reach out to your teen — to thoughtfully consider your response if your child were to ask you that question tonight, no matter how scary or uncomfortable it may be. Chances are, it's a question that's been pestering him already, whether it involves a problem he's facing at the moment, a problem a friend is facing, or something he's simply curious about. Take a deep breath, and trust yourself. Your teen is waiting to talk to you.

Chapter 2:
Communication Problems

*"I always know the right thing to say —
after the right time to say it has passed."*

When troubled parents come to my office for family counseling for the first time, our conversations often come off like this: We sit down, and I offer them some coffee or tea. We work through important stuff like the Yankees, or who is doing what in the NFL this season. We schmooze a little; we chitchat. Then, I turn to the parent who has done the least amount of talking (it throws off the power balance in the partnership a little bit) and ask my first question.

"Okay, Laura," I asked in one particular case, "I'd like you to tell me what the problem is here. What do you think is going wrong? And while you're telling me that, why don't you fill me in on the most recent battle you had with your daughter? Give me the picture starting at that point. Can you do that?"

"Well," Laura replied, "last night she broke curfew for what seems like the tenth time. Ever since she got her new boyfriend, she has changed. Mike (the father) and I fought over that an hour before she came home. He wanted to ground her. I was worried he would scream and start throwing things like he sometimes does. Me — I just wanted to talk to her."

"So," I asked, "how did it go when she came in the door?"

"Well, Mike started screaming. She cursed him out and went to her room and slammed the door. I sat on the sofa and cried."

"And Mike, what was your take of the situation?"

"Well, yeah, I yell and get angry. Her boyfriend is an asshole. A real loser. I won't let him in the house. I do lose it. But she is my daughter. She ought to obey me. I need to find a way to stop her. She's gonna get pregnant or into drugs."

Believe it or not, in all this, I see a huge amount of fertile ground to work with. It's clear that the parents don't have a plan for parenting, they don't agree on how to communicate with their daughter, the boyfriend has been made the enemy (and the daughter is siding with him), and she is actively rebelling. She also, obviously, wants to talk. How can I possibly know this? She is still at home, and she is not in deeper trouble. Better yet, the parents are ready to talk. How do I know? They came to me, amid the fireworks, to begin this work.

My job here is to create a forum for talk and reconciliation between these parents and their daughter, giving her the opportunity to tell her side of the tale without interruption and paving the way for some real communication to begin. No secrets. No closing of the heart. Lots of questions. A few basic rules. Good issues make good conversations.

That is what you, as the parent of a teen yourself, are about to discover firsthand.

* * *

As we begin this chapter — which uses "communication problems" as a broad umbrella to cover topics such as communication (and miscommunication) with friends, dealing with peer pressure, and sorting out who one is and where one belongs — bear this scenario in mind. Here, I hope to address not just the questions kids I've spoken to have raised about the communication problems they face daily, but also introduce to you, the parent, some basic information that will help you to begin communicating regularly and effectively with your teen. Scenes such as the one above are welcome — it means both parents and their children acknowledge problems and want to talk them out — but they can be avoided. The most fertile ground on which good work — and good communication — can be done lies in your own home, in the space between you and your teen.

Key Points to Remember When Discussing Communication Problems

Teens are under a great deal of pressure to conform to and fit into their social world. They're at an age where being popular is everything, and immense tension exists between trying to develop their own identity and striving for acceptance among peers. To make matters worse, pressure is sold through the media — in ads, on television, and in music — and kept alive through the myths generated by the teenage underground. You remember the catch phrases: "Come on, everyone's doing it." "A little bit won't hurt you." "You don't want everyone to think you're a loser" — or whatever the latest term for "hopelessly uncool" happens to be.

Teens are also trying to figure out which social groups they fit with and which they don't. While they may seem to try on peer groups like clothes at the mall, the truth is they want friends desperately and cherish them deeply. Too often, potential social groups take the form of exclusive cliques, which heighten teens' sense of being outcast and give them an inaccurate image of what true, close friendships are. Add to that a teenager's innate ability to say the wrong thing, say it awkwardly, or stretch the truth — which can result in miscommunication and hurt feelings — and you can see why communication problems and damaged friendships are major issues as your teen comes of age. Questions on these topics may be some of the first you encounter as you, too, begin communicating with your teen.

What are the important things you can do to help your teen deal with the struggle to communicate, fit in with peers, and deal with the inevitable peer pressure that results? How best do you keep the lines open so that the vital issues will be brought to your attention when your teen needs help?

To prepare yourself to answer the questions in this section, spend some time reading the following five points. These points will serve as "home base" when your teen raises issues in this arena.

1. The teen years are a challenging time for your child. But if things go well, by the time he is a high school senior, his contrariness and rebellion slow down. He is almost prepared to go out in the world. Still, you won't be exempt from a fair amount of chaos and testing along the way. Remember, this is normal.

2. As your teenager struggles socially and experiments with different ways of communication, she is attempting to figure out her life. Her attempts to do so may look weird and seem strange. Her communication may appear immature or even wacky. Seeing your kid walking around dressed like she bought her clothes at the local donation bin tries many a parent's patience. Having a teen fix his hair in the morning for what seems like hours on end can make any parent feel like he's raised a walking advertisement for hair products. No matter what, take a deep breath and laugh. When facing all these issues, your job as a parent is to comment on substance, not style.

3. Your teen needs your input. At this point, parents often feel their main job is simply to foot the bill. They think that now is the time to stay out of their children's lives, that their children don't *want* them in their lives. Nothing could be further from the truth. The reality is that sixteen- to eighteen-year-olds are finally old enough to have adult discussions about pressure, grades, and friends. They can begin to understand more about what is happening in their lives, and they want your input. Parents need to spend time talking with their teens about their friends, pressure, and the myriad choices and issues they suddenly are facing.

4. The key to lessening communication problems is to communicate more, not less. *More* here means quality *and* quantity. Peer pressure cannot be avoided, but you can help put it into perspective if you spend time, every day, talking with your teen. Maintain your connection, even if you can't always maintain your cool. Especially when your teen is being a major "pain in the ass," stick with it — persevering through this chaotic time will pay great dividends later in life. Make certain you ask your teen every day how his day went — and I mean *every day*. Make that a habit, and when you teen really needs you, he actually will respond if there is a problem.

5. Home needs to be both a buffer and a sanctuary for your teenager as she makes her way in the world. Always make your teen feel that home is a refuge. It needs to be a place she knows she can retreat to, to sort things out. Kids learn to stand strong against peer pressure, deal with their friends, and sort out communication difficulties if they have a secure home life. Knowing that home is a comfort zone makes a huge difference in kids' lives. Parents who will stand with them, talk with them, and support them as they make decisions are priceless for their development. Your child needs to be able to look forward to coming home, talking to you, and lying back in her room every day.

With these points in mind, let's take a look at the top questions teens have about school, peer pressure, and friends today, and consider how best to respond to them when they come up.

Questions and Answers

"What am I going to do with my life? How am I going to figure all this out?"

Sooner or later, your child will have to tackle this question. Often, it surfaces in the senior year of high school. The pressure is on. For many kids, college or work looms large. Leaving home is just around the corner. Life has, so to speak, caught up with your child. Even teens who have a good idea of what career they want to pursue still grapple with this question.

Teens are acutely aware that the world is quickly changing. They know that nothing is "cut and dried" anymore. Permanent careers are rare. The job market tells them — and no doubt they have seen from the lives of adults around them — that they are likely to have three or more careers in their lifetime. Most parents today remember a time — in their parents' generation, if not their own — when it was possible to be defined by the work they did and for whom they worked. Not today. Unlike our parents, we have a rare experience if we go through life committed to a particular company or union.

My daughter, who is a middle school teacher and a part-time actor at Disney told me something years ago: "Did you know that certain 'imagineers' are disappearing at Disney? One of my closest friends there was an imagineer for nearly twenty-five years, and he was just let go. He was the last one left in that department. They are all gone."

I was stunned. Who didn't grow up knowing that behind every Disney creation was a crack team of imagineers — the folk who made their living imagining and creating the Disney magic we thrived on as kids? The world has changed, and even the sacred corporate zone of imagination, Disney, has let that magical era fold away into the twilight of history. Life is tough for your kid. Let me highlight the next sentence for you. *Figuring out what to do with life is very stressful and challenging for your teenager.*

If this is an issue for your child, turn it into a positive. High school and college are times to explore many options in life. This is your child's opportunity to test different careers and ways of thinking. I told my three children, as they went off to college, to pursue as many diverse interests as possible. As a guidance counselor at Yeshiva University in New York, I encouraged students to explore a wide variety of majors. There's nothing wrong with starting and stopping new projects. Trying on different roles and opportunities is the best way for young people to begin answering that question about "figuring out life" — and figuring out who they are. Encourage your child to explore.

And clearly, this is another reason why stressing family values and relationships is critical. In the ocean of life, it is our values that anchor us, not a college major, a job, or a social group.

If you put pressure on your child, pushing him toward a certain major or career, you are not helping him wade knee-deep into his life — unless, of course, he is certain in his mind that this is where he wants to go. As a parent, your best course of action is to support your child. Tell him not to worry or rush into any major decision. Explain to him that answers will come only after he has explored and pursued interesting projects, jobs, and various classes or unique trainings. Explain that you are aware that the world, which he is now entering, is far more complex than when you grew up. Meeting that complexity means being flexible. Good decision making often is best served by trying out new and different interests and pursuing opportunities that come your way.

As a parent, support your child's quest to find out what she is going to do in life. Be a facilitator for her exploration. Creative summer jobs, unique internships, and volunteer opportunities must be top-line agenda items for your teen. Encourage her. In time, she will settle into something and, as we all hope, be blessed with a "something" that gives her meaning. Certainly, that is never a guarantee, but at least your child will always know that opportunities exist for her to chase her dreams.

I often tell students at the university to remember that, after four years, they will be well educated. Even if their college ideals do not translate into the job or life they want, they still will have tasted their dreams. And while dreams may not pay the bills, they often turn out, at least, to be fulfilling hobbies or avenues for community service that will enrich and bring meaning to their lives as adults. In our tough, changing world, I have always reminded my own kids that everything they *need* is provided, and everything they *want*, they have to work to achieve.

"Why are my parents always focused on grades and never on the person I really am? They always are mad at me if I don't measure up."

Make no mistake about this question — it's a serious one, and it's one you can do something concrete about. This question applies to a lot of teens today who are getting the message — often from parents who have only the best of intentions — that they are not good enough. Parents have to be incredibly careful not to let the pressures of society — or their personal dreams for their children — pollute family life. Teens and parents already live under enough pressure. It is not a good idea to add to it by making it doubly hard for kids to succeed.

The teenager who asked this question is really asking, "Why am I not accepted in my family?" He is saying, "You don't see me. You only see what I do wrong. This makes me feel rotten. It stresses me out." Often, parents do not realize how singling out their child's imperfections creates a recipe for anxiety and even depression.

I think that if you, as a parent, think back to when you were a teen, you will vividly remember how self-conscious you were. While teenagers today are very different in many ways, this excruciating sense of self-scrutiny is still there. Teens often feel unsupported and unrecognized, even when they are. Too often, parents slip up and criticize their kids' shortcomings. None of us thought we would fall into this trap when we became parents, but here we are.

Generally speaking, I see too much criticism happening in families. Grades become too important. SAT scores mean more than good deeds. And this can border on the absurd — I have seen parents put down a teen who scored 1300 on the SAT because an older sibling scored 1400. If the situation persists, teenagers may begin to believe that they truly *are* defective. That is a surefire recipe for anxiety and depression.

The root of this all is not bad parenting — it is a by-product of the stress parents live with daily and the ever-increasing expectations that are set for us all at work and at school. Too much work, no personal time, and all the other stressors of our "modern" life shorten many parents' fuses, and the pressure spills into their homes. Yet, teenagers are dealing with enough pressure of their own, including pressure to succeed scholastically, as evidenced by Regents exams in New York and strict school standards. They don't need their parents to point out their shortcomings, too — they are well aware what grades, SATs, or acceptance to a college mean.

If your teen asks you this question, it most likely means she feels you are only seeing her shortcomings. It means she believes that you honor her only if she does well. Teens need their parents' support and encouragement, not constant criticism. Fortunately, this problem is rather easy to remedy. If, in the heat of a battle or in a tearful confession, this type of question appears, here is what to do. The best course of action is to get it all out in the open. From the outset, ask: "What have I been doing (or have said) that has you so upset? I can tell I have been doing something wrong, but I can't read your mind. Please tell me what has been bothering you."

Expect to hear frank and embarrassingly honest answers to that question. Try to resist defending yourself, but instead listen to your teen and understand that this is how he believes you perceive him. And somewhere along the line, something must have been done or said — maybe repeatedly — that gave him this understanding. I suspect you will be surprised that you fell into this criticism trap. None of us ever mean to. After all, what parents would try to prevent their child from becoming the best person he can be? Once your teen tells you the problem, acknowledge it right away, and then tell him you want to change.

Immediately what will become clear is that your teen needs your support, not criticism. Give your teen permission from here on out to remind you if you slip back into your old habits. She can tell you, "You're doing it again. Cut it out." Seldom does this situation ever require counseling. It will, however, if you don't put a stop to it early on.

Your goal in the next several months is to begin to change your expectations — not a terribly difficult task. How is this change accomplished? How do you swallow your pride and admit that mistakes were made? Fortunately, in this situation, there is a shortcut you can take through the minefield of criticism and disapproval that can foster communication as well as understanding between your and your child:

1) Think about your own upbringing and talk to your teen about it. Chances are that you, too, were criticized way too much and strived to meet expectations that were set too high.

2) Discuss, at some length, your own failures and how, ironically, you did not meet the expectations of your parents. Explain what this was like for you when you were a teenager.

This approach results in honesty, openness, and the expression of empathy on the part of both you and your teen. With it, you'll find the whole issue soon resolved. Long-term resolution, however, requires watchfulness of your own actions and words. You must make it clear that you are no longer going to criticize your teen or put him down, and once you have, it's up to you to keep that promise. This approach also requires you to encourage your teen to express himself openly — and the obvious benefit of that is better communication and greater trust between the two of you. In time, you can even find ways to talk about your foibles and pressures with a degree of humor.

"Where do I fit in? What group should I hang out with, and how do I know if this is the right crowd for me?"

Teenagers' relationships with their peers always loom large. Their social needs and need for acceptance can even become a preoccupation. Every parent knows teens are self-conscious. Hours are spent in front of the mirror any given week. A blemish means full-blown acne. Being called on the phone to do anything, or being called about absolutely nothing, is often the day's highlight. Decisions are mountains to climb. Teenagers are surrounded by peer pressure and respond to peer pressure. For better or for worse, it shapes a teen's social life. And while kids might not like it, they must respond to it.

Peer pressure and fitting in are part of an adolescent's rite of passage. The struggle to belong is a psychological step on the path to adulthood. It's a social task kids must fulfill as they shape their identity, deciding who they are and who they are not.

It may seem that this is a period during which teens are best left alone to make deep decisions and learn important things about themselves. Yet this is *not* a time for less contact with parents. Extreme examples of kids left alone during such a tumultuous, vulnerable time are runaways, school shooters, and gang members. As hard as it may be to believe, teenagers need their parents' support, guidance, and love through the emotional ups and downs, the disappointments with friends, and the school pressure. Dr. Frank Pittman said it best when he wrote:

"Adolescents need their parents. It is not frivolous to suggest that children (and they are still children) between twelve and eighteen need parenting more than they did between six and twelve, and perhaps in many ways as much as they did between one and six. There is a tendency for older adolescents to deny their need for parents and for the parents to forget that the adolescents need them more, not less, than a few years earlier." (Frank Pittman, *Turning Points,* W. W. Norton & Co., New York 1987, 176).

Want a motto? *Be in dialogue with your teen, consistently and regularly.* Teenagers have too many quandaries and social issues to figure everything out on their own. They need to talk with someone. It might as well be you, rather than an equally inexperienced friend who happens to be going through the same ordeal.

Friendships are extremely important during adolescence. Teens spend huge chunks of their lives with their friends and are definitely influenced by them. Hairstyles as well as self-worth can seem to be determined by one's peer group. Fitting in, being part of a group, and being accepted are on the top of any teen's emotional list of needs. To make matters more complicated, every kid is different. For some teens, making friends is a breeze. For others, it can be a struggle. And some teenagers, no matter how hard they try, just never fit in during these years.

How do you help your teen figure out which is the "right crowd" for him? Go back and take a look at the motto I gave you a few paragraphs back. You need to begin by cultivating a relationship with your teen in which you actually spend time talking, one in which your teen feels he can bring to you increasingly personal issues without fear of judgment or ridicule. And the key to developing such a relationship is the mantra of this book: The best way to keep the door open is to ask your teen, frequently and regularly, about his life.

In paving the way to conversations about friends, peer groups, peer pressure, and fitting in, I recommend asking some or all of the following questions every day (note that they all can easily fit into casual conversation, then lead to deeper talk):

- *"How are your friends doing?"*

- *"Were there any tough problems you had to tackle today?"*
- *"Did anything weird or funny happen at school?"*
- *"Did you have any good discussions in school today?"*
- *"What was the best thing or worst thing that happened today?"*

Creating meaningful dialogue means asking personal questions regularly. It doesn't matter if nineteen out of twenty times the answer to any of these questions is no, or "Nothing happened today." In fact, every parent should expect *no* to be the regular answer. However, by regularly inquiring about your teen's day, the one time something noteworthy *does* occur, you will get into a discussion. Why? What is the magic? By constantly asking, "How are things going?" the real message you are delivering is, "You can always talk to me if you have a problem."

Think of it this way: We adults regularly talk to our friends or partner about how our day went at work, where we spend the majority of our waking hours. Well, school is where the day happens for your child, so ask her about it. The formula is that simple. And it works. Make it a habit. If you regularly show interest, the interest will be returned. If you follow this simple advice, most problems and quandaries will be brought to your attention. If your child has a question about "fitting in" or picking a peer group, you are bound to be asked about it.

Are there some useful items you can pull out of your Parenting Principles toolkit and use to help your teen answer the question of where he fits in? Yes, and here they are. With them, I've included some important pointers to keep in mind, as well as some crucial questions you can ask your teen to help him consider for himself what friends and groups are best for him.

Become friends with your child's friends. Invite them to your home. Have them over for dinner and sleepovers.

1) Talk occasionally with the parents of your child's friends. This will give you support and feedback to a wide variety of issues that come up about your child's friends.

2) It always takes time to know someone — especially, perhaps, your teenager's friends. Muddy Waters was right when he sang, "You can't judge a book by its cover." Nor can you judge your child's new friends by spiked hair, earrings, or a small tattoo.

3) Do not shy away from discussing peer pressure — even when it pertains to uncomfortable issues like alcohol, sex, or drugs. Talking about tough issues often produces better judgment when pressure situations arise.

Keeping the above guidelines in mind, and turning our focus to the question at hand, begin a conversation about friends and fitting in by using points such as the following:

1. Talk to your teen about what *popular* means to her. Is being popular a real measure of a good person or a good friend? Or is being popular just an image? Does being popular mean being friendly or being cliquish?

2. Ask your teen: "What is a real friend? Who are the kids you think are in the 'right crowd'? Would you put them on the list of what a true friend is or not?" Explain to your teen that to have good friends, you need to be a good friend. Will these people be as good a friend to you as you will be to them?

3. Use real-life examples to help your child make decisions. Take the idea of the "right crowd" out your teen's mind and put it into practice in a situation your teen is likely to encounter. Ask your teen, for example:

- "Would anyone in this new group feel bad if you got into trouble?"

- "If one of your new friends got you into trouble for something she did, would she immediately stand up, take responsibility for what happened, and clear your name?"

- "If your new friend drove you to a party and got drunk, would he turn the keys over to you?"

Scenarios like these demand values clarification. Good peer groups take the right stands on these types of questions.

4. Stress the value of following one's own dictates of right and wrong, not someone else's. Let your child know that it is never acceptable to excuse himself from a wrongful action by saying that someone else

made him do it. Ask your teen whether the peer group he wants to be a part of allows for this kind of individual thinking. Ask whether one particular person in the group makes most of the decisions. Is it possible to be in this group and not follow the leader?

Starting a dialogue with your teen using questions like these puts you in the role of facilitator (not lecturer or dictator) and empowers you teen to make her own decisions, based on her own values, about who she is and where she fits in. What better tool could a parent give a child to equip her for adulthood?

"I want to have my friends over more, but my folks always put limits on it. They think I have too much work to do or whatever. We just like to hang out, talk, and play video games. What's wrong with that? I live here, too."

As you've seen in the Parenting Principles, one of my top "rules" for parents is this: "Open your home to your children's friends." Have them over to dinner. Keep the kitchen stocked with snacks. Engage them in conversation. Be the cool parent.

Assuming everything is basically going okay in your teen's life, I strongly urge you to open the doors wide — on some weeknights as well as weekends. If you want to be on the front line and in touch with your teen, then make it a point to have her friends around regularly.

"Out of sight and out of mind" is not a recommended strategy for raising teens today. "In sight and engaged" is much better. If you want to know what's really going on in your teen's life, then make your home an open house to his friends, where you can witness it firsthand. There's no better way to learn who your teen is hanging out with, what these kids are like, what their personalities and values are, and how they spend their time together. It can also help build trust and open communication not only between you and your teen, but between you and your teen's friends as well.

On that note, remember that many teens do not have warm and embracing families and home lives, and that one caring adult that is present in their life — whether a parent or not — is better than none at all. Therefore, as an added bonus, you can be a positive influence on another child — something that is very worthy indeed.

Think about it for a moment: This is just common sense. To be in the know and to be connected with your teen, open the doors to your home. Kids need a place to hang out that is safe, fun, and nourishing. The easiest way to do that is to provide your home. Don't put obstacles in the way of your child having friends over. In reality, his desire to have friends in his home is a positive statement about his home life. Take advantage of that now.

"Some of my friends have fake IDs. They all like to go to clubs and party. They're not dopers and don't get drunk, but they love to dance. I have gone with them a couple of times, and no one cares if I am underage or ever asks me for an ID. Is there really a problem with that? Everyone does it."

The club scene is alive and well in America, especially in cities and around college campuses. Hot dance clubs are common in urban and suburban areas. It's no wonder that they're a huge draw for young people — the music and the lights and the dancing provide the perfect counterpart for a teen's boundless energy, a means of self-expression, and a kind of escape from the day-to-day struggle of being a teenager.

But the issue here is more than fake IDs and the bending of rules to have a good time. The club scene is also the world of ecstasy and other experimental drugs. Ecstasy, or "X," is so common in clubs that any question about clubbing mandates a discussion of it. Spend a few minutes and read the questions that deal with ecstasy in chapter 6, as well as those on date rape drugs. Clubs, X, and fake IDs go hand in hand in hand.

Fake IDs are simply a click away for any teen on the Internet. In March 2001, the Pennsylvania Liquor Control Board stated the following in a press release on fake IDs:

> Dozens, if not hundreds, of Web sites currently offer fake IDs. Simply by printing and completing a form, and mailing in a photograph and payment, a young person can obtain an ID that might allow him to purchase alcohol. Other Web sites provide a template for a user to create the ID on their own computer.

If your teen wants a fake ID, one of his friends will tell him how to get one. I suspect that even after 9/11 it has not gotten that much more difficult. Also, a lot of underage kids are not carded at dance clubs. This is a problem. All parents need to talk to their teens if they are hitting the club scene.

Here's the bottom-line rule I propose: No fake IDs, period, and no hitting the clubs until a teen is old enough — that means age 18. Using a fake ID to get into a club is in the same category as using a fake driver's license to drive a car — it's illegal, and it's downright dangerous. Even if your teen does not have or use a fake ID, discuss with her the consequences that can happen when she or one of her friends uses one. Teens often do not think about consequences, some of which may include the possible suspension of a driver's license if they get caught — which is sure to get your teen's attention.

I am not recommending a stern legal lecture. But teens usually don't have a clue about what it means to be arrested and have a record. Ask your teen, "Do you know that, depending on the charges filed, getting arrested for having a fake ID can make you ineligible for student loans?" "Do you know that when you fill out a job application, you'll have to list any criminal record you might have?" "What happens if a company runs a background check before hiring you, and this comes up? What do you think they will do? How are you going to explain what happened?"

Simply go over your concerns with your teen. Make sure you mention that you know how much your teen loves dancing, and that you believe he uses good judgment. However, you must also mention that as much as you trust him, it is still against the law. It's a shame, but all twenty-one-and-over clubs are off limits.

It is not that hard to find out if your kid has been partying at an off-limits club. The following questions might seem absurd and obvious, but they will remind you to ask what may seem like the most simple, straightforward questions — you will be surprised at how often you get a straight answer. As I mentioned, dance clubs and club drugs go hand in hand. If you are going to ask about clubs and fake IDs, you also have to discuss ecstasy. Before your teen heads out for the evening, or when she is seeking your permission to go dancing with some friends, ask the following:

- *"Where are you going tonight?"*
- *"What's the club like?"*
- *"Do kids use ecstasy there?"*
- *"Have you seen them use it?"*
- *"What happens when they do?"*
- *"What is the age limit at the club? Do they ask for IDs there?"*
- *"Do you or any of your friends use fake IDs?"*
- *"Have any of them tried ecstasy?"*

I do not recommend you go through your teen's personal effects to find out if he has a fake ID. Parents who have reached the level of snooping through their kids' rooms have reached the level of communication breakdown. My advice is to remember you are a parent, not a private investigator. I am and have been both — there is a difference. To successfully raise children, parents may have to face their own anxieties about, fears for, and dependency on their children, as well as their possible inattention toward their children. Therapy may, in the end, be the best course of action for addressing some of these issues. Communication with your teen is a must, not a maybe. A search through their belongings should not come before that.

How do you deal with your worries and anxieties? The same old advice applies — talk to your teen, every day. While I cannot guarantee "worry-free" parenthood, I can assure you that the basic guidelines for communication we've discussed so far will help lower your blood pressure. To recap:

1. Regularly ask your child about his daily life. A simple question or two is fine.
2. Ask about her friends.
3. Ask if he did or heard anything positive during the day.
4. Ask about the negatives. Did anyone get into trouble today? Did anything distressing happen?
5. Say something if it appears a particular problem is bothering her. Let her know your help is available if she needs it.

Checking in with your teen every day keeps the door open to conversation and dialogue. Following this course of action makes it easier to talk about fake IDs, drugs, and more. Ask enough questions, and your teen will stop and talk with you when it's really important. If your family is already in the habit of discussing issues, when the tough ones arise, they will easily be discussed within the normal context of your family.

"I exaggerate way too much. Lately, I'm having trouble keeping track of my lies. I want to quit, but I don't know where to begin."

We all grew up knowing kids who exaggerated or even flat-out lied. Most of us have likely lied or certainly exaggerated at some point in our lives, too. Corny as it may sound, I'm a fan of the old show *Leave It to Beaver* — not because of the idyllic family setting portrayed, but because the advice of that old Ward Cleaver was usually pretty sound. I remember one episode in particular, where the Beaver got all tangled up in lies. Ward, imparting his great wisdom as he always did at the end of each show, explained to his son the importance of telling the truth:

Let's get something straight. I don't care what kind of trouble you may get into in your life, but you don't ever need to be afraid to come to your parents and talk to them. In the first place, it's always wrong to tell a lie, and in the second place, you just build up more trouble for yourself by not facing the truth. It's really a lot better to tell the truth. That way you don't have to cover up for yourself. You see, Beaver, you tell one lie and then you always have to tell another to cover it up, and then that leads to another and then another, and the first thing you know, you've told so many lies you can't keep track of them. I just hope you don't think you are smart enough to tell lies, because nobody is.

What do you say to your teen when he tells you he has been lying? Right off, acknowledge that it takes real courage to come clean and change. Your child has brought up a concern about his character. He wants to change. To acknowledge this, I suggest saying something along the following lines:

"It takes a lot of courage to admit any mistake. To admit a mistake and then decide to take action is even better. I want you to know I'm proud of you — not proud of what you did, but proud that you are mature and strong enough to do the right thing for your life and find ways to put a stop to behavior that is bothering you."

As a parent, it is important to take advantage of every opportunity to provide meaningful commentary about deeper character issues to your child. By doing this, you pass on your family's values, legacy, and traditions.

Getting back to the issue at hand, untangling exaggerations and lies is not accomplished in one fell swoop. Before your teen gets overwhelmed by the prospect of untying all the "lie knots," I suggest you help him begin with something simple. Small steps that are successful lead to bigger steps. Assuming that nothing else is going wrong in your kid's life, let me share with you a basic method for bringing the lying to a halt and undoing any damage caused by it.

People often exaggerate because of a lack of self-esteem. Basically, your teen needs help from you in two areas:

1. Cleaning up the lies and making amends (making amends will be dealt with in the following question)
2. Building self-esteem

Let's begin with how to start cleaning up the lies. There is no easy way around straightening out a lie. Your support as your teen tackles the clean-up job is critical. Start by straightening out the most important lies — ask your teen which ones she wants to untangle first. Once the process begins, she will take it over herself. Simply asking the question "How do I put an end to my lies?" means that your teen is motivated to effect change in her life. Asking the question also keeps her from falling into the trap of exaggerating again. Or if she does, she will correct it.

Your child might ask what to do if one of his lies pops up in his life. You might say, "Think about coming right out and making the confession that you sometimes exaggerate, and that you know it's stupid, and that you've decided to stop." Explain to your teen that often the simplest, most straightforward approach is the best and the easiest way to clear the air.

Feelings of inadequacy are also behind lies and exaggerations. Building your teen's self-esteem is not complicated. The real secret is taking out time regularly to praise your child specifically for what he's done or said.

This is a basic Parenting Principle. By giving praise, I do not mean complimenting her schoolwork, but pointing out the things you notice in her character — like kindness, good judgment, honesty, or integrity — that you are proud of. Those are the things to emphasize and praise. The shortest and quickest way to build self-esteem is to give feedback every time your teen does or says something important. Do it often and watch how your specific praise helps shape your child into a wonderful adult with strong values. Even if you have never praised your child for her character traits before, begin today. In a few months, you will see the results as she begins feeling better about herself.

"I lied to my best friend. Really messed up. How can I try to get things right again?"

I don't think any teenager makes it through high school without sticking his foot in his mouth or messing up badly with a good friend at least once. Making amends teaches teens the importance of being responsible for their relationships.

Making amends and seeking forgiveness is a lesson parents need to teach their children. It applies not only to personal relationships, but also to the world of work. Most teenagers think a simple "I'm sorry" or "I didn't mean to" passes for a complete apology, when often a more sincere response, complete with an attempt to compensate for harm done, is in order. This is especially true when the harm was done — often unintentionally — to a friend.

Teen friendships are often stormy. Friendships are tougher for boys because their bonds are not formed through talk. Boys get tight with their friends through common projects and activities. "Hanging out" together is more important than talking together. With girls, the opposite is true. Conversation, not tasks, is the glue of girls' friendships. However, both boys and girls need to learn the nuts and bolts of making amends. Forgiveness is core not just to friendships. It is essential for a healthy family life and good work relationships, as well. Adolescents, like adults, need to be reminded that to have good friends, you have to be a good friend.

There is a difference between asking for forgiveness and making amends. Making amends takes the act of asking for forgiveness one step further to do, say, or perhaps even give something to make up for the harm that has been done. Making amends is a very important life lesson, and now is the time to learn it. Teens kick each other around a lot. They make mistakes all the time with their friends. When such a mistake threatens the life of a friendship your teen cherishes, you may be faced with the question "How can I get things right again?" You can begin by explaining some of the reasons why seeking forgiveness is important. Say something along the following lines to your teen:

"You do not make amends simply to make yourself feel better. Amends are to correct the wrong done to your friend. Even if a friendship cannot be fixed, making the effort to correct a mistake is still required. Forgiveness does not bring you back to where things were prior to what you did. Don't count on your friendship going back to what it was. Don't count on even staying friends after you do this. If your apology is accepted, that will be wonderful. No matter what happens, though, you will have done the right thing. Doing that will make you feel better."

Then, I suggest you discuss with your teen the following six points, which cover the essentials of making amends. Each point is preceded by a question. Go over each one with your teen and have her tell you how she plans to carry it out. Breaking down the process into a series of questions, followed by answers, makes it much easier to learn how to make amends. Not only will these questions help your child understand what is involved in making amends, they also will help her understand that, even when amends have been attempted, friendships sometimes get broken.

1. *What happened?*

Write down or talk about what you did that caused pain and harm to your friend. Make certain that what you did is what you *really* did and not what you later decided happened. In other words, be accurate.

2. *Why did you do it?*

Now is the time for a little "moral inventory," as they say in the Twelve Steps. Why did you do what you did? Was it a knee-jerk reaction or a thoughtless mistake? If so, promptly admit it. Was it a seemingly logical response to something that happened, or something your friend did? Keep in mind that even if you believe the reason for you doing what you did seems valid to you, your friend may not accept it. Try to understand your friend's point of view, and how what you did was hurtful. Finally, consider what "character defects" might have been involved (to borrow another Twelve Step phrase). Did your quick temper get away from you once again? Did your desire to be popular cause you to slight a less-than-popular friend? Consider ways that potentially harmful behavior and habits can be changed — this will come in handy when it's time to make amends.

3. *What are you going to do?*

Decide what you are going to do as a result of the mistake that you made. How you are going to change your behavior so a similar mistake isn't made in the future? Look at those character defects you might have identified — how can you work on them to prevent future problems? How can this unfortunate event help you to become a better person? What do you have to do, specifically, to make yourself a better person?

4. *What amends do you have to make?*

Plan your amends. Begin by assessing what damage was done, and how best to make up for that. Will you write your friend a letter? Will you admit your wrongs and pledge to make up for them? How? Will you talk to other people involved to clear your friend's name? Was physical damage done to property that needs to be repaired or replaced? What if your friend is now distrustful of you? How are your amends going to reassure that person that what you are saying and doing is sincere, that you are different than you were when the mistake was made?

5. *What needs to be said in your apology?*

Prepare your apology. Offer amends with no conditions attached — no excuses, no rationalizations, no "I'm sorrys," and no "I didn't mean to's." Write down the specific things you are going to do to make amends. Be sure to clearly state exactly what you did and how you are going to change. Make certain your apology is directed at precisely what you did wrong.

6. *What if your apology is not accepted? Will you try again?*

Your attempt to make amends can end in one of two ways: Your friend may accept it, and carry on as your friend (though it still may take time to rebuild trust fully). This is what we all hope will happen. However, your friend may be hurt too deeply, or simply be too angry or distrustful, to continue your friendship. If your apology is not accepted, that's okay, too. Don't get angry with your friend for not accepting it. After all, you hurt him. Leave it alone for a while. Learn from the damage you caused, and do follow through on your plans to change. Grow from this experience, and in time, you may want to try again. In time, too, your friend's anger may mellow, or he may see that you're changing and decide to give you another chance. Accept this as a gift of grace.

Making amends is one thing you earn and pay for at the same time — but it is worth every cent.

* * *

The theme of this chapter has been communication — not only between your teen and his peers as they navigate the labyrinth of peer pressure, friendships, and self-identity, but between you and your teen as you begin opening the doors between yourselves and engage, openly and effectively. Much of what we've explored here will serve you well in the chapters and questions that lie ahead. Remember: You can lay the groundwork now for any question or issue that comes your way by doing one small thing, starting now — talking with your teen, consistently and daily.

Chapter 3:
Sex, Sexuality and Relationships

*"Ships are safe in the harbor.
But ships are not built to stay in the harbor."*

We all want to know that we've made progress with our life challenges. Sometimes, the best way to measure this progress appears when we're forced to confront them once more. While none of us wants to revisit our troubles — or worse yet, see them re-emerge in the lives of our kids — when we face them, we find we *have* learned from our mistakes.

I was sitting at my desk, trying to organize my day, when the phone rang. The mother calling identified herself as Ruth, and she was worried sick about her daughter. "Rabbi," she said, "something bad happened between Kathy and her boyfriend. She's really depressed. She spends most of her time in her room. It's been going on about a month now. I don't know what to do. How can I help her?"

I asked the obvious: "Do you know what happened?"

"I don't have the whole story," she replied, "but she was beaten up by her boyfriend during a fight. She came home bruised and crying. Ever since, she's been real depressed. She dropped out of college this semester."

"How depressed is she?" I asked. "Have her eating habits changed? Does she cry constantly? Is she sleeping all day?" While I was ready to refer Ruth to a psychiatrist, I couldn't help but wonder what else was going on. Each family has a unique history. There are always issues that have never been resolved. Each crisis brings up challenges from a buried past that cry out for resolution. To my surprise and good fortune, Ruth offered a critical piece of information about hers.

"Rabbi," she said after a long pause. "I also want you to know — you see, when I was her age, I had a boyfriend. We were, I guess, in love. I got pregnant. We got married, and — well, it didn't work out. He left us when Kathy was a baby. I raised her alone, and — I don't know — I've got this feeling, kind of a mother's intuition, that she's pregnant. She hasn't told me, and I don't want to push it — but I remember what I went through. Things happened so fast. I had no one to talk to and no way to sort things out. I'll stick by Kathy no matter what, but I don't know what to do. I told her if she wasn't ready to tell me what was going on, I'd find someone she felt she could talk to. That's why I called you. I don't want her to go through what I went through."

I smiled to myself. Ruth was one impressive mother. "Does Kathy know you're talking to me?" I asked. "Is she willing to see me?"

"She said okay," replied Ruth. I dealt myself in.

* * *

In any one of my seminars, nervous laughter erupts the instant I shift the questions to sex. Embarrassed laughter always is a signal that means, "I am interested, but don't know what to do." The initial titters and giggles soon evolve into powerful and revealing questions, not just about teens' confusion over information about sex, but also their concerns about deep and tragic problems that have taken or are taking place. After my talks, I try to spend another hour meeting individually with students. Someone always sits down with me and tells me an incredibly sad and disturbing story about some sexual incident — involving abuse, abortion, incest, date rape, and more — but what bothers me the most is that these teenagers spilling their secrets to me feel they have nowhere to turn in their darkest hours. No one should have to hide part of their life. Buried secrets are like time bombs that are guaranteed to go off later in life. No one can convince me that suicide rates and divorce statistics in this country are not, at least in part, tied to early "sexual secrets."

Wherever I go, teens are astounded that I really am willing to talk in-depth about sex and relationships. My recommendation to parents: Astound your kids by asking them about sex and relationships, too. Most of us grew up with parents who never spoke to us about sex. I certainly never had any sex talk with mine. I would like to think that times have changed, yet time and again, I hear from students:

"I really would like to know what my parents' experiences were sexually. You know, what are their stories? What was tough for them? It would help me understand what is going on."

"Can I really talk to my parents about sex? I would like to say yes, but I don't think so."

"It's not a cool situation, never being able to talk with my folks. It sucks. I wish this wasn't the case."

"I don't know why it's this way; it just is. We just don't talk. I sometimes try, but I don't really know what to say."

Indeed, that last comment is one that comes from the mouth of a parent just as often as a teen. And no wonder. It's easy enough taking your little boy to Little League, teaching him to ride a bike, or curling up with him for a bedtime story. Then, one day, you look across the kitchen table and are shocked to see a hulking sixteen-year-old looking back. "*Now* how am I going to talk to him?" you wonder, wishing you could go back to the simpler topics of his childhood — like bugs and baseball and where clouds come from — instead of ones that make you sweat, like sex and secrets.

Let me bring you up to speed on discussing the sex issue: Most teenagers know a lot about the biology and the nuts and bolts of sex. They know about condoms and birth control. They are not strangers to words like *STDs, HIV,* and *AIDS*. If you ask them about high-risk sexual behavior, most teens will give you some credible answer.

Still in all, when it comes to high-risk sexual behavior, teens need more direct, blunt information, simply because many of them do not think trouble will visit them. They assume the statistics apply to others, not themselves. Furthermore, they have watched plenty of R-rated movies and TV, and they have formed their opinions about what it means to be in a relationship based on what they have seen, not what they or others close to them — like you — know to be true.

It should come as no surprise, then, that teens do experiment sexually. There are even new twists in the sexual revolution. Some kids today have adopted a concept called "hooking up," in which kids partner up to have casual sex. Hooking up does not mean being boyfriend and girlfriend. Hooking up means getting together to have sex. With the younger teens, hooking up means girls giving oral sex to boys, often at parties.

While it is true that teen pregnancy rates have dropped recently, "fooling around" certainly hasn't, especially — shockingly — among very young people. Studies have shown that rates of oral sex among twelve- and thirteen-year-olds have gone up (Barbara Cooke, "Oral Sex and Young Teens," Chicago *Tribune*, 2001). In fact, according to a 2003 report by the National Campaign to Prevent Teen Pregnancy, about 20 percent of adolescents have had sexual intercourse before their fifteenth birthday. In addition, only about a third of parents of sexually-active fourteen-year-olds knew that their children had sex — and while most parents said they had spoken to their kids about sex, far fewer teens reported having had such conversations (Tamar Lewin, "Study Finds 1 in 5 Youths Have Sex Before Age 15," *New York Times*, May 19, 2003).

    Such data should leave us all wondering who, if anyone, *is* talking to teens about sex and relationships, what they mean, and how they affect others. Too often, parents leave discussions on topics like having sex while wasted, oral sex, or sex in general to movies, television, and the teen underground. For many underinformed teens, much sexual activity falls into the benign category of "fooling around" — this includes oral sex — and is not considered "real" sex. Real sex, they think, is having intercourse. A lot of teens are under pressure to perform sexual acts, rationalizing them with this faulty distinction. And remember, the teens who carry these misperceptions are not just somebody else's kids — they're very likely *yours*.

    A bit tough to hear, isn't it? Hang on — I will get you through this anxiety-laden minefield. Give me a few more paragraphs, and you will see the how you can make a real impact in the sex life or potential sex life of your teen.

    For a parent to make progress in discussing sex, you must turn the discussion to the most important issue — and surprisingly, that's not abstinence or pregnancy or birds and bees — it's relationships. Teens are hungry to know the ins and outs of relationships — what makes them successful and what does not. Want to make a dent in the sex advertising tossed at your child? Sit down and talk to your kid about relationships, love, treating others with dignity, and how you expect them to behave with the opposite sex. Yes, I sound old-fashioned in that last sentence, but read and on and you will see how on-target your conversations can be. Sex discussed in the context of relationships can change kids' attitudes and habits.

    And bear in mind that this is information they're not going to get in science class, from TV, or from their friends — only from caring, trusted adults who have real experience in real relationships. As informative as The Discovery Network's Dr. Drew or any other sexologist might be, they are no substitute for a parent's words, answers, standards, and values. Now, don't think for a minute that some good conversation will keep your kid away from "fooling around." It's likely it won't. But it will slow her down and get her to think, which is definitely something every parent wants. Talking with your teen about sex will also make him more willing to come to you if he does get into trouble. If sex talk is off-limits, then your teenager will form his own opinion based on what he sees, experiences, and hears from others. Putting family first means that when it is time to talk about sex, you talk with your teen about sex *and* relationships.

Key Points to Remember When Discussing Sex, Sexuality, and Relationships

Sex, secrets, and *teenagers* — three words that, when joined together, can make any parent cringe. What mother or father doesn't want to know the secret sex questions and issues of their teen? "How do I discuss this?" they wonder. "How can I create an atmosphere at home that will give my teen the freedom to talk to me?" Here's a little rule to remember: In life, there are no slam-dunk answers. There are, though, solid ways to transmit values, discuss embarrassing issues, and ease both your and your teen's anxiety about sexuality.

It sure was no cakewalk for me when I had to "talk sex" with my three teenagers — two sons and a daughter. In fact, if you ask my kids how I did, I bet I didn't get more than a passing grade in at least a few areas. But despite that fact — or maybe because of it — I've come up with five points that can help you get started and make you feel capable when you have that inevitable sex talk with your own teen.

1. If you are nervous or embarrassed to talk about sex, it's okay to tell your teen so. Sex talk is just as embarrassing and difficult for your teenager. Most parents today, I suspect, never talked about sex with their own parents. Admitting your discomfort is a surefire strategy to get you started talking with your teen. Doing that will lower your blood pressure and knock out most of the "hems" and "hahs." It will make you less anxious. And it will also teach your teen that difficult issues in life are not to be avoided. They can and must be faced, even when your insides are churning.

2. You don't have to have all the answers. In fact, a better strategy is asking questions. This encourages your teen to think through her own feelings about difficult topics. It also signals to her that she can come to you and really talk, not just receive a lecture or pat replies.

3. It is more than okay to share some of your own sexual and relationship experiences. Stories bring out emotions and put facts and choices in a real context. Tell your teen about your first love. Discuss your first long-term relationship. Talk about what happened and how it felt to break that relationship up. Tell about how you fell in love and got married. And if you got divorced, tell what went wrong. Telling these stories connects thinking with feeling — which is extremely important when dealing with sex. At the same time, don't go into all the embarrassing details. Not only is that inappropriate, but your teen does not want to hear it. Still, do share your mistakes and what you have learned from them.

4. Daughters need special attention. Teenage girls' first loves are very serious and important to them, and it is important to honor and acknowledge that seriousness. Talk to her about virginity and what it means to lose it to someone who doesn't take a relationship as seriously as she might. If she is no longer a virgin, make certain she knows that doesn't mean she has lost what makes her special.

5. Sons also need special attention. Give them the standards and values you try to attain. Don't shy away from discussing what it means to take away a girl's virginity, and what it means to take advantage of a girl sexually.

Now, take a deep breath and fasten your seat belt. It's time to address your teen's questions about sex and relationships.

Questions and Answers

"A lot of my friends talk about sex. It kind of embarrasses me. I mean, I know all the health class stuff, but not so much about the other stuff. So I don't know what I should say when this topic comes up. I would like to talk to my parents about it, but that seems weird, too, and could be really embarrassing."

As I've mentioned, most teens already know quite a bit about the basics of sex, from health and sex ed classes. But there's an important distinction to be made. What's covered in these classes is the biological aspect of sex, along with how-tos on condom use and preventing STDs. What teens *don't* get is education about relationships. This realm is up for speculation — and boy, do teens speculate.

Teenagers spend a good deal of time talking about sex with their friends. They make jokes about sex. They hear and participate in crude put-downs of gays and lesbians and yet are mostly quiet about this in front of adults. They hear and pass on rumors about the sexual activity of their classmates. They often share, down to the last detail, their sexual experiences with their friends. They often lie about them, too. They share locker-room sexual fantasies or at least dream about them. And nearly every teenager in America knows another teen who is sexually active.

Sound normal? It is. Yet posit this against the sexual backdrop of rising HIV rates and a high rate of teen pregnancy in this country. Make no mistake about it, teenagers are under enormous pressure to engage in sexual activity, and the risks accompanying it are higher than ever. Still for many teens, the question is not *whether* they are going to have sex, it's *when*. Why do teens spend so much time thinking and talking about sex? It's really quite simple: Sex is the forbidden taboo, the topic all the adults in their lives dance around and warn against.

In addition, many teenagers assume that having a good sex life just might be the major determinant in whether they are in love. Put another way, in many teens' minds, sex is the gateway to love. They believe that love is nourished first through sex, not the reverse. Why? Clearly, they lack frank information and sensitive discussion about the meaning of being in a relationship.

Teenagers have so many questions about love. However, over and over again they remind me that it is not sex they are interested in discussing, but rather what it means to be in a caring, nurturing relationship. This is where you come in.

When you sit down and have a talk about sexuality and relationships, what are the most important issues for you to emphasize? I would suggest you begin by sharing your experiences and failures in love. Explain to your teen how you see the difference between love and sex. Make certain you let them know that you understand they have strong sexual feelings and that those feelings are normal and okay.

Wouldn't it be easy if you could just continue by asking your teen, "What do you want to know?" and have her pull out a list of straightforward questions? That's probably not going to happen — most kids are way too shy or embarrassed to delve into something so personal with their parents. I recommend that you continue the discussion by asking your teen questions along the following lines:

- "What do your friends talk about when it comes to sex?"
- "What are their questions about sex?"
- "What are the most outrageous things that they have heard about sex?"
- "What did you think about that when you heard it?"
- "What do you think you would like to know, or what do you think your friends really want to know about love and sex?"

These questions are a good way to break the ice, to even laugh, and then get down to discussing the important issues involved in sex, love, and relationships.

"What are the benefits of having premarital sex versus waiting until I get married? I'd like to talk to my mom about this, but she has already been married twice, so I don't think she knows what to say about sex and waiting."

I am always asked some version of the "to have or not to have sex" question, but this one has an added wrinkle. Not only is this teen struggling with whether to keep her virginity, she is also wondering if her mother is much of a resource. When she writes, "I don't think she knows what to say about sex and waiting," it is clear she feels they do not communicate very much. As you, I hope, are learning, you are in fact your child's most valuable resource, no matter what your personal history.

Years ago, girls were encouraged to "save themselves" until marriage. Boys might have been "winked at," but they were told the same thing. Today, by the time teens hit puberty, they know a lot about sex. Even if your teenager never has brought up the subject of sex with you, I can assure you he spends a lot of time thinking about it.

Please do not think you can rely on a health class at school to teach your kids about sex. Lessons in anatomy and how to put on a condom are not at the core of a teen's quest for sexual information. I am not denying that teenagers are bristling with sexual feelings and immense curiosity, but their questions go way beyond the sexual act. Teenagers want to know about love and what makes a relationship work. Like the teen who is asking this question, they are wondering: "Can I talk to my parents? Do they have anything relevant to say to me?"

A question like this is actually contains the seeds of good news. As I explained earlier, teens can learn a lot from understanding their parent's mistakes — especially sexual mistakes. Admitting your mistakes, blind spots, foolish choices, and misconceptions as well as why your relationships failed is actually a gold mine of information for your child. When children have real information about what their parents learned from their failures, they are not nearly as likely to repeat their patterns.

Teens want to know what makes relationships work. On the other side of the equation, they want to know what makes them unravel. Share your successes as well as failures. Whether you are married, divorced, or remarried, you can provide firsthand information about love and relationships. While part of that discussion has to include sex and how you made your decisions about sex, ultimately the sex act cannot be separated from love and relationships.

For example, it you had sex before you were married, I do recommend you tell your teen. Teenagers are old enough to know about certain family secrets. Use good judgment; your whole past need not be put on display. Your goal is to explain what it meant to give up your virginity then and what you understand about it now. Core to this discussion should also be what it meant to give away your body to someone with no future commitment. If you don't think that will get your kid's attention, then think again.

After you have gone through your story, get right down to the big ethical issues that spring from sex and your relationships. After all, that is what your teen wants to know about. Use these seven points as starters:

1. Discuss what you think you have learned from your experience.
2. Describe how the loss of your virginity affected your relationship and future relationships.
3. Tell your teen what you thought you were doing when you gave yourself away the first time.
4. Let your teen know whether you were pressured or not.
5. If drugs were involved, that too should be discussed. How did that affect your relationship?
6. Discuss what your boyfriend/girlfriend said to you when the issue of sex first came up, and what you said to him/her.
7. Why did you break up, and what did you feel when you broke up?

Then ask:

- "Do you think there is a difference between having sex and being in love?"
- "Why do you think some people wait until they're married to have sex?"
- "Do you think guys see having sex differently than girls do?"
- "Do you feel pressured to have sex? If so, who is putting on the pressure?"

These are just a few sample questions — add your own. Still, remember: No matter how good the discussion is between you and your teen, do not assume that she will not experiment sexually, though studies have shown that the more parents discuss intimate issues with their teenagers, the more likely teenagers aare to wait to have sex. Even after all your advice, your teen may still go out and make mistakes. Teens do have sex, they do get pregnant, and they do get sexually transmitted diseases. If any of these do happen, your teen will need your love, support, and understanding more than ever. Families must stick together. You don't have to approve of your child's sexual choices, but your love must remain.

One further item to note: If you are a parent who has had a life filled with troubled relationships, do not despair. The litter pile of failed relationships and serious events that shattered lives can become a new garden where strong and wholesome relationships can flourish for you and your children. Whatever limitations you had in the past do not have to be present in your future. Limitations, in the end, are nothing more than opportunities to open new doors.

Let me remind you that *who you are is good enough*. To dream of the person you would have liked to have been is to waste the person you are now. I assume, of course, that you are now attending to your life, have gotten any help you need, and are heading in a new direction that includes your child. You have to trust me on this one. I have seen far too many family successes to steer you wrong. Perceived negatives can be turned into positive messages and lessons.

When the day arrives and your teen comes to you to talk about a mistake or serious problem they are having, you will receive the blessing of parenthood. Being blessed as a parent is being blessed with a child who genuinely seeks you out and values your advice.

"Why is sex considered the most important part of a relationship?"

I would put this question among the top ten things kids ask me, and aside from it being one of the most popular ones, it is also one of the most troubling. Many teens do believe the most important part of a relationship is sex — that it is the gateway to love. How has this happened? How do kids end up thinking this is the case?

While teens today do talk to each other about sex, they have few discussions about relationships. And it's no wonder. Parents rarely talk to teens about what is behind good relationships. TV, films, and the music industry, on the other hand, sell a lot of sex. Since no one is really talking about relationships, and since nature abhors any vacuum, that vacuum gets filled — mostly — with sex. Adding fuel to the fire is the adolescent's powerful, awakened drive of reproductive biology. Yes, we have made sex very popular in our society. And to what end? We're raising a generation of kids who think sex is the main feature of relationships — and whose own adult relationships will be in danger of heading to the statistical pile of broken marriages in America.

If this is your teen's question, what can you say to get a conversation going? You might want to use some version of two questions I ask teens:

- "Why do you say sex is the most important thing here?"
- "Does anyone talk to you about sex and relationships?"

What are kids' answers to these questions? When I ask them, they generally comment, "Sex is what we see and what we know about," or "What relationships? My mom and dad are split up," or "All my folks do is fight and seldom talk to me," or "My folks are just too busy."

If you think about it for a moment, you will see that by asking your teen questions — even just these first two — you are already way ahead of the curve. You are showing your teen that you are not too busy. You are not always fighting. You are talking. Just by asking a few questions, you have gone against the trend of noninvolvement with your teen. You will be able to get to the issues that are important to you and your child.

The real dope is that your teen wants to talk to you, wants to find out what you know. How do you get this across? Give your child a message that lives, breathes, and speaks about your own experiences with sex and relationships. You don't have to be a relationship expert, not at all. You only have to share what you know, what you have learned in your own life. Let your teen in on what has worked for you — and what hasn't. Share experiences that helped you understand the difference between sex and love. Always remember that having these conversations does not necessarily mean your child will remain chaste, but it may help her understand what is real in a relationship, and what is simply a high feeling.

Continue your discussion by asking some of the following questions. They are blunt and go straight to the issue. Use your own words, but get right to the point. The idea is simple: If you ask some of the following questions, you will end up talking about relationships. There are a lot of questions here, and you probably won't ask all of them. Use them as your guide.

- "Do you think, or do your friends think, it is okay to have sex on the first date?"

- "What does sex mean to you?"
- "How do your friends view sex?"
- "How do you know someone loves you?"
- "Does having sex mean you are in love?"
- "Who has to 'put out' first to show their love?"
- "Who should press for the sex?"
- "Does having oral sex mean you are in love?"
- "Does having sexual intercourse mean you are in a relationship? Does that mean you love each other?"
- "How do you think you'll know you are in love?"
- "Does it matter if you are in a relationship, or it is just okay to have sex and forget the relationship?"
- "Where do your friends stand on all these issues?"
- "Where are relationships in all of this?"
- "Who talks about relationships?"

I trust you see the point here — it is to ask as many questions as you can each time you have a discussion. Questions, in the end, drive the point home. They will make your teen think. You can also take each question your teen asks and break it down into more questions. Kids who have the opportunity to talk issues out are informed kids. Your job is to keep plugging away with the questions — which will help your teen exercise her own wisdom and explore her own sense of right and wrong — and add in bits and pieces of your life experience. In the end, that will make the difference.

"When is a good time to have sex? My friends say I'll know when I'm ready, but that doesn't help at all."

All questions dealing with sex are eye-openers, but some more than others. This is one of those questions. It also happens to be one of the top ten questions teens ask me.

If you are a parent who is extremely uneasy speaking about sex — and there are probably few of us who aren't — remember the tip I offered earlier, which has always allowed me to push forward in spite of fear. If you can't at least *act as if* you are not afraid, simply admit that this topic is embarrassing and hard for you — then talk about it anyway. And if your teen approaches you with this particular question, first and foremost, be thankful you have the opportunity to discuss sex with her before she has lost her virginity.

It is clear from the question, and the popularity of it, that teens feel pressured to have sex. What is also clear is that your teen's friends are the first avenue for advice in this category. Now you, as a parent, have your chance.

If your teen comes to you with this question, keep in mind that he really *wants* your opinion on whether or not he should have sex. He also wants to know the reasons why he should not have sex. Otherwise, he wouldn't have asked the question in the first place.

Here's another hint for you as a parent: Never take a question at face value. Always assume it will be the starting point for talking about many issues. It may be that right now your teen is being pressured to have sex. You won't get down to basics if you do not ask, "Why is this question coming up now?" Still, don't expect your teen to openly discuss her sexual habits. I only mention this because often parents try to pry everything out of their child, and I want to remind you that lectures and interrogations are off limits. Parents have to work hard to maintain a two-sided discussion. Heading in the other direction effectively cuts your teen out of the conversation, decreasing the chances she will seek you out for further dialogue.

So, how might you start a conversation on this question? How do you discuss losing virginity, having sex, and what all that means? First of all, every discussion needs to start with you asking more questions. I recommend asking ones along the following lines:

- "Do you think you need to have sex now? Why?"
- "Who told you sex is important, and why?"
- "What do you think your friends mean when they say you'll know when you're ready?"
- "Is someone pressuring you to have sex?"
- "How important do you think being a virgin is?"
- "Do you think you can be in a relationship without having sex?"

The purpose of these questions is to get teens to begin making choices and thinking about sex on their own. Every parent wants their kid to make positive choices in life. Parents want their kids to live by positive values. Values do not arise in a vacuum. Issues of sex, unattached to values, mean nothing more than the sexual act. Virginity, when not attached to values, is nothing much more than a biological term. We cheapen life by not talking about what important events mean, and I encourage you to raise this with your teen. What *is* love? Why *is* virginity important? How can sex, when not experienced within the realm of a respectful, trusting relationship, be harmful?

I hope you'll notice that these are not questions that have a tidy, "one-size-fits-all" kind of response. Instead, in order to discuss these topics effectively and honestly with your teen, you'll have to search your heart and consider your own experiences to find your responses to and feelings about these questions. What have *you* learned to be true? Were you harmed by losing your virginity? How? Have you had your heart broken by someone who took advantage of your willingness to have sex in hopes of finding love? It's this information that teens will find most useful in making their own tough choices. What has happened to others? How did that make them feel? Could that happen to me?

By sharing your experiences and opinions, and showing your teen how they guided you and helped you make decisions, you are not only giving him practical information, but you are also passing along your values — *real* family values tested by and built upon true experience, not just a glib catch phrase like those peppered throughout political campaigns. These values, passed down from generation to generation by transmitting the real experiences and stories of your family, are critical to any discussion with your teen.

Since every family is different, every family's values are different, too. It's up to you to decide what information is important to you and what will help your teen make the best, most responsible decisions she can. Make clear your values and be precise as you talk to your teen about sex and relationships. Let her know where you stand, what you believe, and why. In your discussion, always bring up not just your opinion, but important events or incidents in your life that relate, as directly as possible, to the issue at hand — in this case, when it's "time" to have sex for the first time. It is in telling these stories that you will have the opportunity to transmit your values. For emphasis, I like to add at the end of any story the statement, "And that is why we value _____," which very clearly drives the point home. I conclude by saying, "This is what our family believes, and that is why I told you that story when you asked me your question."

By using stories to emphasize values, you will be able to give your teen the independent strength to make strong ethical decisions. Naturally, some of your stories will be about mistakes you made. Every parent wants his or her teen to learn from mistakes. Your mistakes are the best example to teach this very point. The more you emphasize that in your conversations, the more your teenager will understand that he too can thrive and grow with life despite — and often because of — making a wrong turn in the road. And most of all, he'll know that when he stumbles, he can come and talk to you.

"Is it wrong to want sex right now, as a teenager?"

This question is another one of the most common questions I am asked by teens. Its variations are many:

- *"What age should I have sex at?"*
- *"Who should I have sex with — someone experienced, or a virgin, like me?"*
- *"What if I don't want to have sex? Is that okay?"*

Why is this one of the top ten questions? I think most parents know the answer. All you have to do is travel down memory lane back to puberty and the first time you had a heavy crush on someone. Do you even remember the person of your fantasy? Probably not. The point is, you and your friends thought a lot about sex. The teen years are a time when sexual desire makes its debut on center stage. Sexual imagination almost grows in lockstep with puberty — it's as if biology downloads the whole issue of sex. It is then sold by the media and endlessly discussed and joked about by teens. Sex is all over the place.

Certainly, wanting sex is not wrong. Yet consider this: My informal survey of thousands of high school students around the country reveals that nearly 100 percent of teenagers know someone who is sexually active. However, when asked, about 40 percent of those same teens say those friends (or they themselves) regret giving up their virginity. When asked why they regret it, they simply say, "There is more to relationships than sex," or "I thought sex would mean more, and it doesn't." You can preempt some of this regret by getting your teen to think about these issues ahead of time — by looking at sex in the context of one's *feelings,* not just the act.

As you begin your discussion with your teen, ask some questions to get her thinking along these lines and to help her consider what she already believes. Here are some suggestions:

- "What does it mean to have sex with someone?"
- "How do you think that would affect you? The other person?"
- "What do you think happens to your feelings when you give up your virginity?"
- "Do you think there is any difference between casual sex and sex in a relationship?"
- "Do you think it's okay to be in a relationship and have sex, yet know you are never going to marry that person?"

When talking with your teenager about this question, you also need to ask:

- "Why is it important for you to want sex now?"
- "What would it mean to you to have sex now?"
- "What do you think you want in a (or this particular) relationship?"
- And finally, "Do you think having sex now will mean you'll get those things? Can you think of ways it might not?"

Parents need to remember their own teen years. They also need to remember that on a very basic level, their teen is keenly feeling his sexuality. Teens' bodies pulsate at times with sex. It can be embarrassing and even annoying, especially to boys. Of course it is not wrong to *want* sex — it's perfectly natural, especially at this age. But the question your teen is asking is actually part of a much bigger issue. The real question is when, under what circumstances, and with whom to *have* sex. So share: What did you learn from giving up your virginity? Do you wish you had waited to do so? Why? Did having sex help your relationship or hurt it? Did you think having sex would mean more than it did?

Discuss these issues with your teen, and she will be able to see sex in a new context. Having such discussions does not mean that teens will never experiment sexually. However, if they do, they will tend to do so at an older age and will have a greater capacity to learn from any mistake or inevitable broken heart that occurs.

"How do I know if I am truly in love?"

Teenage romance is alive and well. It may seem like a cliché, at this point in your life, to insist there is a difference between love and infatuation, but it's a distinction that is still lost on young people today — and not-so-young people, for that matter. The intense, crushing feelings that come with attraction — and the rejection of affection — are so powerful to young people hit with them for the first time that it seems they cannot be anything less than love. The tidal wave of emotion caused by desire — the almost-physical pain of yearning — surely must be more than infatuation. Just try to convince someone in the throes of such intensity that love is really something deeper, quieter, less thrilling perhaps, but deeply rewarding and satisfying — who wants that? It's this heady, exciting delirium that must be love.

This is a very important question, especially for kids who are "hooked up" in what they see as a serious relationship. It's also a very important question for teens who may be trapped in a serious relationship. On the outside, this question may seem about love, but on the inside, it might also be about questioning or "breaking up" the love. (If that turns out to be the case, read the questions on the following pages, which deal with effectively breaking up with someone.)

Some teens really do believe that their current love will last forever. Yet how frequently do high school relationships last much longer than graduation? College and other plans pull young people in opposite directions. Especially at this age, self-discovery and an awareness of a world beyond what they have grown up with lead to lasting change and development. It's not often that teenage relationships survive this — and that's fine. Heartbreaking, sometimes, but usually for the best. Perhaps the best thing you can offer a teen who is asking about love is acknowledgment that this happens, and if it happens to him, assurance that this is a natural part of finding lasting love, and that more, much more, is out there to be found.

Many kids are keenly aware of the fragility of relationships already. Maintaining a successful relationship is not an easy thing to do, and people in general are not very good at it. The divorce rate hovers around 50 percent, and the fallout from all this divorce takes a toll on children. As I've found in my surveys of teens, while most teenagers do want to get married, only about 20 percent think they will have fulfilling marriages.

Too often, I have found that teens think that one of the keys to successful love and marriage is having the best or "hottest" sex. I have had hours of talk with groups of teenagers on this very topic. Why do they make that connection? Why do so many believe the relationship they may be in now, as a teen, will last forever? The answer is simple. No one has sat down and talked personally with them about love, relationships, and married life.

Whether your teen is in a serious relationship or not, it is important to talk with him about these things. Begin your discussion by asking your teen:

- "Do you think you're in love?"
- "What do you think love means?"
- "What do you think a good, loving relationship looks like?"
- "How do you recognize it?"
- "Do you think you are going to spend the rest of your life with your current boyfriend/girlfriend?"

Tough questions for sure. A lot of parents do not really know the key to lasting relationships — they may never have experienced one themselves. Who sat down and talked to you about your loves? Did one of your parents spend a few hours with you talking about what makes a good relationship? Or did you learn, through trial and error, just what love *wasn't*? Be assured that no matter what its source, you have important information to give your teen.

In this question, your teen is really asking you, "What do you know about love and relationships?" He wants to know the connection between sex and love. Whether you are or have been in a successful relationship or not, you have an enormous amount of life experience to contribute to this discussion. If you are divorced, you have a wealth of information to share with your teen about what you have learned about love, about thinking you were in love and finding out you were not, or about being in love, then having something go terribly wrong.

Your teen generally knows about your successes. What she needs to know is how you handled your mistakes and failures in life. She needs to know what you learned and how you grew wiser from your failures. Your experience won't preclude her own inevitable process of trial and error, but it might help prevent a divorce down the road.

If you haven't sorted through your own understanding about love, now is a good time to do it. Thank your teen for bringing up such an important issue. Be bold. Tell him you want to share with him your mistakes, and that you hope your discussion about love and relationships will be something that will benefit both of you, for a lifetime. Teens do not expect from you the ABCs of love. They do, however, want to understand what makes a good relationship and what doesn't.

I hope that this question will evolve into ongoing discussion between you and your teen. An absence of discussion leaves children only with what they have seen in their home, with no interpretation or explanation. They will absorb and basically use as a yardstick what they saw you do — healthy or not. Surely every parent has time to comment about his or her views on love, whether their own experiences have been positive or otherwise. It will teach your teen, and remind you, that we can count the lessons learned from negative experiences as rungs up the ladder of progress.

"Why are guys who have sex looked upon as being 'cool' and girls who have sex called 'sluts' or 'whores'?"

It is tough to see this question staring at you and then realize that your kid's peer group generally does relate to girls as "sluts" or "whores." It makes you wonder how successful we have been in getting away from sexual stereotypes and demeaning language. This kind of talk can be found in any school. And interestingly, this is another one of those top ten questions that always generates a huge discussion.

Teens tell me some interesting things about calling girls *sluts* and *whores*. First of all, seldom has anyone — adult or student — challenged teenagers to lift their language and attitudes out of the garbage. You occasionally hear a politician bring up the issue. But kids tell me this is not an agenda item discussed at home. I challenge kids to step up and refuse to let low-down, demeaning language be used in their circle of friends. I suggest you do the same.

Interestingly, teenagers tell me that no one really likes calling girls *sluts* and *whores*. So, why do they do it so regularly? Believe it or not, a lot of parents speak this way. Slippage occurs everywhere. Going along with the crowd — or the family — is always the easy route until someone says, "Hey, stop and think. The ones you're hurting are you and me" ("Gangsta's Paradise," performed by Coolio, *Dangerous Minds* Original Motion Picture Soundtrack, MCA Records, 1995).

A lot of rap music and rock music that demeans girls makes its way onto MTV. Record stores are filled with this music. We have gone from locker-room culture to mainstream culture quickly and easily in the past decade — it is now a huge, lucrative industry. But as you may be aware of by this point, I do not believe in making culture the culprit. To me, culture simply reflects our values or lack of them. I am interested always in empowering families. No concert or rock station can overtake the values of an involved parent.

It is up to you to set a standard. And be assured that if you are asked this question by your teen, what you're really getting is a covert signal that he does not want to fall into the bad language trap. Obviously, telling him, "Watch your mouth" or "clean up your language" is not going to accomplish anything. He will, however, welcome discussing the whole issue with you. Ironic, isn't it? While the media leads us to believe that teens live and want to live a life apart from parents, the truth is that you are the most important person in your teen's life. Not only that, but your teen eagerly awaits talking with you. Not necessarily all the time, but definitely when an important question like this comes up.

Now let me ask a question of you: What do you do if *you* are the one who is guilty of using offensive language? Simple: Cut it out. You do not need to see a counselor to wash out your mouth. Change your language, and your teen will tone down what is coming out of her mouth, too. If you let her know you are willing to change, she will try to do the same — in fact, she will mark your change as an important lesson in her life. Remember: every situation you find yourself in with your child is a new opportunity to teach her something positive about life.

If your teen uses this offensive language or, as this questions asks, wants to know why people are speaking this way today, here is what I recommend asking to bring the issue into focus:

- "Do your friends use the words *slut* or *whore*? Have you?"
- "Why do you think they do that? Why do you do it?"
- "What do you think about it?"
- "Why do you think guys get away with being 'saints' while calling girls sluts?"

Questions like these generate a profound discussion about sexually stereotyping others and hurting others' feelings. You don't even have to wait to bring this up. Just turn on any local rap station and have your teen sit down with you and tell you what the singer is saying. The discussion will flow with ease. Next, take your questions to an even more personal level by asking, "What do you think happens to someone's feelings or reputation when *you* call them names like that?" The goal is to get your teenager to think about the direct impact of things he regularly does or hears. The goal is to get him thinking, "Is what I say or what others say important?"

Another way to drive this point home is to ask questions that might shock them. Shock value questions really get teens to think — I use them all the time at my seminars. As the discussion deepens, consider asking

- "Do you think it's okay to call your mother a slut or a whore?"
- "Do you think it's cool for your friends to call your sister, or your best friend's sister, a slut?"
- "What do you think it's like for a girl to be called that to her face? Could you do that? Have you ever done that?"
- "Has someone ever called one of your friends a slut? What did you do when that happened?"

Not only do personal questions like these make abstract issues clearer and more real, but they also allow you to bring in examples from your own life. I guarantee you that these types of questions will reveal how words hurt others. Your teen will get it. The conversation must be personal. If not, nothing much will be accomplished.

The idea here is to support and challenge your child to put a stop to using demeaning language with her friends. Even if she never uses these words, you can empower her, as I do at my seminars, to make a pact with her friends to clean up their language.

And again, if you are a parent who uses words to hurt others, this is a wonderful time for you to tell your teen that you, too, are going to stop using words that hurt, demean, and put down others. I truly believe the reason these kinds of nasty comments have become so common is that parents simply have not taken the time to set up the standard for their children. Teens know words hurt others. To empower them to change, parents have to bring these issues out of the darkroom and into the light of day. This will only happen through open discussion with your teen.

So let your child know that in your family, you do not use or no longer will use words to hurt others. Teens might be surrounded by despicable language in today's culture, but if they know they come from a family that does not use that kind of language, they will never feel that they have to completely give in and follow the crowd.

"What is wrong with wanting sex when you are wasted?"

In my work, I find it refreshing that teenagers trust me enough to say what is on their minds. This is not to say that their questions don't disturb me. I'd be terrified if one of my kids asked me this question — it would make any parent wring his hands. Difficult as it is, though, no issue should ever be avoided. Real trouble happens when you ignore your teen's questions.

Please do not start panicking and lecturing when you are faced with a very tough question, like this one. Remember, you can always let your teen know how hard or uncomfortable it is for you to discuss sex — I guarantee that revealing your discomfort will make it easier for you both to talk. It will take some of the pressure off you. However, it is also okay to fall apart and feel helpless for a while. I confess that happens even to me. It's okay to tell your teen you need a little time to think before you discuss such questions — but make sure the communication doesn't end there. What is important is that you actually have that discussion.

Teenagers do indeed have sex when they are stoned or drunk. When they do, the risk for sexually transmitted diseases, pregnancy, and host of other problems goes up. The myth that sex is better with drugs still persists. Kids tell other kids, "Sex on dope is a big high. It's the best."

Some teens use drugs to take advantage of others and get what they want sexually. With the rise of "date rape" drugs like Rohypnol, it even makes the headlines. Keep in mind that in my survey, nearly 100 percent of teens have friends who are sexually active. Nearly 100 percent of them have friends who have oral sex regularly. And nearly 100 percent of them know someone who uses drugs or even has a drug problem. Clearly, there are kids who mix sex with drugs.

Mixing chemical cocktails with sex is risky business. If your teenager has asked you this question, fasten your seat belt — there is a lot to discuss. Let me first talk about the issue in general, then give you suggestions about what to say and ask.

Why is your teen asking this question? Do not assume it's because he *likes* to have sex when wasted. If it does turn out that your kid is *regularly* getting wasted and having sex, you need to seek professional help — a chemical dependence issue may need to be dealt with. Regardless, any child involved in high-risk sex is blind to his own personal safety, as well as the risk it places on others. Therapy is needed. And remember, I am not talking about a one-time mistake: Trouble means a *persistent* pattern of behavior.

Mixing sex with drugs means taking sexual advantage of another. As we've already seen, the whole issue of having or not having sex is a big one for teens. Adding drugs makes it even bigger and more troubling. Teens know about rape, but there are myths about date rape. Teens know about high-risk sex and some of its consequences, but they often don't see themselves as fitting the profile of someone who engages in that type of behavior. In addition, any discussion of sex they might have regarding the dangers of engaging in chancy sexual behavior is often too clinical, lacking in personal impact, or becomes a morality lecture that does little more than shame and blame.

This question has many layers. Before you panic, remember that it's very likely that it's one of your teen's friends, and not your teen herself, who sees nothing wrong with having sex while wasted, and your teen is trying to develop her own opinion on this issue. In order to dig deeper, ask the following:

- "Who is telling you it is okay to have sex when you are wasted?"
- "Is this something you are doing? Is it something you have seen or heard about?"
- "If not, is there a particular reason you want to know about this?"

Where are these questions heading? Toward a discussion of ethics and consequences. What do I mean by discussing ethics? I mean that here, your job is to get your teen thinking about what he says and does. Personalize all discussions as quickly as possible, placing your teen in various scenarios. Don't hesitate to use very tough and attention-getting questions, like the ones that follow. They will drive your

point home, get your teen to think, and get right to the heart of this issue:
- "Let's say you, your friend, or someone you know thinks it's okay to have sex while wasted. What about the partner involved in this? Does she have a say?"

- "Imagine this partner is your sister. Do you think it's okay for some guy to get your sister loaded and then have sex with her?"

Parents must open the door to real-life conversations with their children. If you don't do that, how will your teen ever wrestle with real-life ethical issues? By dropping a bombshell question into the discussion, you will have a basis from which you can talk with your teen about the entire issue. I do this all the time at my seminars with students. It works. If you want your teen to think about important issues, make the discussion hit home.

There are other ways to discuss sex and ethics. You do not have to wait for your teen to ask you. At the dinner table or in the car, for example, take advantage of stories that appear in the newspaper. If you see a court case about date rape, or an article on high-risk sex among teens, talk about It. Ask your teen for her opinion. Have her tell you what she knows about the issue. Also ask her what her friends are saying. If her friends are over, bring them into the discussion. What you will discover is that this kind of talk is welcomed and valued.

My three kids often have told me how our discussions were helpful in their life. Teens like to be in the know. They like to make a difference in their friends' lives. Let them know they are being raised in a family that takes the time to talk about key issues.

"What is wrong with oral sex? I mean, we are not having intercourse."

Parents, take a deep breath. Yes, this is another one of those questions you did not want to hear and certainly do not want to answer. But parents *do* need to talk to their teens about oral sex. More kids have oral sex today than sexual intercourse — kids as young as twelve and thirteen. It is extremely common, and it can be just as risky as sexual intercourse if done without protection. In a recent survey of teens by the Centers for Disease Control, it was reported that approximately three million teens, or about one in four sexually experienced teens, acquire a sexually transmitted disease every year (*Newsweek,* May 8, 2000). There's no way around it. You are going to have to talk about oral sex with your kid. Remember that sexual intercourse is not the "in" thing; oral sex is.

Like so many others, this topic does not fall into any comfort zone. Before we go any further, let me remind you that the key to discussing tough topics is to rely on the Parenting Principle that says, "Admit your feelings of discomfort in discussing the 'hot topics.' Talk about them anyway." Sharing your vulnerabilities builds your teen's character. It helps him learn to make wise decisions. Even if you feel you can't do it, you have put your toe in the water and talk.

Where do you begin? First, find out who is encouraging the sex. This is important. Often, sexual relations between teens are the result of demands for sex or pressure to have sex. Bearing this in mind, ask your child:

- "Have you ever felt pressured to have oral sex?"
- "Have you ever felt your relationship depended on having it?"
- "Has anyone ever talked to you about oral sex?"

If it's clear your child already has been having oral sex, you might want to move along to more direct, engaging questions like the following:

- "Do you feel okay about 'going down' on your boyfriend or girlfriend?" (Yes, that's the common term.)
- "Who asked for it first?"
- "Is it important for your relationship to do this? If so, why?"
- "Are you having unprotected oral sex? If so, why?"
- "Are you at all worried about sexually transmitted diseases?"

At some point, your discussion will focus on your concerns about your teen's health. AIDS and other sexually transmitted diseases are contracted through unprotected sex, including oral sex. Many teens think sexually transmitted diseases are only acquired through unprotected intercourse. In fact, many do not think oral sex is sex at all. To them, only intercourse is sex. Everything else is just "fooling around."

Your goal is to open the door for an honest and frank talk about relationships. Again, I recommend that you bring in some of your own personal experiences regarding dating, pressure to have sex, and choosing to have sex — or not — in whatever form it may take. Why are these stories important? They get your teen's attention. They make your discussion relevant and meaningful. When facing tough decisions, your child will know what happened to you, what you did, and how you understand your experiences today. Will your personal disclosure stop him from having sex? Perhaps. Teens who have some knowledge about how their parents handled their personal relationships are more likely to make strong ethical decisions for their own life. And don't forget to tell your child your hopes and dreams for his relationships.

Finally and most important, remind your teen that if she gets into trouble or crosses a barrier in a sexual relationship that puts her at risk, she can come and talk to you. You want your teen to speak to you about anything and everything, anytime and anyplace — especially after a major mistake has been made. While you might not change your teenager's sexual relationships, you can at least know that if trouble strikes, it will not remain a secret. Secrets are toxic.

"I was at a party, and I saw one of my friends go upstairs to have sex when I knew she didn't really want to. What can I tell her next time? She could have gotten raped or something up there."

Rephrased, this question reads, *"What do I do if I or one of my friends gets into a sexual situation that could be real trouble? How can I get out of it?"* Kids can and do get in over their heads. Even with all your good advice, bad things can happen. The most tragic situation is one in which your child gets into serious trouble and does not feel she has permission to call you or speak to you about it.

When addressing this question, be straightforward and to the point. Guys *can* get out of control. Booze and drugs can distort situations. Sexual assaults are way too common. Before giving your daughter some pointers, make sure let her know how strongly you love and support her. I would say something like the following to the teen who asked this question:

"I am really proud of you for worrying about your friend. If you ever get into a situation where a guy won't stop and something happens, make sure you come to me. I know it will not be your fault. I love you, and I will help you. Call me in the middle of the night if you have to — I will come and get you."

In this question, your daughter is asking for more than conversation: She wants some clear-cut advice from you. She wants to know what she or her friends should do if they are getting pressured to have sex. I suggest you tell her the following:

1. If the guy starts to force you to do something sexual, say "No!" Sometimes loudly and firmly saying "No!" can be enough to make him know you're serious. Don't smile or joke about it. *No* means *no*.

2. If you can, get out of there. Make excuses. Say you have to use the bathroom or get something from your bag or your coat. Then leave and get to a safe place.

3. If you are stuck, start talking. Try to get him to see you as a person, not an object. Talk about your family or friends, your pet, anything that will humanize you in his eyes. Go on and on. Keep talking. When you have a chance, get out of there.

4. Don't panic. Use your head. When you have a plan, act quickly.

5. Last but not least, try never to put yourself into a compromising situation. Don't go up to a guy's bedroom. Avoid parking with him in out-of-the-way places. Know your limits and keep to them.

Parents often ask me if I think it is a good idea for their daughters to take a self-defense course. It is. Knowing a few quick, devastating moves puts the element of surprise in your favor. It builds confidence, too, even if you never have to use it. I also recommend you read books by Gavin de Becker. His advice about handling fearful situations is invaluable.

"I'm pretty sure I'm gay. I need someone to talk to about this. How can I tell my parents?"

This is one tough spot for any kid. Teens who are confused about their sexuality and who suspect they are gay desperately ask, "What am I going to do? Who can I talk to?" These are valid questions:

Who *can* they talk to about their confusion? How are they going to decide if they are gay? How are they going to find some peace with their sexuality?

I understand that this is a difficult issue for any parent to deal with. However, as hard as it may be for a parent, it is worse for a child. Gay kids live in a social nightmare. Gay jokes, gay bashing, and pointed, off-the-wall comments fill school hallways and teen conversations. Words like *faggot* and *fag* or simple joking comments such as "That's so gay" are prevalent. To make matters worse, everywhere gay kids turn, they regularly hear — even from their parents — that being gay is bad. They deduce that if you are gay, you'd better keep it a secret.

But secrets are dangerous. Sexual secrets are especially toxic, and they can become deadly. The isolation gay teens experience is extremely profound and dangerous — their life is a secretive living hell that often includes depression and suicidal ideation. Gay teens, or kids who think they are gay, have a need bordering on desperation to talk to a parent. But too often, their parents either give negative signals or, worse yet, openly express hatred toward gay people. Make no mistake about it. Gay kids "in the closet" are tremendously at risk.

Most parents have such a hard time dealing with their kid's sexuality anyway, that I wish there were something I could say to make this issue in particular easier. But my best advice, hard as it may be to take, is this: If your teen comes to you with this question, I urge you to be a parent who does not turn away, shut the door, or condemn your child through negative stereotyping. Of course this is tough. But your child needs you. All children need to know they can come to a parent in their desperate hours.

A few years ago I decided that, at all my workshops, I would bring up the gay teen issue and try to lend a hand to parents who truly are silenced by cultural shame. Put bluntly, gay teenagers are dying because of negativity and silence. It is time that parents stop being manipulated by slogans and by people who demonize children. History has taught us enough lessons about what happens when we label others "defective."

However, I have no solution for parents who truly believe anyone who is gay is deviant and evil. All I can do is warn you not to alienate your child. Kids ought to be able to turn to parents for help. Sadly, with gay kids, this does not often seem to be the case. Still, families *can* find common ground that is acceptable to parents and gay kids alike. The key to making that happen, however, is this: Families have to be respected enough to be left alone to work out their own problems. Anti-gay bias from communities, extended family members, political groups, and religious organizations needs to be left outside the house. Parents and kids must have the privacy to talk and work out their own dilemmas.

Parents, do not be ashamed if your child is gay. The only real shame should come from not making room to discuss this issue with your child, and not allowing your child to stay part of the family. I am not saying that you have to be thrilled if your child tells you she is gay. I understand that it changes much of the family vision. But to face the inevitable struggles ahead, your child will need your support and understanding. It does not mean you have to completely understand your child's sexual orientation, either. It's okay to have problems with the whole issue — but you still need to love and accept your child.

What that means is that you strive to have a loving relationship with your teen. In healthy families, anything and everything can be discussed. Do not hesitate to get counseling for the entire family. Social service agencies in every city have competent counselors who can assist your family. I want to warn you, however, to avoid therapists that claim they can change your child's sexual orientation. They only put your child at further risk by underscoring the idea that being gay is bad, that your child is not acceptable as he is. Not only is that unethical, it is dangerous. For research documentation, query the American Psychological Assocation.

I am not naive enough to believe that every child who thinks she is gay is indeed gay. However, in the hands of a good therapist, most everything that needs to be will get explored, including sexual orientation. Your job as a parent is to make room for your child to discover who she is. Do not make her have to choose between herself and your family.

Even if you are terrified of discovering your child is gay, it is all right to communicate your fear to him. Loving your child does not mean you have to accept with open arms everything he does. No parent ever adores all their kid's attitudes and actions. Fear, however, should never undo the ties of love between parents and children.

If your child is gay, get some assistance. Stay open. Take time to really understand the issue. Make room for your child to explore and understand her sexuality. Will it be difficult? For many families, yes, it will. Don't expect much support from most social quarters. Be constantly aware of how important your acceptance and love are to your child. The life of a gay teen in many American high schools is not pleasant. It can be demeaning and even dangerous. How you support your child through this time will make a huge difference in your teen's life. Search your heart, and do not let your child down.

For those parents who cannot accept their gay teen, there is little I can say to you in this book. Rejection of your teen leaves him at a terrible risk. As hard as it may be for you, take six months — or better, a year — and get some therapy. Seek out a support group to help you cope with your struggle. Read and read and read. Try to educate yourself. Keep anyone who has negative and dangerous attitudes toward gays out of the loop. You devoted years to raising your child. Don't let someone else's opinion negate that.

"How do I tell my friends I'm gay? How will they react?"

First of all, let's be realistic. There are a lot of gay teens in America. Unfortunately, most gay teens are underground in their families. Being a teenager on a daily basis is hard enough, but being a gay teen puts life stress off the charts. While generally, in society, things may be getting better for gays, being a gay teen is still dangerous today — so dangerous that the suicide rate for gay kids is extremely high.

If you are the parent of a gay teen, please read the previous section, which discusses the question "I'm pretty sure I'm gay . . . how can I tell my parents?" Please do not use religion or politics to lay down the law in your discussion with your teen. Do not let anyone, under any circumstances, move you away from your relationship with your child. This is a private family matter and not to be worked out in public.

Having said that, I think I can safely assume that the student who asked the question raised here has already told his family. Now, the question is about telling his friends. This student has probably sought some counseling and worked through some of the basic issues. Despite all this, be aware that this is one tough question to tackle.

Many quarters of our country do not accept gay or lesbian kids. My experience in discussing this issue with teens is that they are more open in their acceptance of their gay peers than society in general, although I certainly haven't traveled and spoken to students everywhere. At the same time, most teens tell me that while they personally could accept a gay friend, the general school environment for gay teens is not a place where "coming out" would be welcomed with open arms.

If your child is gay, it is important that you do your homework with your teen before he decides to "come out" to his friends. By homework, I mean reading up on other families' experiences in these situations. There are many articles available on the Internet that discuss the issue of gay teens coming out to their friends. Literature and support can be found in various gay alliance groups and social service agencies in most major cities. I suggest using them.

There is no simple answer to this question. Fear constantly feeds anti-gay sentiment in this country. Gay bashing is still far too common. If your teenager decides to swing open the door to her friends, there will be consequences. I am sorry this is so, but it is the reality in which we live today.

I firmly believe, however, that you can help your teenager understand the potential danger and velocity of reaction that can leap out and threaten him. Talk to others, seek professional counsel, read up on the issue, and gain a solid understanding of the social milieu that you live in. Teens pretty much know their friends' and their social circle's attitudes toward gays. But teens do not know everything. You must step in and add parental guidance. If you live in a community where acceptance of gay people is widespread, you are indeed fortunate. I hope that will be the case. But my job is to raise the "what ifs" and to help you, as a parent, do the same. Clearly, be very careful. I am not an alarmist — I'm speaking about the possibility of real danger.

If your teen brings this question to you, your first conversation ought to be about your child's friends. Be direct and ask:

- "How do you think your friends will react?"
- "Who do you think will stick by you? Who might not?"
- "What will you do if things go badly?"
- "Do you think there is any possibility this might put you in danger?"
- "What will happen at school?"
- "What kind of talk do you already hear in the hallway regarding gays?"
- "Are you prepared emotionally to handle the fallout from 'loose lips'?"

- And finally, "What kind of help and support do you want from me?"

Spend time talking about what might or might not happen at school. Do not be fooled or lulled into a sense of security simply because you and your child have seen TV specials on gay teens and their positive relationships with straight friends. In my experience, this is not generally the norm.

Again, there is no simple response to this question. But hard as it may be, by facing it, you will doing much good where much potential for harm lies. Not only are you discussing this with your teenager, but you are also giving him the opportunity to see you wrestle with your fears and at the same time affirm your love. Both of you are in this together. I know you will have sleepless nights. I know you will endure dark hours. All I can tell you is that the darkest hour is only sixty minutes long.

Difficult as it is, this is a profound and rare opportunity for you, as a parent, to step up to the plate and show by words and deeds how deep support runs in your family. This is a wonderful opportunity to show your child the real meaning of justice, courage, love, understanding, and compassion. Even if you cannot totally accept your teen's sexuality, your assistance is a clear message of your unconditional love. You can demonstrate that real family values translate into action. What a wonderful gift to give your child.

"I am getting ready to break up with my girlfriend. I am afraid she is going to freak out. What should I do to make sure she leaves me alone and doesn't hassle me or get all weird and clingy?"

Teen romance and breakups cause upheaval and often depression. How many popular songs have been written on this very subject? This student not only wants advice on breaking up, but is concerned that the breakup will be difficult. Your goal is to teach your teen to live in the solution, not the problem.

A lot of teens will not come to their parents when they are about to break up with their boyfriend or girlfriend. So if you suspect a breakup is on the horizon, talk to your kid. Explain to her that she needs to be 100 percent clear that the relationship is over. Let her know that leaving the door open — even a little — is not only unfair, but also creates problems and real confusion. Here are some tips to give your teenager:

1. You must make it clear to your boyfriend or girlfriend that the breakup is for real. Tell him or her that your relationship is totally over.
2. When you speak with your boyfriend or girlfriend, don't dwell on how sorry you are to be ending the relationship. Don't make apologies for splitting up. Simply say that the relationship is over.
3. Also make it clear that there is no chance of getting back together. Even if you think that getting back together later on might be possible, do not, under any circumstances, say that.
4. Tell your friends that this relationship is totally over.
5. However, don't gossip about the former relationship. Don't put the other person down. Just make it clear to everyone it is over.

I mention friends in these tips because there are specific things that need to be said to them. They will want to know what happened, but your teen should keep details to the minimum. Gossip is poison. Remind your teen again and again not to stir things up. The ancient adage "Don't throw a stone in the well from which you drink" (Baba Kamma 92B) is very good advice. Self-righteousness is character assassination, and so is gloating over or boasting about "dumping" another person. Tell your teen that when friends ask what happened, she can simply tell them something along the following lines:

1. The other person's feelings in the relationship were stronger than yours.
2. You stopped being happy in the relationship.
3. The relationship is definitely over.

It's also important to cease communication with the ex-partner, again, to make it absolutely clear the relationship is over and there's no chance of reigniting it. No more talking also means no instant messaging on AOL and no e-mail. Emphasize that months later, when things have cooled down, it might be possible to have some kind of communication or even friendship with the ex-boyfriend or -girlfriend, but not during the breakup.

What if calling or e-mailing continues? Tell your teen that if that happens, simply make sure he tells his ex not to call or write again. Remind him that it is over. If his ex writes or says, "I just want to be friends" or "Why can't we be friends?" tell him not to get into a deep discussion. At most, send one more e-mail, and that is it. An emotional response from the ex, involving crying and begging, can be very unsettling. If this happens, encourage your child to stand firm. Remind him simply to say, "The relationship is over. We have broken up. There is nothing more to say."

Of course, this is not easy. Most people naturally want to explain their actions.

But make the point to your teen that the quickest way to get back into trouble is to get into a long conversation. Keep everything simple and clear. No detailed explanations are required. "Silence is a protective fence for wisdom" (Pirke Avot 2:15).

"I broke off my relationship, and no way do I want to get back together again. But I still feel bad that it ended. Why do I feel this way?"

The loss of any relationship requires a time of mourning for everyone involved, even the person who initiated the breakup. Crying and feeling badly is normal and healthy.

Tell your teen that it's normal to feel the way she is feeling. Emphasize, however, that it's not a good idea to share how badly you feel about breaking up. Make it clear to your teen that when a relationship ends, everyone benefits when the breakup is final and complete. By definitely ending her relationship, she makes it easier for everyone to get over it and move on.

Don't be surprised if your teen feels sad after breaking up. He may, in his mind, believe he's the "bad guy" because he ended it. All of this is normal. However, none of these bad feelings mean that he should be back in the relationship. Tell him so. And naturally, if you have been the one who ended a relationship at one time, or have friends who have been in similar circumstances, now is the time to tell that story.

"My ex-boyfriend won't leave me alone. He calls all the time. Shows up in the middle of night. Follows me when I am out with

my friends. I've told him I just want to be friends, but he is beginning to scare me. What should I do? How can I get him to stop?"

When I first went out on the road, I was surprised to see how often teenagers asked me this question. Milder versions get asked, too:

"I went out with this guy just a couple of times, and now he is calling all the time and bothering me in e-mail. I told him to stop, but he just keeps doing it. What should I do?"

I get similar questions from guys:

"My old girlfriend just won't leave me alone. She is always showing up at parties I am at. Writing me notes and slipping them in my locker or leaving them on the windshield of my car. The other night, when I came home late, she was waiting for me. She just won't go away."

Love obsessions that border on stalking don't have to hit the evening news to be a problem. Teenagers who break up with their boyfriends or girlfriends occasionally run into this kind of trouble. Any form of harassment, including stalking, is a problem.

If this is happening to your teen, it is critical that you talk to her right away and put a stop to the harassment. In all but the really scary cases, it is rather easy to put an end to this kind of behavior.

First, let's back up a moment and take another look at the first question that's been raised here. Why has this ex-boyfriend become a problem for this teen? Reread the question carefully, and you'll see there's a preventive step that was missed. "My ex-boyfriend won't leave me alone," this student writes. *"I've told him I just want to be friends. How can I get him to stop?"* As we've already discussed, breaking up should never include the words, "I said it was over, but I still wanted to be friends."

In the world of teen romance and breakups, any mention of "being friends" during the ending of a relationship leaves the door open — in the mind of the jilted lover — to the possibility that they might get back together again. As long as that hope flickers, there is a possibility that harassment will begin and cause trouble in your child's life. If real friendship is to surface, it will surface much later, long after the relationship is ended once and for all.

Let me state this as clearly as possible: *Whenever a breakup is not final, then the message at breakup time was ambivalent.* Leaving the door open to false expectations is at the root of the trouble. This is what precisely has happened here. The door was left open. It has to be closed.

What should your teen do if she is in the middle of this problem? Explain that she has to break up all over again. As the parent, you need to help her do this. You need to step in and guide your teen through some basic steps that will put an end to the relationship and this behavior. The key word, as I've mentioned before, is *clarity*.

Sit down with your teen. Have him first review with you what he said to his ex when they broke up. Pay particular attention to precisely what he said or *thought* he said to put an end to the relationship. You will hear words like, "Well, I said we still could be friends," or "I told her we still were going to talk," or " I said we still could go out sometime, but only as friends." If he said something to this effect to his ex, then the message he gave at breakup time was that the relationship wasn't really over.

Tell your teen that she has to confront the situation all over again. Only this time, she has to state, simply and clearly, that the relationship is over. No long discussion is necessary. It does not have to be done in person. The telephone will do. Be supportive to your teen. Make sure you are home, just in case things do not go well. Your support will add punch to the breakup. It makes it clear that you also know what is going on, and so it adds finality. The relationship is over.

If, however, you have a real stalker on your hands, I strongly suggest you get hold of the authorities, a rape crisis center, or a battered women's shelter for information as to how to proceed. Furthermore, if it continues, get a good lawyer. Go on the Internet and read up and plan a course of action and response. There are many Web sites filled with good information that will help you develop a plan. Do not take this lightly and simply assume it will go away. Most of the time it will, but when it doesn't, the situation can become scary and dangerous.

Above all, make certain your child does not talk to the stalker. Never open the door to communication. If for some reason that door gets open, and your child is confronted by his stalker, tell him that under no circumstances should he get emotional or try to reason with that person. No discussion is going to straighten this out. In fact, any discussion that has even a small emotional content will only encourage more trouble. No contact is the best. However, if your teen is in a situation where he cannot avoid the stalker, he should not try to reason, appeal, or say anything emotional. Close the door, walk away, call 911, and get your friends over to you.

I have made the very mistake that I am counseling you to avoid. I once tried reason with a person who was stalking me back when I worked on the street. It only made things worse. I made most of the mistakes I've mentioned here, and it took months to get my stalker out of my life. Not only that, but he returned for another round a year and half later. I was miserable and scared, and I felt like a fool. But once I really had the door completely shut, all communication stopped. While the street is not the same as a broken relationship, the important point is to cut off all contact. If you want this to go away, *you* go away. And if it does not go away, then the proper authorities need to be contacted.

I thought I'd finish this chapter with a lighter question for you — but one that you will no doubt hear at some point in your parenting career, and one that needs to be addressed just as surely as some of the more hand-wringing questions:

"I am trying to get a date for the junior prom. I asked two girls and they turned me down. What should I do?"

For most teens, dating has gone by the wayside. Kids today are more likely to go out in groups. They meet at the mall. They go out to dinner or to a movie, but more as an opportunity to hang out with friends or each other, not as a date. This magnifies the importance of the prom, homecoming, spring fling, or whatever event the school or youth organization holds as their big annual event.

For a lot of teens, especially girls, this is a huge event. It involves renting limos and tuxedos. It means finding the perfect gown. The corsage is still mandatory. Pictures are taken. Dinner reservations are made. Hopes and anxieties are high, and hearts are sometimes broken. The sense of rejection that looms when one is not asked or turned down as a date lurks at the back of many a mind, and sometimes it becomes a reality.

What do you tell a child who is having trouble getting a date for the prom or a similar high-stakes event? What do you tell any teen who is summoning the courage to ask someone out for the first time? When some of us were in high school, we could read about the "dos and don'ts" of dating. Kids today do not have such a manual.

What's the best way to answer this question? First of all, ask, "Who did you ask out? Is there an obvious reason that person said no?" You need to find out if your teen is even in the ballpark. He might have asked out someone he does not know or someone who is already involved with someone else.

Next ask, "What did you say when you asked for a date?" I know this sounds like a no-brainer, but remember, most teens have no experience in the dating game. She might have mumbled something incoherent, and the reply was taken as a no when it might have been a yes if the question had been asked properly in the first place. Review what your teen said and what was said to her. From that, you'll probably be able to give her some pointers on asking someone out, or even encourage her to call back and ask again.

Another simple thing you can tell your teen to do is to ask one of his friends to help set up the date. Friends can recommend or even ask someone they think might want to date your teen. If there seems to be any interest, he can call that person.

There's another possibility that can help ease the tension for your teen or help him consider other options. In years past, the prom or formal was most heavily populated with couples. Now, it is much more likely to be attended by groups of friends or pairs of good acquaintances who simply want to go to the event. They want to enjoy the formality, get their picture taken for memories, and afterward head out to a late-night dinner or party at a friend's home. Of course there are still couples, but not exclusively. Encourage your child to use her network of friends — if she doesn't end up going on an actual "date," she can still have a wonderful time with people she cares about.

There is more good news here: These evenings are formal ritual practice runs for teens as they socially come of age. Not every tradition has vanished.

* * *

Every parent wishes that they could hand over their most important life lessons to their teenager. Parents dream that these hard-learned lessons — including mistakes — will be understood by their children and seldom repeated. Wouldn't that make parenting a breeze? Unfortunately, it doesn't happen that way. If I may again quote *Leave It to Beaver,* I'd like to remind you of an episode in which Ward Cleaver gives a very timely reminder to parents, one that still applies today, perhaps more than ever:

"I guess you can't wrap your childhood up in a package and give it to your kids. Sometimes when a person's made a mistake or done something wrong, that's the time when they need understanding the most." (Irwyn Applebaum, *The World According to Beaver,* New York: Harper Collins, 1998, page 167)

Good advice from a classic dad, and while those words likely were spoken in the aftermath of a fairly innocent dilemma on the show, they are deeply resonant in light of the very serious issues that surround teenagers, sex, and relationships today. Swallowing your discomfort, sharing your stories, and opening the doors to honest communication with your teenager are the first steps toward cultivating that understanding so crucial to helping teens navigate through their most complicated questions about sex.

Chapter 4:
Family Problems

*"Experience is a great teacher.
Unfortunately, it's something you don't get until after you need it."*

Steve and Gloria arrived early for their appointment with me. Steve presented himself as a guy you'd find on a golf course Wednesday afternoons: Dressed in khakis and a designer cardigan, he was tall, fit, and confident, with a firm handshake. Gloria was petite and stylish in a tailored suit. But her makeup was a mess, and she kept wringing her hands. They wanted me to help them find their son, Michael, who had recently run away. Since they seemed to be no-nonsense people, I cut right to the chase. "Help me understand what happened when Michael left home," I said. Gloria took the stage.

"Michael was out of control," she began. "He got involved with this group of kids" — she shuddered — "and everything changed." She glanced at Steve, who took his cue.

"I came home late from work one night, and Michael was up in his room with a couple of these friends," he said. "Gloria had reminded him he had to be up early for school the next day, but at 11:30, the friends were still there. I went up to tell them to leave. Michael told me to get out, and he shut the door on me. I pushed it back, and shoved him and one of his friends to the floor in the process. All hell broke loose. Michael shoved me, I pushed him back, and I threw his friends out. Later that night he packed up and left."

"Let me get this straight," I interjected. "Gloria, you help me with this. Make sure I don't miss anything." She shifted uneasily. I turned to her and said, "Okay, so Steve comes home and goes to help you parent Michael. Michael is obnoxious and out of control. As a result, he gets into a shouting match with Dad and splits. Is that it? Have I got it right?"

Gloria looked at the floor for a long moment. Then she looked at Steve and said, "I've got to tell him everything. I can't take what's happening to us."

Steve looked at his hands. "Well, I was pretty angry when I went upstairs," he said. "I probably also had one scotch too many — "

"You went up there looking for a fight!" Gloria interrupted. "You cursed him out and attacked his friends! You were yelling, 'Get them out before I kick your ass!' What did you expect Michael to do? That wasn't the first time you attacked him."

Steve snarled back, "Well, maybe I was drinking, but I was sick of having to come home and clean up your messes with Michael."

"You're never around!" Gloria snapped. "You've never been around for him. What am I supposed to do? Our whole life is falling apart. You don't even care. You just work, play golf, and drink with your friends." She started to cry.

A lot of reckless collisions like these are a response to the desperation people experience when they sense their family crumbling around them. Something needs to change, but paradoxically, everyone responds by emphasizing old patterns of behavior. "I know it's not easy waking up every morning and being filled with anxiety and despair," I said. "I think we all agree that up till now, the way you've communicated with Michael hasn't been too effective." They both rolled their eyes. "Look," I continued. "You have a choice. You can continue what you're doing, realizing that adolescence does end eventually. Or you can take a risk and try something new."

Gloria moved a little closer to Steve. They glanced at each other and then looked at me. "Okay," Steve said, an edge still in his voice. "What can we do differently?"

* * *

It's no secret that families harbor secrets. Take a moment and reflect on your own upbringing. Chances are, at some point you heard the words, "Now, this doesn't leave the dinner table," or "Don't share with your friends, but..." Such phrases may have surrounded disclosure of a parent losing a job, an uncle being hospitalized for drinking too much, or a rebellious sister being "in trouble." Or perhaps such phrases and whispers were absent in your family, and while problems were never spoken of, they lurked about the house like angry ghosts. Maybe your parents fought so much you laid awake at night worrying they'd divorce — or wishing they would. Maybe your mother cried all the time, which made your dad uneasy or even angry, but no one ever asked why. Maybe something unimaginable happened to you — or your sister, or your brother — but you were sworn to secrecy at risk of further danger to you or someone you loved.

Silence isn't the rule in every family, however, and maybe it wasn't in yours, either. Some families seem to communicate by fighting. Even the smallest of incidents may explode into unresolvable shouting matches; throat-wrenching screams of "I hate you!" punctuated by a door slamming frequently rattle the walls. Objects fly and family members leave, but somehow these things are never spoken of. They're all symptoms of instability in a home.

Most teenagers have secrets — that's perfectly normal, even healthy. It's important, especially during adolescence, to have a good amount of privacy in your life. And families need privacy, too — there's no need for family concerns to become public knowledge, offered up to gossip vultures eager to pass along a juicy tidbit, regardless of who might be harmed. But there are secrets, and then there are *secrets* — the serious, dangerous ones that can't be spoken of, so they sit and fester, eating away at one's soul and poisoning one's future.

Fighting in families is also pretty normal — put any number of people in a confined space at once, and you bet the tempers are going to flare as boundaries are crossed, possessions are ruined, and promises are broken. But again, there are fights and there are *fights*. The fury of some fights evaporates after a walk around the block or a few hours alone. Others are never resolved: The screaming continues, the doors keep getting slammed, people keep leaving in a rage, and sometimes, they're physically or emotionally hurt.

It's those family problems — often stemming from secrets and often manifesting themselves in fights — that will be addressed in the questions in this chapter. And because it is so often the cause — or the result — of unspoken family problems, we'll also raise here the numerous questions teens have about divorce. As you will see, it's taking the risk to do something different *now* that will teach your teenagers a better way to relate to others (including you), show them how to make changes, and give them a better chance to have healthy families of their own. Let the problems stay underground, and your kids will only repeat the mistakes you've made.

Key Points to Remember When Discussing Family Problems

If you are part of a family (and as a parent, you most certainly are), you're familiar with these givens: Every teen keeps some secrets; fighting is part and parcel of family life; divorce is a matter of course for half the families in America — and likely yours, too. Successful parenting requires dropping any fiction about your life and taking a real look how you raise your child in the midst of secrets, strife, and separation. Honesty and openness with your child is key. Problems and secrets not dealt with will always make an appointment with you at a later date.

If you have been harboring troubling secrets that you haven't faced yet, deal with them now — the chance that your teenager will grow into an adult who can maintain healthy relationships depends on it. The first step is becoming honest with yourself, then determining which issues are appropriate to share with your teen. Perhaps you spent some time in drug rehab when you were your teen's age, and you're worried about his chances for addiction now, especially after he came home drunk the other night. Or perhaps you had an abortion when you were sixteen, and your own daughter's flirtatious, impulsive nature makes you fear for her own fate. Or perhaps you cheated on your wife when your children were small, but ended the affair quickly, got some good couples therapy, and enjoy a healed relationship today. Not *every* secret needs to be shared with your teen — but ones that are clearly having a negative impact on your family's life today, or ones that might help your teen learn a lesson or heed a warning, are good candidates.

The following four points will guide you as you answer the many questions your teen has about secrets, fighting, and divorce.

1. Some secrets are toxic to family life and toxic to children. If I could think of a stronger word than *toxic*, I would have used it. These secrets may deal with physical or sexual abuse, current or past drug or alcohol abuse, infidelities, mental illnesses, even money. The more secrets you, as a parent, keep, the more secretive your teen will be with you and others. Secret keeping, fighting, and upheaval from divorce take a big toll on your teen's life. If you are a parent carrying a major secret, I strongly suggest you seek proper professional help to determine what you are going to do with it,

whether it is appropriate to come clean to your family about it, and how.
2. Some secrets are easy to deal with. Teens are aware when parents lie or just change the truth a bit. If the lie is not serious, teens laugh about their parents' attempt to camouflage their actions or their past. Most mistakes, lies, and fights in relationships, when confessed and discussed, can become remarkable character-building opportunities for your teen. Never be afraid to sit down and talk it out.

3. Parents who carry secrets of infidelity, abuse, and the like should never one day lower the bomb and come clean to your kids. Some secrets need never be revealed, and especially tough issues must be dealt with in a therapist's office. However, most of the questions raised in this book address problems you can immediately tackle.

4. How do you deal with all those secret issues? How can you dig yourself out of a secret hole you have dug? Dr. Evan Imber-Black, a senior training therapist at the Ackerman Institute for the Family in New York, has some great suggestions. Set aside some time to think about or write down the answers to the following questions. They will make dealing with your secrets easier. They will also help you keep your presence of mind when talking with your teen and trying to deal with her tough questions. Take a moment to reflect on your life as a teenager:

- As a teenager, were you able to keep secrets from your parents?
- What were the secrets you kept?
- How did your parents respond if they discovered one of your secrets?
- Were there differences in the kinds of secrets you kept from your mother and the ones you kept from your father? What accounted for the difference?
- What was the relationship like with your closest confidant?
- Did you keep secrets from your siblings?
- How would you compare the secrets you kept with the ones you imagine your teen keeps from you now?
- How would you compare the secrets your parents kept from you with the ones you keep now from your teen? (Evan Imber-Black,

Ph.D., *The Secret Life of Families,* New York: Bantam Books, 1998, 246)

A final note before we begin looking at questions: One of the biggest things unresolved secrets and problems lead to in families is divorce — and with it, sometimes, plenty of fighting. Kids absorb the dangerous fallout from all this bitterness, and you bet it affects their chances of having healthy relationships with others, now and in the future. If you are in the middle of a divorce, work hard to not let the fighting spill over onto your children. It does and will hurt them. If you are unaware of this, read the questions about divorce included here especially closely. If you are fighting all the time, not only must you work to stop it, but you must also be prepared to ask for forgiveness from your teen. Don't let unresolved big issues — especially yours — follow your teen into adult life.

Questions and Answers

"Why do my parents never admit that they have problems? Why does it seem that they are keeping secrets from me?"

As we've discussed, secrets are one of the main catalysts for trouble in families. It should come as no surprise that some parents keep secrets, avoid discussing most problems, and sometimes simply don't want to be involved in their teen's life — or want their teen to be involved in theirs. In this question, it seems the parents are trying to hide their real lives from their teen — a fiction is being played out in the family. The details of the secrets might not be known, but the fact that there are secrets is obvious.

What might a teenager in this family feel? *Rejection* is the first thing that comes to mind. I would follow that with *disinterest* from the parents, and then *confusion*. Teens in these families feel shut out, and they eventually realize there is no benefit bringing their problems to their parents (which is exactly what I am trying to prevent with this book). They think, "What good does it do? They are never straight with me anyway." If nothing changes, teens start keeping their own counsel. In a word, they go underground. Life is lived below their parents' radar screen. Their own problems become secrets, some toxic.

Adolescents "living underground" can get into all kinds of trouble. What makes matters worse is that they can be in trouble and their parents never notice. Kids in this predicament easily can have secret abortions, develop drug problems, run away, forge report cards, gamble, and even run a small drug business out of their bedroom. Underground adolescents often are bored, chill with bored friends, and pass the time smoking dope, hanging out, and doing nothing. These kids are not out of control; they are, as Dr. Frank Pittman points out, "under-controlled." (*Turning Points,* New York: W. W. Norton and Company, 1987).

Occasionally, these teens make the headlines. When you read about girls having a "prom baby" in the bathroom or watch a talk show where a nine-month-pregnant daughter is finally telling her surprised mom that she is about to have a baby, you should no longer find it a mystery how these things happen. Kids growing up in families filled with secrets and disinterest are simply not noticed, even under extreme circumstances. While they live at home and take their meals there, they are living a separate life. Their parents, it seems, have no involvement.

Spend even a small amount of time in a family like this, and the first thing you'll notice is that no one talks to each other. Often, what creates this behavior is the fear of revealing the family's secret issues. The parents do not want to speak of them, let alone resolve them. Only the teen seems to comment that nothing gets discussed and secrets abound.

Parents in these families also don't want to discover their teen's problems. Why? Problems might demand their attention and force them to parent. When I speak with these parents, often they tell me they are tired of being parents. They want the whole parenting business to end. Ask them about their secrecy and their teen's underground life, and they will interpret it as something entirely different. To them, noninvolvement with their child is seen as proof of that child's maturity and independence.

All of this is very troubling to teens. The message they receive is twofold: (1) "Don't bring your problems to me," and (2) "Don't bring up any important issues. I'm not going to talk about them anyway."

This is a serious problem. I confess that I have never found it easy for uninterested parents to get interested in parenting again. It seems they want to keep things the way they are. When a crisis erupts, they may get involved for a time, but as soon as the "all clear" has been sounded, they disappear again. Often, many of these parents were not themselves parented as teens. They, too, lived underground lives.

But teens need parents to be involved and to actively check in on their lives. If the pattern of behavior described here is one you recognize in your own house, how do you go about turning things around? How do you break the pattern? Three things need to happen:

1. Everyone has to come to an agreement that problems must be brought into the open.
2. No one in the family must keep any confidence a secret.
3. A "what to do" list, detailing how problems and secrets will now be dealt with in the family, must be agreed upon by the entire family and taped to the refrigerator door.

This is easier said than done. For one thing, this requires the family to talk, which may never have happened before. In addition, there will likely be resistance. Often, parents want things to stay the way they are. It's easier not to be involved. For these parents, to come back out of retirement, actively parent, and really help their child grow up is very frightening. Furthermore, it is no simple task for a parent — or a teen, for that matter, particularly one that's spent some time underground — to expose a long-held secret.

Having given you all the gloomy news, let me now tell you what, in fact, generally *does* occur. Good things happen when problems are finally spoken about and secrets are no longer kept. Most parents, in the end, are willing to turn their attention back to their children. Rules can be made that are fair and agreeable. Parents, if given some support through counseling, will reveal their insecurities and secrets. Furthermore, they can and will be involved enough to set standards, even punish their kids, and, especially, talk about the important issues in their lives. Teens will come along with them. They will tell their secrets, accept consequences, follow the family rules, and even adjust to the fact that their parents are not perfect, but real people with real problems seeking real solutions.

"I really try to avoid talking to my mom and dad. They're just way too serious. If I try to talk to them about anything important, they either get hysterical or lecture me."

I vividly remember a family I called the Crying Gang. The parents operated in two gears: lecturing or crying. Their daughter also operated in two gears: running away or crying. There were, of course, a host of other problems, but this was one serious crying family. By the second session, I was amazed at how systematic they were. When I brought up an important issue, Dad would, on cue, blow up or start another ineffective lecture. For his finale, he would cry. Mom would start bawling her eyes out. Their daughter sat and watched for a few minutes. Once Mom got the tears rolling, that was her signal. She would either join in the crying or angrily walk out. The drama was stupendous. I had to figure out a way to turn off the switch. By the third session, I was prepared.

As soon as everyone sat down, I reached down to the side of my chair and handed each of them their own special Kleenex box. On each box I wrote their name. I handed the boxes out and told them that since we had an hour together, I was going to step out the room for twenty minutes. "While I'm gone," I instructed them, "I want you to cry. When I come back, you will have finished crying for the session. That way, we can use the rest of the time to talk."

Dad, as usual, got angry at me. Mom started crying. But their daughter burst out laughing. And I mean she was really laughing. Her laughter was so outrageous that her parents stopped and stared at her.

After a moment, they turned and stared to me. They were waiting for me to give them some kind of pithy comment. I simply said, "You're never too old to do goofy stuff," then added, "I learned that from *Leave It to Beaver.*"

Dad took one long breath and then burst out crying. Mom looked at her hubby, then at me, then at her daughter, and suddenly burst out laughing. The daughter didn't need any more tuning up. She laughed even harder. They both used their Kleenex boxes to wipe away tears of laughter. Dad looked around and finally smiled.

After that, we got down to basic family business. No more lectures. No running away. No more melodrama. And yes, the crying stopped. There wasn't a need to hold on to that anymore.

As kids grow up, parents do, too — often to become overly serious adults. The problem here is, in a way, the opposite of the previous problem. Instead of trying to avoid having to parent, some people take parenting a little too seriously. Fortunately, this problem is much easier to fix.

Parents often ask me, "You mean, it's okay to joke around with my kid? Don't I have to make sure he respects me?" But being a "stuffed shirt" with your kids only keeps them from being touched by the real you. If you are always serious and giving lectures, how is your teenager ever going to feel able to approach you? Lighten up. A little dash of humor and goofiness cuts the tension and lowers the anxiety in many families. Your kids will come to you because they are drawn to the real you, not the distant, serious parent you think you are required to be.

It really is okay to be involved in your teenager's life, and to have fun while doing it. It's okay to go to ball games, take in a movie, and hang out a bit with her. They say, "Those who laugh, last." Maybe this is good advice for your family.

Of course there are no families without struggles and problems. It is, though, a lot easier to work through them knowing we can be ourselves, not trying to adopt the image of someone we are not.

Changing your attitude it is not as hard as you might think. In fact, it is quite easy to do. If you want to parent differently, begin by doing things differently. Change your actions, and your thinking will follow. You can't think your way into a new way of living. But you can live your way into a new way of thinking.

> *"My mom says one thing and punishes me for another thing. My dad gets home and changes the punishment. Sometimes it's worse, or sometimes nothing happens. This drives me nuts. It makes me mad at my parents. What is going on with them? They never seem together when it comes to me."*

Staying on the same page with your spouse is extremely important when raising children. It is very important, especially with discipline, to be consistent. It's crazy-making for any teen to get confusing and mixed messages. Fortunately, there are things you can do that in time will bring about some positive changes. The following four points help parents get on the same track. If you cannot come to some agreements in how you parent, then I recommend you seek therapy.

1. You *and* your spouse don't need to react to every issue. Plan out in advance which issues need team effort and which ones don't. You probably don't need to confer on whether your child can go to a friend's house after school, whether he can cut homework time a half-hour short to watch TV, or what she can wear on a date. Pick and choose the incidents you want to discuss — it doesn't have to be all of them.
2. Always make certain you and your spouse are together on issues that affect your teen. Make an agreement to trust each other's best judgment on minor issues and back each other up. On more major issues — like when she can date and whom, what parties he'll be allowed to attend and with whom, and other standard rules, like those surrounding curfews and punishment — come to an agreement and *do not waver* without further discussion for special circumstances. The key is to discuss first, implement later.

3. Always present a united front. Unified parents create calm in the household and reduce confusion. For teenagers, consistency is key.
4. Try to say yes more than no. The power of 'yes' makes for real adult conversations around the 'no's of life.

> *"I want to add a couple more piercings to my ears. My mom says no. This really makes me angry. I mean, I am not piercing my tongue or anything. I love earrings and think I will look really good with some more. Why is she fighting me?"*

Maybe this question should be titled "How to Pick Your Battles." Body piercing, in some circles, has become a fashion statement. The same holds true for tattoos. However, I must also distinguish between relatively minor body piercing and tattooing and the excessive piercing and tattooing that's also popular today. There is a different world surrounding kids who engage in self-injurious behavior — those who have multiple tattoos or who pierce body parts like tongues, genitals, and nipples. I will discuss the problems surrounding those kids at the end of this question.

Parents need to provide expertise in matters of substance, not style. In most cases, you have to let you teen be the expert in style. As a parent of a teenager, you already know you differ on a lot of issues. One of the keys to effective parenting is figuring out which battles are fundamentally important to you and which are not. It is best to tolerate annoying teenage habits and fads and conserve your strength for the big issues, where you have little flexibility and must get your opinion across to your child.

Drugs and high-risk sex are examples of issues that cannot be ignored. Think for a moment — is an extra piercing in the ear really in the same category? If you choose to fight over clean rooms, hairstyles, clothes, or a pierced ear, how well will you be heard when you need to put your foot down for a curfew or need to talk about alcohol or drugs at parties?

I strongly recommend that you let your child win sometimes. Or better yet, simply give your kid room to be a teenager. Is it really necessary to fight over the small stuff? Pick instead the big issues where you have to put your foot down. It is important to be selective.

Choose where you must take a stand. A good rule of thumb is to think long term, not short term. Ask yourself:

Will it make any difference in a few years if my daughter has an extra ear piercing? Will his messy room interfere with his long-term goals? Is my kid's spiked hair going to affect his job prospects when he gets out of college? Is that eye shadow going to prevent her from getting into graduate school? The answers to all of these, most likely, are no.

You certainly can comment or even laugh that you are annoyed, but let then it go. If you frequently get locked in petty fights, later, when you have something really important to say, it might be very hard to get your teen's attention.

I think most parents are aware that body piecing and tattoos are definitely a big fad. They're glamorized by the media. Watch any pro sports team or rock star and you can't miss seeing some kind of tattoo. Kids will tell you it is all about personal empowerment and expression. It is also about having control. However, there are times when the so-called fad gets out of hand.

Often people get multiple piercings or tattoos as a way to reclaim themselves after suffering from physical or sexual abuse. I have been around too many kids who have suffered from abuse and who also have multiple piercings and tattoos not to pay attention to the reasons behind their decisions to alter their bodies. My concerns go way up when kids tell me they have pierced their private areas. Style is one thing, but self-inflicted injury is an entirely different matter. Kids whose piercings reflect the pain and wounds of abuse need to get professional help.

For more information, research material about kids who cut themselves or engage in other forms of self-harm.

"My parents always tell me I am out of control. Things have gotten really bad at home. I hit my mom last week. I really blew it. I think my parents are going to ship me off to some boarding school or something. Why don't they just leave me alone?"

"Out-of-control" teens need attention. They are not just going through a phase. If you believe you have an out-of-control teen at home, you need to get professional help. This is not something you can handle by simply talking with your teenager. Kids spinning out of control bring too many issues for any parent to handle alone. Help — good help — is available and prevalent, but let me begin by offering you a warning.

In recent years, getting help for unruly teens has become rather treacherous. Let me explain why. In every community, there are able professionals in social service agencies, at clinics, and in private practice that specialize in working with rebellious kids. However, in the last decade, an entire industry has grown up catering to families with out-of-control teens. In other words, you have to be aware that a large business market now specializes in assisting parents by shipping their rebellious teens off to "boot camps" and other reform-focused institutions. They are expensive and can be unscrupulous. Books, organizations, and even talk-show hosts push self-righteous formulas and ineffective hard-nose approaches for dealing with teens. My advice: Keep your money in your checkbook, stay away from formulas, and turn off those kinds of talk shows.

Finding good and competent help is not always easy, but it is available. It requires research and unwavering focus on your teen's best interests. Where do you begin your search? Besides asking your clergy, family physician, or friends, your local social service agency is a good place to start. Even if you do not avail yourself of their services, they certainly will have a good local referral list for you. These agencies will know which clinicians and programs are experienced in dealing with your type of family crisis.

They may recommend that your child does need a residential program. Most reputable residential programs also have an accredited high school attached to the therapy. Your child will not only get the counseling she needs, but she will also be able to complete high school. Residential programs are full service and often offer a host of amenities that add positive fuel and drive to the program.

An educational consultant who specializes in matching teens with the right residential program is extremely helpful. These consultants have a combined background in therapy and education. They have the ability to evaluate your teen and your family and find several schools that might end up being a good fit. I recommend you contact a competent clearinghouse for residential treatment programs. This is essential. There are unscrupulous treatment centers all over America. Teens have even died at some of them. You must seek trustworthy advice and guidance.

Still, while many of these programs are quite good, they are often very expensive.

Keep researching local services — you do not necessarily have to pack your kid off to a program. Use your community and dedicate yourself to counseling. That is the key to effecting some lasting positive change. Many parents try to use residential programs as a quick fix to get their teen out of the house and out of their hair. When the child returns home, chaos returns. Ultimately, there are no magic formulas. Get help for yourself at the same time as you're getting help for your teen — better yet, be involved in your teen's therapy. That way, you'll have a better chance of being a healthy family when your teen's program is done.

"I am having trouble at home with my mom and dad. They are always fighting. Then they fight with me over their fights. I don't listen to them anymore. What should I do?"

This is not a question from an out-of-control teen, but a deeply concerned one who recognizes trouble and wants something to change. Even though he claims, "I don't listen to them anymore," which makes it sound like he's tuned out his parents and "gone underground," there's more to his response than meets the eye. The key line in this question is "What should I do?" Often, when teens challenge their parents, it's not as an act of rebellion or disrespect, but of hope or desperation — they want something to change for the better.

Teens challenge their parents in an attempt to get their attention. It is always important, when your teen flings a challenge at you, to pause for a moment and rein in the impulse to defend yourself or attack back. Ask yourself, "What is my child trying to tell me?" If you are at a loss and cannot pick up the clues in an accusation or question, you can simply ask your teen, "I am not certain what you are trying to say to me. Please tell me more." If a question along these lines is thrown at you, your work, besides dealing with the fights with your spouse, is to get the lines of conversation back open. You don't need a therapist to do that.

This question is a call to action. It requires you to sit down and ask your teen, "What is the most recent thing I've done that upset you the most?" Always start with an immediate problem rather than drag up the past. You can always work back.

Next ask, "What do I do that makes things worse?" That usually will open the door to your teen's laundry list of complaints. Of course, what she will say probably will be hard for you to hear. But this is the time to listen. You, your spouse, and your teen have some difficult work ahead, but it is work that will make a difference. As tough as it might be to remember, you are working toward progress, not perfection.

These first steps are designed to get you started talking about how and why you are fighting, and what the impact of it is on your teen. Remember, the issue is that your child has decided to not listen to you anymore, and that is linked to your fighting with your spouse. Change that fighting, and you change your kid. I am assuming here that you and your spouse can also sit down and discuss ways to keep your fighting to a minimum. If not, seek some couples therapy.

Of course things are not going to improve overnight. The key to reestablishing calm in the household is for you to make the extra effort. Think of this way: In order to discipline, you must first establish love and trust. None of that will ever happen if there is incessant fighting.

"I hate my mom and dad. I want to run away from home. What should I do?"

This question is a cry for help. When parents are fighting, or when a brother or sister is in serious trouble, a kid will often do something very dramatic to bring the family back together. They will run away. Kids who run away don't handle family tension that well. Dr. Frank Pittman commented, "It's really not a bad trick, unless the runaway stays away too long... get[s] into trouble or expose[d]... to dangers... I've seen kids run away during a family fight, a family funeral, a sister's abortion, a financial crisis, a parent's affair, as well as after an embarrassing failure of their own" (*Turning Points*, New York: W. W. Norton & Company, 194).

There is also a darker side to the world of runaway teens. Often teens flee from violent parents. Emotional and physical abuse of children in America is all too common. Normal teens from time to time tell their friends they hate their parents, but runaway talk is not idle chatter, and it should be treated seriously. If you suspect or know your child is thinking about running away, things have to change. As a therapist, I am not interested in hearing about who is to blame or how much everyone has tried to help this kid talk. Let's cut to the chase.

What are you going to do about this? What steps need to be taken? First of all, you know that runaway talk means that your teen is anxious or angry. Your first move is to sit down and tell your child you need to talk to him. Make it clear that *you* need to talk to *him*, not the other way around. If your relationship has been filled with tension, or if some kind of family crisis has brought on talk of running away, now is the time to start straightening out the mess. If you have done something wrong, and you suspect that is at the root of the problem, it is okay to tell your teen so. Use I-statements like "I have," or "When this happened, I responded in the wrong way." Never use accusing words. Attacking or blaming your teenager for "the problem" will send him packing. Need I remind you that it is a dangerous world out on the street?

Ask your teen point-blank something like the following: "I know you sometimes seem to hate me and want to leave home. Will you please tell me what is going on?" Then, hang on to the sides of your chair, as you might be hit by a firestorm of words or a waterfall of tears. Be prepared to hear a lot of anger or anxious words. Whatever comes out of your kid's mouth, let her say it. It may be painful, but this pain is necessary to begin healing. You are starting a process to mend your family and get things out in the open. The next step in the process is to seek therapy — get some professional help. Remember, runaway talk must be taken seriously.

If you are a parent who has abused your child, you have to take a different approach. Basically, your first conversation has to include your admission of guilt. No excuses. Tell your teen, "Please hear me out for five minutes." These five minutes will not solve anything. I know that. But it is your beginning. Go forward and talk. Admit what you have done. Admit your remorse. Tell your teen you are going to seek professional help and you need her to lend a hand. That is how to start the process of healing the wounds. Then, make the arrangements to get the help and stick with it.

I have spent a good deal of my adult life working with children who are survivors of abuse. Most parents who abuse leave that as their children's legacy. It can ruin their lives. When I worked with hard-core teen prostitutes in New York City, most of them died on the streets. Nearly all of them fled from violent, abusive parents. Nearly every one of those children told me that if their parent would actually track them down and speak with them about what happened, they would forgive him or her. I heard this dozens and dozens of times, even from kids dying of AIDS. They were out on the mean streets, being abused and ravaged by other adults. Yet they were willing to forgive their parents, who were the ones who gave them their tragic life.

Even in the worst-case scenarios, you can turn things around. You simply will have to trust me on this one. I have spent more than a quarter century dealing with families and people who have suffered terribly. I can report that help does bring about positive change as long as families have courage and stay the course in treatment. My advice is to do whatever it takes. And do not measure change in months, but in years.

And ultimately, you always will be better off if you remember that teenagers do grow up. It might take a while, but it does eventually happen. While teens tend to see everything as permanent and parents see them as impermanent, real problems develop when parents freak out and suddenly think their child is never going to change. Every teen on some level is a "pain in the ass." But even out-of-control, pain-in-the-ass kids grow up. Use this time as an opportunity to really effect lasting change.

A child's love for his parents is so deep. So too is a parent's love. Bitter anger and big divisions between parents and teens can be bridged. Often the very first step is to clear the air. Admit the problem and start talking about the secrets behind the current family tensions. The approach must be two-pronged: therapy and family conversation. The combination does work. Difficulties are opportunities to open new doors.

"My parents are divorced, and my dad always talks bad about my mom. Every time he calls me, he goes off. I've tried to tell him that I don't like it, but no matter what I say he does not seem to get the point. What should I do?"

This question is one of the most common ones I hear. You will encounter several variations of this question throughout the rest of the chapter. I chose to put in as many as I could because each one presents a slightly different issue and an opportunity to discuss several different points relating to divorce, fighting, and forcing kids to pick sides.

With divorce rates so high in this country, it's no wonder that teens have so many questions about what to do when a divorce gets ugly. What kids really want is some semblance of family and relationship with both parents after a divorce. Kids may be able to adjust to divorce, but they have a terrible time adjusting to the fighting between parents that so frequently follows divorce. In fact, in my opinion, they do not adjust. It can create lifelong trouble.

In this particular scenario, the father is stuck in the blame game. He's making a full-time job of getting back at his ex-wife. His list of grievances from this marriage is long, sharp, and deep. He is an angry man. But instead of finding a way to blow off his steam and deal with his issues constructively, he's firing all that frustration and anger straight at his child, who has no idea how to deal with it.

The key to successfully raising children after divorce is having a respectful, working relationship with your ex-spouse. That is one of the Parenting Principles. Teens depend on their families for security, love, and protection. Families that provide security and refuge for their children build self-confident teens who draw on the strength of their home to go out in the world, take risks, and pursue dreams. Even if the family is split apart, children need both parents. If they cannot have both, then one solid, loving parent is a huge plus.

If you are a parent like Dad in this question and are "carrying on" to your teen, it's time to stop. Seek professional help. Your anger and frustration is leaking all over your child. It is corrosive to her mental health. Something decent brought you together in your marriage, and though it has failed, it is not your teenager who caused it to do so. Don't throw your child in your anger. You are still her parent, and she needs you to be stable.

What do I tell teens who ask me what they should do? Straight off, I tell them to tell their parent to stop, a few times if necessary. If that doesn't stop the vitriol, then I tell them to get angry. I make it clear to them and support them by saying: "No one should have to put up with all that anger. Why should you have to drink poisonous words? If your parent will not stop, tell him or her that conversations on the phone will end as soon as the bitter words start up, and visits will be cut short if negative behaviors continue."

No child should have to try to discipline an angry parent. Someone has to be the adult here, and it is not the teenager. I also want to warn you of this: Constant complaining and bad-mouthing can become hard-wired into your child's behavior, and by the time he reaches adulthood, he runs the risk that your current nightmare will be repeated in his own marriage.

If you, as a parent, can step back from the bad behavior for a moment, surely you can see that hidden in your teen's request for help is her need of you. Otherwise, why would she ask, "What can I do?" Do you really want to turn away from your own teenager because of personal bitterness over your failed marriage?

If you, the noncustodial parent, will not calm down and cherish time together, then, in the end, you will lose or diminish your relationship with your child. It's that simple. Calm down, work out your problems elsewhere, or lose a chunk of your bond with your kid. Most people can learn from their mistakes. Experience is a great teacher. Unfortunately, it's something you don't get until after you need it.

"My parents keep fighting all the time. They're divorced. They keep trying to use me to get at each other. It makes me sick. Is there something I can do?"

Negative fallout is not rare after a divorce. I often tell families I wish I could simply wave a magic wand and make all the fighting go away. Believe me, if I could, I would, but unfortunately, there's only one thing that will work: One or both of the parents has to let go and stop the fighting. Not doing that will eventually rupture their relationship with their child. In many cases, it already has. Sometimes teenagers tell me they wish they could "divorce" their parents.

There will be negative consequences in your relationship with your teen if you do not put a stop to your fighting. Your teen will make decisions in life that don't include you. Kids stuck in this mess will not turn to you in their time of need. As adults, they often conclude that their parents are too toxic for them to be around. Furthermore, they too are eventual candidates for divorce. Yes, the sins of the parents can visit the children. I don't think any parent wants that for themselves or their child.

What can you, the parent, do in this situation? How do you dig out from this mess? Begin by facing the situation. Even though your marriage is over, you surely are aware that the fighting is not. Obviously, much has not been dealt with. To get to some of the causes of these nasty squabbles, you'll have to do some thinking about what went wrong. I always tell parents who will not stop using their kids in their battle, "If you resist dealing with difficulties, you antagonize them, and they just keep on biting you back. The nightmare will only get worse, and you will lose in the end."

The causes you uncover as you reflect on what went wrong need to be shared with your teen, if appropriate. Contrary to popular belief, your willingness to discuss some of the difficulties that arose in your marriage is a plus, not a minus for your teen. Yet, it is very important to remember not to justify your fighting and using your teen as a weapon; there is no justification for that. Share some of these causes with your teen, explain what has happened to make the fighting so bitter, and emphasize that none of it is his fault. Tell him you are deeply sorry that you have used him as a pawn in this battle with your spouse. Tell him that you are going to make the effort to end it. Even if it means you going into counseling, communicate that you are serious about not dragging him into your problems. It is your job to stop the fighting, not your teen's.

This may all sound too simple to be true. How do you really sit an angry teen down and go over this very difficult material?

Begin by making an appointment with your teen. Naturally, that will get her attention. Tell her why you want to do this, saying something along the following lines: "I need to talk about some of the problems that have been happening. I am aware that my fighting been driving you crazy. I need to talk to you about that." While it is best if both parents come together to discuss the fighting, often that does not happen. You can, however, turn the tide with your teen by yourself. Here are some suggestions to help you get started:

1. Avoid simplistic explanations. Don't just say, "Well, we don't love each other anymore." A message like that is meaningless. Get to the real issues and explain what you think happened to you without anger. Admit that you have let it get out of control. Explain what you plan to do to stop your bad-mouthing and fighting.
2. Get right down to the issues that caused the separation. Again, do this without anger. Bring up some of the toughest issues you faced, being cautious to be age-appropriate in what you share. Bring

relevant secrets into the open; the truth is your child does sense them. (Remember, though, that affairs should only be discussed with your children in a counselor's office, and/or only after you have discussed it fully in private with your own therapist.) Most secrets that dissolved a family cannot remain secrets. Telling your secrets is difficult, but not telling them creates an unspoken imbalance in your teen's future relationships. This is a hard and difficult process, but this is how you start to clean it up.
3. Talk about everything. You will know you have made progress when your teen sees there were two sides to the divorce. When everyone knows the price paid for separation, tensions will ease.
4. The whole family has to become the protector of the divorce. Set in place rules that give permission to everyone to remind you, the parent, if you step over the line and start bad-mouthing again.

If you are not making progress, be prepared to seek therapy. I assume fighting will continue with many couples, but progress still can be made if you are at least committed not to respond to attacks. Again, if you cannot let go, for the sake of your child, fight somewhere else or in someone's office, not at home. You will have opened the door to meaningful communication with your teenager, and eventually all will be allowed to move on with their lives. Nothing is better than that.

"My parents just got divorced. I know a lot of my friends live with only one parent, but I still really feel depressed about it. I go to my dad's house, and every time I'm there, he has to say something mean about my mom. My mom is no better. I tell them to cut it out and leave me out of it. Why do they keep doing this? I'll be a senior next year and just plan to go away to college and come back as little as possible."

Let me be frank. Divorce has side effects. Everyone pays a price. Kids stuck in the middle of the battleground grow up witnessing family relationships that lack trust, appear treacherous, and do not, in their eyes, provide stability. As a result they often do get depressed — who wouldn't? At every seminar I give, some teenager always tells me how *depressing* it is to see their parents attacking each other.

While the topic of depression will be addressed more thoroughly in chapter 7, it's worth mentioning here that teens already have much to cause them concern and hopelessness in their day-to-day lives. Divorce — more specifically, ugly post-divorce fighting — only adds to their burden, and can be an ingredient in a recipe for depression.

Read the question carefully, and you'll also see that this teen is heading underground. "I plan to go away and come back as little as possible," she writes. Any parent reading that should become quite concerned about how his or her actions are affecting a future relationship with this child. Remember too, "underground" teens are at a higher risk of suffering negative consequences from their problems — simply because they feel they have no one to talk to. I'm quite certain this teen feels her parents are too preoccupied with their own battles to listen to her concerns — or secrets — about sex, or drug use, or depression. They may be shocked to hear her say she believes they don't care, but their actions are showing her otherwise.

A final concern: This teen is learning profound — but wrong — lessons about relationships, facing problems, and resolving problems that could lead her to make some of the same mistakes her parents have. Over and over again, teens report to me that they are nervous about making any commitments in relationships. When I ask them why, they respond by saying, "Because I went through hell when my parents divorced. I want to be careful." As a result, many young people hedge their bets and live together before they get married. It makes no difference to point out that couples that live together first have a higher divorce rate. The fighting has already affected their lives. They are in confusion over relationships and certainly marriage.

In addition, two of the worst ways to deal with problems — both of which are being modeled for the teen right now — are fighting about them incessantly, with no effort made toward identifying or resolving them, and simply avoiding them altogether. Knock-down, drag-out fighting is simply a noisy way of not facing a problem, and the teen's own choice — leaving as soon as she can — is an obvious form of avoidance. Neither is healthy. What is? Bringing these issues to the light, talking about what caused them, then deciding what to do about them.

If you are a parent in this situation, you must first bring your child back from the underground and let him know that you are aware this is hurting him. Let him tell you exactly what he experiences, how it makes him feel, and what he wants to have happen. Make it clear that you are committed to putting an end to the fighting, and will do whatever it takes to make that happen.

It is a good idea to set up some ground rules with your teenager, beginning with a contract proclamation that declares you will cease attacks on your ex-spouse. Begin this proclamation with a pledge. Have it declare that you are now committed not to involve your teen in your squabbles. After the pledge, make a specific series of declarations. Each should begin with the phrase "I will no longer . . ." Put it on the fridge.

Put your teen in charge of reminding you when you cross the line. Once a week, take a few minutes and have your teen read your proclamation out loud. Failure to adhere to your proclamation will be noted by your teen. You will have to admit guilt for any violation. This kind of contract is very effective. It can even bring some humor back into the family, and it definitely can put on the brakes on your mouth.

If you cannot control your attacks, then you will know you need counseling. Be sure to make all of this clear with your teen. Divorce is tough on everyone — not the least of whom is you. Getting counseling also is a way of taking care of yourself and your needs during this difficult time. I recommend going to the bookstore to find a useful book or two that will help see you through. Try *Coping with Teenage Depression: A Parent's Guide* by Kathleen McCoy, for starters.

"My parents are divorced, and I live with my mom and stepdad. My dad lives in another state. He never calls me. If I call him and leave a message, he doesn't call back. Do you have any suggestions about what I should do?"

It is hard to read a question like this. Even after all the years I have spent seeing the results of some version of this question — on the streets and other out-of-the-way places — my first thought is still, "How could a parent just dump his kid?"

Still, it happens. I have seen parents abandon their children. They just go missing in action. I have picked up kids as young as ten years old on subway platforms, miles from home, at two in the morning. I have met hundreds in Times Square, wandering around with a suitcase and a backpack full of schoolbooks. I have found teens who came home after school only to find a note saying, "You're old enough to take care of yourself." And, of course, most of us know some type of deadbeat parent like the one mentioned in the above question.

When I sit down and talk to a teenager in this mess, I discover that the noncustodial parent usually has a new family and has abandoned the old one. Things, over time, have just gone on drift. Finally, the parent stops visiting, and the calls stop, too. Messages from the child are not returned. Birthdays are forgotten. In the beginning, such parents keep making excuses about why they are not in touch. In the end, they simply drop off the radar screen. If alimony is in the picture, the only contact will be a monthly check. These "dads" often fit the profile of "deadbeat dads." Of course, I am aware that fathers have rights. I am not describing that situation and this is not the question at hand.

By the time this question has arisen, I assume you, the custodial parent, have exhausted every avenue. You have called your ex-spouse. Yelled. Pleaded. Told her to get into therapy. Sent reminders a week before your teen's birthday. Nothing has worked.

Please, however, make certain that your teen is aware of or even present as you try to straighten things out with her absent parent. That, in itself, is a powerful lesson. Let your teen learn that even when facing a tough problem that may not bring a successful resolution, you still try to straighten things out. As a parent, you don't want your teen to end up a victim in this ugly rejection.

The lesson here is that you are not going to be further victimized. Seeing you in action, your teen will learn that in life there are no victims, only volunteers. He will see a mom or dad who is not going to sign up for any extra pain.

When you feel you have exhausted every option, level with your kid. Since you have told her what you have been trying at every point along the way, she is up to speed on your efforts. And now, after she too has tried by making phone calls or sending letters, for the time being, it truly is over with good old Dad or Mom.

Finally, you must spend time with your teen talking about his feelings, worries, anger, and sadness about not being able to have a relationship with his other parent. Never assume that "he'll get over it." No one really ever gets over something like this. It leaves in its wake bitterness and a residue of anger. Any time a parent abandons a child, it creates a hole in any kid's heart.

It is your job, though, to help fill that hole. How? With understanding and love. Every parent wishes they could keep the dangers of the world away from their child. Since that is not possible, you can help her cope and understand. Even negative actions can have positive results if put into the light of understanding. Use this situation as an opportunity to teach your child about the importance of commitment in relationships. Explain to her what went wrong in your relationship. This will help her see that even wrongs done to her can strengthen her resolve to make good choices and strong commitments for her life.

The bottom line: It is important for teenagers, as they emerge into adulthood, to know that while it is not easy to find happiness in ourselves, it is impossible to find it elsewhere. Use this tough question as an opportunity to help your teen grow, mature, and understand what makes relationships work. Through someone else's failure, great lessons can be learned about life's commitments. As a parent, seize the opportunity to bring as much clarity and understanding to the situation as you can. The more open you can be about the issue, the better it will be for your child.

One small note here to stepparents: Stepparents are very, very important. And, of course, stepparents love their stepchildren. However, stepparents are not birth parents. As such, it is well advised to keep out of the discussion in matters involving your spouse's problems with the noncustodial parent. Get involved only if asked by your spouse and your stepchild. Make sure your involvement is agreed upon and welcomed by all.

"My mom got remarried. I am seventeen and can't wait to get out of the house — it's a mess all over again. I mean the fighting and the screaming, this time with the new husband. What is going on here? I tell my mom that this is bothering me. All she says is, 'Girl, we will work it out.' Is she blind or what?"

Teens from divorced families or in families trying marriage for a second or third time around often tell me, "No way am I gonna fight and hurt my kids like my parents. I'm gonna be careful not to get too close to whoever I marry. You just never know." Translation: "I am not ever going to let myself be that concerned with the emotional welfare of my partner." Teens also tell me that they see nothing wrong with tying the knot for only ten years. "Make a contract to end it," they say. "Redraw the contract for a few more years if it is going okay." Emotional debts from childhood do spill over into a kid's adult life.

In troubled families, the pain and fear is very real. Divorce is never easy on children, but it goes off the charts when separation is nasty and bitter. When that happens, everyone gets hurt. Furthermore, couples who cannot work it out in one marriage often make a repeat performance in their next marriage, and drag their kids through the fighting all over again. If screaming and fighting is the style of marriage number one, then odds are that in marriage number two, the brawling is not likely to stop, even if the children ask for it to. Divorce rates for second marriages are even higher than the first.

It's no wonder, really. Divorce and remarriage can throw family dynamics way out of balance, especially if no help or counseling has been sought and if no effort has made to talk to the kids about what is happening, hear their concerns, and make changes for the better. After divorce, the standards of living often change. Kids are embarrassed to talk to their friends about the divorce. Court fights surrounding a divorce can go on for years. The parents may start having new affairs and new relationships. And then, the "new love" shows up. Marriage is again attempted. And unfortunately, sometimes, the anger and tension from the first marriage rolls over into the next one. Old problems from the previous relationship were never resolved. A vicious and hurtful cycle continues onward.

This cycle is precisely what this teen is questioning. *Why* is this happening again? Hasn't Mom learned anything? Why doesn't she respond to her kid's pain and frustration? In the worst-case scenario, as your teen gets older, the fighting may actually drive him out of the family. This should come as no surprise. What the teen sees, clearly, is that the parent has been working hard to make sure nothing changes.

This is not a situation where simply sitting down and talking with your child will change the situation. Things have spun too far out of control for that to be beneficial. For a situation like this, I recommend counseling *in addition to* taking a "time out" and at least minimally explaining to your teen that you are aware of what is happening, you are aware of how it is hurting him, and you are going to try to put a stop to it. I must admit that I am not optimistic that this particular parent will go into counseling. There is no indication by the mother's response that she is willing to change anything. The prognosis is not good.

What I tell teens in this situation is that they are on their own. I recommend that they seek help themselves. It is now up to them to break this vicious cycle in their own lives. Sadly, not every situation has a "family remedy."

"My parents are divorced. My mom and dad are constantly fighting. Then they end up fighting with me. I get so pissed off at them that I fight way more with them than they even fight with each other. I want to the fighting to stop, but they won't get off my back. What should I do?"

This question serves to illustrate a point I have made repeatedly in this chapter: The very fact that this teen is now fighting is a surefire signal he is becoming just like his parents. If you and your family are in the middle of a divorce war zone, and you find your teen is now hurling the blame bombs as much as or even more than you, stop and take a good look at the situation. Two things are happening here: Your teen is obviously acting out against a situation that is unbearable to him, and he also has clearly learned — from watching you — that the way to react to an unbearable situation is to fight. Not talk. Not seek help. But fight. The cycle we discussed in the previous question has picked up another victim, ensuring it will continue another generation, at least. Kids who grow up in the war zone get the wrong message about love, commitment, and caring. They have nothing but negativity modeled for them as they cross the threshold into adulthood.

However, there's hope. If you can see it happening, you can stop it. And change, as always, begins with yourself. If you want to guarantee the gift of failure in marriage to your children, then keep the fight going. If you want no relationship with your kids when they leave home, then keep the battle raging. However, if you want to pass along a legacy of love and hope to your children, if you want them to believe that a marriage can succeed (even if yours didn't), if you want them always to come to you with their troubles and questions, then make a commitment to start modeling positive behavior — now. All of this begins, as I've pointed out over and over, by ending the fighting and talking with your teen — acknowledging your behavior, listening to her concerns, and pledging to change.

I have asked thousands of teens, "How many of you think you will have a marriage that does not end in divorce?" Only around 20 percent of them do. When I asked further, "Why do you think this is the case?" they universally reply, "We have never seen it happen." And it's true — most of them haven't.

Whether or not your marriage works out, you can always — always — model positive, respectful behavior for your teen. Even when you are deep in the war zone, you can save bitter words and accusatory tones for settings in which your teen is not present. When you talk about your ex-spouse in front of your teen, you can choose to do so with respectful, fair words and a calm voice. You can be up front about the issues you and your spouse could not resolve; you can acknowledge your part in the problems.

When talking to your teen, your best course of action is to be direct. Ask her, "How has the fighting confused you and messed you up? What else is it doing to you?" This accomplishes two important things: It lets your teen express her feelings, and it immediately lets her know that you are aware of how bad things have gotten.

You must also tell your teen that you are going to try to stop the bad-mouthing and fighting. Even if your ex-spouse will not stop, you can bring about positive changes. In family therapy, there is an unspoken understanding that when either parent hangs up the gloves, it helps immensely. In addition, you may want to draw up some rules or agreements between you and your teen, underscoring your willingness to change and also empowering your teen to hold you accountable — which may help him feel that he *can* do something to help the situation. Following are some suggestions to include in your new "relations rulebook."

1. Give your teenager permission to tell you when you get out of hand.
2. Develop a sense of humor over what has transpired. Crack jokes about yourself after apologizing for a mistake. Don't become defensive. When your teen says, "Hey, you blew it again," reply by saying things like, "You're right. Sometimes I think if I didn't have someone to fight with, I'd fight with myself."
3. Put a chart up on the refrigerator. Have your teen give you a gold star when you've had a good day, a black mark when you blow it.
4. At the end of each week, let your teen decide on some kind of award or demerit for your overall behavior for the week. If you were

good, you and your teen go out for pizza or do something fun. If you've been bad, perhaps your kid gets the pizza, and you don't.

Remember, humor and the ability to poke fun at ourselves helps to make us more accessible to our kids, particularly when we have run the risk of alienating them by negative behaviors during divorce strife. It opens the door to communication, paving the way to talk to about other troubling issues. As time passes, share with your kid how painful the breakup was for you. Explain as best you can why you have been unreasonable and at times irrational. This will take time. And remember, if at first you don't succeed, you are running about average.

* * *

Let's face it: Life in families is rarely easy. Relationships require hard work. Even in the best of circumstances, secrets and strife will sometimes abound. There will be stretches where life runs smoothly; there will be times when it all hits the rocks. The most important thing to remember, though, is to keep those lines of communication with your teen open. If they're not currently open, take a deep breath and make that appointment to talk with your teen. Get your foot in the door. Your goal, always, is to communicate to your teen that no matter how hairy things get, no matter how troubling a secret he is harboring, he can always come to you. And your behavior has to mirror your words.

If you have secrets that affect your family's life, or if fighting — whether fallout from divorce or otherwise — is obviously causing your child pain, then stop it. If your child point-blank asks you to stop, by all means stop, and thank her for taking the initiative to change the situation for the better. Focus on how you can set a positive example for your child. Never, never be afraid to ask for outside help. The health of your children — and all your future generations — depends on it.

Chapter 5:
Violence and Abusive Relationships

*"The past is history. The future is a mystery.
This moment is a gift."*

When a kid makes a special appointment for a chat with me after one of my talks, I rarely expect that it's because he has a happy story to share with me. Sometimes I can sense a dark, dangerous secret looming long before it's spilled to me. It's hinted at in the quick way kids avert their eyes, the little shake in their voice or sometimes in their hands.

The afternoon I had a cup of coffee in the school cafeteria with seventeen-year-old Stacey, all the ingredients were in place for a long-withheld secret about to be revealed. She, too, had a hard time making eye contact — she'd glance at me from time to time from between layers of cheap drugstore mascara. As I stirred my heavily sweetened "cup of joe," I wasn't surprised to see her hand shake as she extended it toward me, asking if I'd pass her the sugar. I was shocked, however, to see what happened next.

"Thanks," she said as I handed her the sugar. The second I let it go, she gasped in pain and nearly dropped the container. "Now, how much did that jar of sugar weigh?" I wondered. Then I saw the scars and bruises on her wrist, and the perfectly matched set on her other one. I looked in her eyes and said, "What happened?" Tears flashed up fast. Mascara ran down her cheeks.

"How did you know and why are you asking?" she said.

"Well," I said gently, "I am in the business to know. You wanted to talk, and I figured from the get-go you had something important to share."

She eyeballed the stained acoustic-tiled ceiling, then pushed out both her arms across the table, exposing her wrists. "Okay," she sighed. "Take a look."

With great care I took both her wrists in my hands. With my thumb and index finger, I turned them over and took a look. Under the skin, I could see old and new break marks and twisted-up bones. "How long did this go on?" I asked.

"Just until a few months ago," Stacey said. "My dad started tying me to the bed when I was eight. He tied me so tight that he would sometimes snap my wrists when he used me. They don't work so well anymore, and they hurt all the time. Someday I will have the money to get them fixed. Maybe when I am out of college."

"Is he still alive?" I asked. "Still at home?"

"Are you kidding?" she said. "He's in max doing time for assault. I waited to move out of the house till he was sent up. I couldn't leave him there with my little sister, could I? But now it's cool. I'm finally safe."

I just smiled at Stacey. In the midst of living with the horror of her father's unreported sexual abuse, she also became a heroine. No one, including her mom, came to her rescue, yet she had survived, and in doing so had also protected her sister. Yes, it was horrible, but the saga had ended. She was finally talking to someone about what had happened, and finally beginning to heal.

I told her that even though her father was in prison, she needed to talk with someone besides me so she could finally exorcise the pain out of her mind and her heart. She needed help to understand that the memories of her abuse were still riding shotgun with her, and they would her entire life unless she dealt with them now. I explained that her work was to make peace with her heart and with the trauma that visited her life. She took a referral for counseling on the spot.

At every talk, I try hard to explain what happens to people who have suffered abuse and violence. I also let them know that these kinds of hurts are so bad that even though the bogeyman has gone away, the movie often has not ended. The pain can revisit them any time their entire life — even in future generations. Abuse is a serious matter.

* * *

A parent reading the above scenario may breathe a sigh of relief. "Thank goodness," you may think. "That's never happened in our home. Our children are safe. This chapter doesn't apply to me." Think again. Your child doesn't have to come from an abusive family life in order to be concerned about and affected by abuse in countless forms. Abuse can happen in homes and in dating relationships. It can be administered by parents, family members, boyfriends, or girlfriends. It can be as obvious as a punch in the face or as subtle as mind games and manipulation. It can take the form of love withheld, violence threatened, or rape.

And a teenager doesn't have to be abused himself in order to care deeply and raise serious questions about abuse. About 40 percent of all the questions I'm handed on abuse during my seminars are asked out of concern for a friend in a questionable or downright dangerous situation. As a parent, you need to be able to address your teen's questions about abuse whether or not it is happening under your own roof. By doing so, you may be helping your teen to avoid being raped or teaching her how to know it's time to leave a potentially violent relationship. You may be in a position to help a friend of his who is suffering abuse or at least help your teen find ways to support such a friend. In all cases, you'll be communicating something deeply important to your teen: That even in the midst of the most desperate situations, she can come to you for support and help.

It's this last point that may be the most important of all. Abuse thrives on secrecy, which we've already seen can eat away at the health of a family. And I'm not talking about long-held secrets that can help shed light on a current family situation — I'm talking about the elephant-in-the-living room secrets that teens in abusive situations live with every day but feel powerless to do anything about for fear of bringing about even more violence. These secrets *must* be brought to the light of day — meaning, at least, that the proper authorities must be informed — in order for teens to emerge into adulthood intact. When these secrets are never faced, when the pain of abuse is never rooted out and talked about (with professional help, if necessary), the abuse is often carried into the next generation, and the next, in a continuous cycle.

Some of the questions in this chapter will deal with situations you'll recognize in your own home. Some you'll hear when your teen confides in you about a friend, or possibly a relationship he is involved in himself. Or perhaps you'll hear them from another teen — a neighbor, your child's friend, a niece, or a nephew — who will seek you out as a trustworthy non-parent adult. Abuse touches all of us — including our children — in more ways than you may realize. It can be dealt with and, better yet, it can be prevented. But it will require your involvement. Read on, and you will see how.

Key Points to Remember When Discussing Violence and Abusive Relationships

Teens have lots of questions about violence and abuse in relationships. Many teenagers report to me that they have friends involved in violent dating relationships (this may also be a sideways manner of reporting that *they* are in one themselves). Others worry about their friend's home life (or perhaps their own). Abuse is more common than you might think — or that society likes to admit. A study published in the *Journal of the American Medical Association* (July 2001) states that up to 50 percent of all women in America have been involved in a violent relationship at some point in their lives.

Unfortunately, abusive relationships are hardly ever discussed with teenagers — who, as we'll see, are in prime positions to end existing cycles of abuse and prevent new ones from beginning. Abuse in families and dating relationships is not a topic frequently discussed in health class, yet at every school I visit, I am always asked questions about family violence and abuse. And any teen is vulnerable to stumbling into a dating relationship with an abusive person — or having a relationship with a seemingly safe, nonviolent person suddenly go bad. You must be vigilant and prepared if your child gets involved in an abusive dating relationship. You must be prepared to acknowledge and get help for abuse that is happening in your own home.

Here are the key points to remember as you prepare to answer these kinds of questions:

1. Family violence is too often kept a secret. If parents start paying attention to the issues surrounding abuse, it will be possible to begin to root out this cancer that infects so many teens' lives. You, as a parent, need to be aware that you are probably the only adult who ever will discuss this volatile issue with your teen. Regardless of how positive and stable your family life may be, your child's happiness beyond the home can truly depend on the input you give her now.
2. Violence in relationships is not often discussed among teens, either. It may be noticed, but the taboos surrounding abuse are so great that teens seldom bring up the issue among themselves. Parents must step forward and discuss this issue with their teen, whether or not they suspect it is affecting his life.

3. Kids growing up in abusive families often carry the wounds of abuse and incest into adulthood. Family violence is rooted in family history. If you grew up in an abusive family and are now in an abusive relationship, get help immediately. If your children are being abused in your family, get them help, too. Help does not necessarily mean leaving your home or getting out of your relationship. It means going to an expert who can assist you and your family. There are no quick fixes to tough issues.
4. Your teen may need your help if one of her friends is in an abusive home. Up to 40 percent of the students I have surveyed are worried about the home lives of their friends. Encourage your children not to ignore what they suspect and perhaps see. Parents need to lend a hand to both their teen and her friend. Three things must happen:

- Encourage your child to remain steadfast as a friend. Too often kids in desperate trouble also lose their friends — their only support — along the way. Explain how important it is to stick by friends during their time of need.
- You have a responsibility to report abuse; it is the law. However, do not simply call the police (unless an immediate danger is reported). Also contact a battered women's shelter, a professional counseling agency, and/or a member of the clergy who understands the issues of incest and violence.
- Emotional abuse is just as devastating as physical abuse. Make it a point to mentor any one of your teen's friends who is in trouble. Have him over to your home regularly. Build his self-esteem. Refer him to the school guidance counselor or his clergyperson. Demonstrate how being a parent means being involved in your teenager's life. Demonstrate that there are adults out there who care deeply. Set the example and get involved.

Questions and Answers

"Why do parents abuse their kids?"

There's no better place to begin than with this question. Why does abuse happen? How could a parent harm a child? How does family violence spill over into violence in other relationships?

Teens ask these questions because they are keenly aware that some of their friends live with a parent who abuses them. When I ask students if any of them are worried about what is happening to one of their friends, the hands go up, and the looks of concern make my heart miss a beat. I see this everywhere I go in America.

There is no question that adult violence is rooted in childhood violence. Sadly, it becomes a tradition in many families — each generation takes their turn at hitting their own children, carrying on what happened to them. Some parents justify their heavy hands as being character building. Some families even use religion to justify hurting their children. Naturally, all this does not mean that every child growing up in an abusive family becomes an abuser. However, kids who are hit or molested sometimes do become abusive parents themselves — or, more often, they grow up to repeat the cycle by becoming victims, heading into relationships where the familiarity of abuse is comforting.

Family violence comes in many forms. Physical abuse might be the most obvious — it's manifested in hitting, pushing, kicking, choking, shaking, or using a weapon, among other things. Emotional violence can be just as devastating as physical violence, but it's a little more insidious. It can include playing mind games, withholding love or affection, constant criticizing, threatening, manipulating, or name-calling. Sexual abuse might be the toughest one to think about: rape, unwelcome or inappropriate touch, fondling, oral sex — any sexual act between a child and adult. All of these types of abuse can be incredibly damaging to young people. All of them, also, can become repeated behavior for generations to come.

Why isn't the cycle is broken? I truly think that not enough people know they can get help. Recent studies note that 50 percent of women today are hit by their husbands at least once during their marriage, yet many of these violent families live in fear and secrecy, and so incidents go unreported. Often, shame is so great in these families that it is taboo for the "outside world" to be notified. Drugs and alcohol also can play a big role in family abuse. It is a tragic, ongoing, dangerous mess. Yet it can be stopped — or better yet, prevented.

I remember reading the following statistics in the late '80s: Some degree of physical violence occurs in 30 percent of engaged couples. Sixteen percent of couples have experienced some form of marital violence in the past year. Fifty percent of high school seniors are hit by their parents. Eight percent of them are actually injured (Frank Pittman, M.D., *Turning Points,* New York: W. W. Norton & Co., 1987, 283). At that time, I was working with street kids in the dark world of Times Square. Those statistics opened my eyes to the amount of family violence occurring in America. Most of it goes unreported.

But here's the good news: Most physical violence in marriage can be stopped *before* marriage. Since violence begins in relationships, rooting out violence also needs to begin in relationships. If teens make good choices in relationships, the violence will be reduced.

At every one of my seminars, I speak bluntly and openly about violence in relationships. I tell teens if and when they are in a serious relationship — or even engaged — if violence surfaces, even just once, *immediately* break up. I am serious when I say this. It always launches every group into a discussion about the root causes of violent relationships. I tell teens, "If you don't want to get hit, then break up *as soon as* violence begins — or is even threatened or hinted at." I expect you, as a parent, to tell your teen the same.

More than 90 percent of the time, violence in relationships rears its ugly head before the wedding bells sound. In other words, most couples already know, going into a marriage, whether their partner will be abusive. It is rare for abuse to begin after marriage — unless, of course, a couple dated a short time, got married quickly, and never got to know each other. To put a stop to potential marital abuse, talk with your teen *now* about not getting into an abusive relationship. Here's how to address this question if it comes up (and if it doesn't, include the topic when you sit down with your teen to have that "relationship talk"). Ask your teen:

- "Why are you asking me about this now?" (If the question hasn't been asked, perhaps raise the issue by saying something like,

"Now that you're starting to date (or have a girlfriend or a boyfriend), I want to mention one thing you should always keep in mind...")
- "Are you worried about one of your friends?"
- "What concerns you about family violence and abuse?"
- "What do you think causes abuse? How do you think it can be prevented or stopped?"

The first question you always need to ask your teen is "Why are you asking this question right now?" It is important to know if there is a pressing issue that needs to be addressed. Perhaps a friend of your teen's — or your teen herself — needs immediate help.

Whatever the reasons, your teen most likely has seen abuse, heard about it, or read about it. What do parents have to do? If your teenager has a friend in trouble, encourage your child to get his friend help (a later question in this chapter will discuss just that). Your teen cannot do that alone. You must lend a hand. Anytime children are at risk, the proper authorities *must* be notified. Experts in family violence need to be brought into the picture. Tell your child that as a friend, he needs to stick by his friend, but it is not his responsibility to be a counselor. Please emphasize that point. Leave the tough stuff to seasoned professionals.

If your teen is herself involved in a violent relationship, read on. The remaining questions in this chapter deal with different facets of violence and abuse in relationships, and how to deal with it in specific cases.

"My best friend told me that she was raped by her father. She also has had a lot of boyfriends who have used her for sex. She told me that she hates herself. She feels that somehow she is to blame and doesn't know what to do. What should I tell her?"

Reading questions like this used to make me shudder. I still shudder, but now I have a clearer picture of what some teens face in their families and relationships. It is troubling to know that these kinds of problems are not rare. All the way back in 1978, 20 percent of girls reported some kind of sexual contact with adults. Today, we know that one-third of high school girls and college-age women experience violence in an intimate or dating relationship. Fifty percent of all rape victims are teens. And the vast majority of these rapes were perpetrated by known acquaintances (National Clearinghouse for Battered Women).

Furthermore, I have seen, over and over again, that there is a connection between sexually promiscuous behavior in teens and deep, disturbing trouble and/or violence at home.

Let me give you a quick tour of the world of kids who have been abused. Abuse in any form leaves in its wake emotional confusion and self-doubt. It can even make the victim think he is to blame for what happened. Families in which incest has occurred often look very normal to outsiders. The abusive parent — whether the father or the mother — does not appear to be a tyrant. In fact, he or she is often seen as mild mannered, eager to please, hardworking, insecure, anxious, and frightened by failure.

As Dr. Frank Pittman noted in his book *Turning Points,* there is a double standard at work in these families. The father (assuming he is the abuser) "feels the man should offer the sex, but it is up to the female to set the sexual limits...no matter what age, to say 'no' or say 'how much.'" These men see their children as having invited them into sex. When the foreplay starts, the child becomes the "little whore," and hence he no longer has responsibility for what happens. The father does not experience much guilt, but may be ashamed when the story comes out (pp. 308–309).

Clearly this is very confusing to the victim. Living through this nightmare leaves kids wounded, angry, confused, filled with self-doubt and self-hate, and depressed. If you think for one moment that kids just get over these things once the abuse stops, think again. They don't. When intimacy has been violated in any family, life falls out of balance. Family is the place where children learn to love and trust; sexual abuse tears this apart and inevitably affects their other intimate relationships. Too often, years later, after several failed marriages and children in tow, people finally wake up and decide to tackle what happened to them. It's far better to deal with this problem in high school rather than middle age. Help a teenager resolve this issue now, and it will not haunt him later in life.

In this question though, there actually is some progress. Abusive sexual relationships have stopped for now. The girl is aware that she has been hurt, but the best news is, she wants to find some way to heal her heart. All of that is a positive. She clearly has the support of a friend, your teen. That's positive, too, and in the next question, we'll talk more in-depth about the help a friend can provide.

Still, this girl needs to be in therapy. Counseling will sort out the whys and hows of what occurred. In this case, friendly support is not enough. One important thing you can do is to tell your teen to strongly support her friend to see a sexual abuse specialist. How do you go about doing that?

Most teenagers do want to help their friends and, as a matter of policy, parents need to empower their children to assist their friends. Kids do well with support and guidance. Start the process by contacting the school guidance office, local social service agency, or your clergy to get a good referral. Suggest your teen go with her friend to the first session (if her friend wants her to). Make certain the friend sees someone who will involve the rest of the family in therapy. Then, leave the rest up the to the professional. At the appropriate time, the counselor will contact the mom and bring in the whole family.

"My best friend was abused by her stepfather. Her mom threw him out of the house, but she still feels like she is dirty. How can I help her let go of these bad feelings and feel better about herself?"

The first step in dealing with this question is similar to that of the previous one. As a parent, you ought to make certain your child's friend gets into counseling. The school guidance office or local social service agencies are good places to start. Be bold, make the phone call. Find a good referral. Make certain that whoever will see the girl knows to also see her mother. Even though it is clear from the question that the mother is aware of what happened, when there is sexual abuse, both parent and child need therapy. If the friend is nervous about going to speak with the guidance counselor at school, have your child go with her to the first appointment. Make certain, though, that the friend's mother is aware that her daughter is going to a counselor for some assistance. Only in extreme cases should parents ever be kept out of the loop, and this is not one of them.

Any child who has been abused needs to be in counseling. Every parent should know that to be true. Support groups are also very helpful. But what can victims do beyond this? And how can a friend, like your own teen, help?

There is a certain kind of ritual I have found to be extremely helpful for victims of abuse. It is helpful not just for teens, but also for adult victims of abuse and child abuse. Victims of abuse generally have a lousy self-image. Letting go of all the dark images of self-doubt takes a great deal of courage. Confronting the pain rebuilds courage.

What follows is a wonderful adjunct to the counseling process — though it in no way supplants the need for therapy. In fact, this exercise should only be undertaken after a good deal of time in therapy has passed. Still, it is one that I have used extensively to help victims let go of the anger and pain that haunts their life after abuse. It works best if a friend is involved in step two of this exercise.

Step one:

- Buy a diary or spiral notebook. Keep it private. Do not show it to anyone.
- Set aside a half-hour every third day. During that time, write a very personal letter to your abuser (in this case, the stepfather).
- Repeat this process every three days for one month.
- In each letter, make certain to write down, in vivid detail, everything that happened to you. Spare nothing. Describe how the abuse made you feel and what it did to your personal life.
- Spill out your emotions in your writing. Do not avoid your rage. Let out your anger in the letters.

Once you have completed the letters, one more thing must be done. This is where you might involve your best friend. Step two:

- Find a very special spot that you love and where you feel especially nourished. Go there. It can be a park, your backyard, a stream, a lake — any place you feel is special. Once the spot is picked, your friend may accompany you. I believe it is better to have a witness to what happens next. Bring a box of matches with you also.

- Upon arrival, stand for a few minutes in silence. Then, even if you are alone, announce out loud something like the following: "Behold, I prepare myself to let go of all the dark feelings and pain expressed in the letters. I have suffered enough. By destroying these letters, I am making them dust of the earth. As I destroy them, I will release my pain and anger. It will no longer haunt my mind and heart." Say this with great concentration.

- Take out the letters and read them aloud. Read slowly. Do not hold back any emotions. Crying, moaning, wailing, or yelling is permissible and recommended.

- When you are finished, gather the letters together. At this point, you can decide how you wish to dispose of them. If you like, you may rip them into small pieces. If you prefer, take out the matches and burn them (make sure, however, that you are in a place where burning is allowed). If you are by a stream or lake, you can toss the pieces of paper or the ashes into the water. If you are at home, you can throw them into the toilet and flush them away (use your best judgment, though — don't litter or plug the toilet). You can also bury the pieces or ashes in a special spot, if you wish.

- The goal is to let go of your pain. After you have disposed of the letters, declare the following: "Behold, I am free in my heart of you. I am now free of what you did to me. I know what happened. What you did no longer is a part of me. I have let go now of what you did. I will not forget what happened, but I will not let it hurt me anymore!"

This last statement is very important. Too often people who have been hurt carry the pain of what happened long after the event. They feel it as if their injury happened yesterday, not years before. And worse yet, they carry their wounds long after the person who hurt them is no longer in their life, even dead. Yes, the pain can be so real that even if the abuser is deceased, his or her presence still lives on in the victim's mind and heart.

Often, this exercise needs to be done more than once. It is a good idea to repeat it once a year for a few years. How will the victim know when the self-hate and bad feelings are basically gone? He will know that healing has occurred when he sits down to write another letter and no longer feels any need to pour it all out again. At that point, it is over. I also suspect that the therapy will end right around the same time.

Reading this last question, as a parent of a teen, you might be thinking, "Gosh, this is just too heavy for my kid to handle or be involved with." You might, at the same time, also think, "This is too tough even for me to handle."

Sorry, you have to be involved — all the way, as best you can. No holds barred. Any child who is a victim of abuse needs the best parental advice and support you can muster. Many tough years always lie ahead for victims of abuse. Any measure of comfort requires rigorous honesty and support. If you are the partner of your child's abuser — whether or not that person is still in the picture — face up to what happened now. Do not abandon your child. Not getting fully involved is a form of passive aggression toward your child, and passive aggression is devastating. Denial only leaves your child wounded, hurt, and angry. Sexual abuse just doesn't magically get better.

"I am in serious trouble at home. My father gets scary drunk. Every few months, he beats on my mom and threatens me. I am old enough to get out of the house, but what about my mom and my little sister? There is no stopping my dad, so don't tell me to talk to him."

This is admittedly a complex question and a dangerous situation. I always tell the student who writes this question to get immediate help. In fact, when questions like this come up at my seminars, even though I have no idea who wrote the question, I make it a point, in front of the whole group, to say that help has to be secured before the end of the school day. Fortunately, at most of my seminars, the school guidance counselor or another seasoned social service veteran from a local agency is with me. I have them explain what the student needs to do, how they can help, and how they can be contacted.

It is beyond the scope of this book to adequately answer this question. You will see why when I explain a few important points surrounding questions of this nature. However, there are things you must do if a teen drops a question like this one into your lap.

This is a dangerous situation. The father is a violent binge drinker. On any binge, he might harm his kids. I imagine you are wondering, as many people unfamiliar with this situation do, "Why hasn't the mom picked up and gone to a battered women's shelter with her kid?" or "Why hasn't she called the police and the had the father arrested?"

Let me explain to you why this is a very complex and dangerous issue. Alcoholism is a disease of denial, and denial often includes the entire family. Families caught in cycles of violence are often too afraid for their own safety to take action, and the flip side of taking action — staying in the situation — obviously also means danger.

Everyone is caught in the drunk's frightening world. Alcoholics tend to lose all sense of reason and judgment when they are drinking, and if they have violent tendencies, this is where they come out. Alcoholics also can be extremely unpredictable. The father who brings his kids treats and his wife flowers one night can be a rip-roaring, fist-swinging drunk the next. It's like living with two different people: one who is relatively normal and caring, and another who will expend any amount of effort to destroy all that is good in his life.

Why haven't the police been called or shelter sought? With family violence, nothing is as simple as it seems on the surface. Ask any police officer who deals with domestic violence or any professional at a shelter, and they will tell you that not every family who is in danger should go to a shelter, nor do they call and request real help. How could that possibly be true?

Well, it turns out to be a very dangerous paradox. If a family goes to a shelter before they are totally committed to get out of the house, then decides to return home, it can turn out to be a deadly decision. A move to a shelter must be a final move; no turning back. If the family does return to a violent parent, they may face wrath turned up exponentially. Yet staying in the house can also be deadly. Either way, there is danger. Police, shelters, and therapists deal with these kinds of situations all the time.

What should you do if your teen tells you that one of his friends is in this kind of trouble? Or if you are "Mom" in this scenario? Involve the authorities immediately. Trained professionals need to be involved, not concerned neighbors or friends.

What happens to kids growing up in families like this? What lies ahead for the student who asked this question? The good news is that most kids who get help end up just fine. However, there are victims, and the picture is not pretty. Children of alcoholics carry a tremendous amount of guilt. If you read between the lines of the question, you can almost hear the confusion, guilt, and pain. In addition, when children of abusers don't get help, they often go on to become abusers themselves or spouses of abusers (as we've seen).

The brunt of the trauma is often carried by the oldest child, who often tries hard to make things appear "normal" at home. These children live with the continual false hope that if they make things appear normal enough, then somehow Dad will stay away from the booze. Keeping the family secret is very important, as any exposure might set Dad off or harm the family in some way. In the end, invariably, their efforts fail. I have worked with dozens of teens from these kinds of families who ran away or threatened to kill themselves. These are desperate ploys to draw attention away from the violent drunk; their action is a cry for help.

Often in the end, they give up and go underground. As they grow older, they sometimes join in the drinking and turn into drunks themselves. In the end, their lives are destroyed. Pretty grim tale, isn't it? However, I feel that, as parents, you need to know the unvarnished truth. I think you now understand why the authorities, not you, need to be involved. Again, make the phone call. But how do you find the best or right agency?

You can start with the school counselor. I would also open up the phone book and call your local police department and speak to an officer. Usually, they will have what they consider to be the best referral in town. If there is a battered women's shelter nearby, you need to give them a call. Your search will pay off. One of more of these professionals will get involved. Give them as much information as possible, and then let them handle it. I do not recommend calling the family; I think it is obvious how dangerous that might turn out to be.

If a teen in this family has run away or attempted suicide, odds are that an agency or some professional is already involved, which is a good sign. Remember, crisis does open doors to solutions. Often, they turn out to be the best doors. If someone is already involved, then your job is finished. Since your teen is a friend of the child in trouble, make certain he reaches out to his friend. Let the power of friendship and support flower. Open your home by making it a normal and safe haven.

Too often, when families or friends get into sticky situations, friends disappear. Make certain that is never the case in your family. True family character means standing by friends. One of the lessons your teenager will take away from this situation is that problems require that something be done; they can't be avoided — that only makes them worse. Alas, facing crisis is never easy. Teaching your teen that she can make a difference simply by being a good friend is a powerful lesson.

"My mother is an alcoholic. I always have to watch out for her. It's hard 'cause I also have to take care of my little brother a lot of the time. What should I do?"

As we've seen from the previous question, addiction creates nightmares in families. When a parent or other family member is an alcoholic or addicted to another substance, the entire family is thrown into chaos. Yet while this question addresses the concerns of a family fractured by addiction, it's mainly the story of the oldest child — the child who takes charge when his parent is incapacitated by alcohol.

To fully understand the impact of a question like this — and the seriousness of the situation the child is beginning to disclose — you must learn how to probe for more information. This question, revealing as it is, only uncovers the tip of the proverbial iceberg. You quickly sense there is much more to the story. What do you do when a teen — maybe even your teen — tells you a story that is clearly filled with a lot of unspoken issues? How do you fill in the blanks? Let me spell out the procedure.

The secret is always to begin by asking more questions. The rule is, when you are confused, sense unsaid complications, or feel you're only getting a portion of the story, ask as many questions as you need until you understand. Not only does that create good conversation, it clarifies issues and gives you the bigger picture. Follow your intuition. Get as much information as possible. This will pay off great dividends later. If therapy is recommended, you can save literally hours of session time if you have the basics of the story and the presenting problem. In addition, when you understand the issues, you will stay on message when you talk with your teenager. This is a great help to you and your child. Making assumptions will only lead you into a thicket of difficulties.

I did spend some time speaking with this student after my seminar was over. My short conversation revealed the following: His mom comes home and drinks herself into oblivion regularly. She refuses to get treatment. Dad is long gone — missing in action for at least ten years. The young man is eighteen years old. He is a senior in high school. He does all the shopping and cleaning. He has a younger brother to look after. His aunt helps out occasionally. His grandmother, who lives across town, is frail and housebound. He is now the adult in charge of the family. He is exhausted and burned out. He feels powerless to stop his mother's addiction. His grades have suffered and so has his social life. Finally, he always feels very responsible. I got all this information in less than five minutes, and it helped immensely in the following weeks as he sought help. I asked and he answered. You can do the same.

When you are confused, keep asking questions. Information is critical in understanding the mental health of the entire family, including the problems that underlie the obvious issue of addiction. Often, even when an addict or alcoholic cleans up, only the drinking or drug problem has been tackled. Predrug problems and unresolved issues remain intact — they've only been hidden behind a self-medicating smokescreen.

Dealing with the alcohol or drugs, then, is only one part of the puzzle. Getting clean is only the first step. Rehab is also necessary. The children need to get help, too, otherwise the whole process can start up again. The alcoholic will return to a home where nothing has changed. The old problems will surface, and then the alcoholic is at risk to pick up the bottle and once again star in this sad family drama.

Rephrased, this question really means: "My mom is an alcoholic. She is ruining my life. I can't handle it anymore. Everything is in turmoil. What do I do?" This child, because he is the oldest, has been forced to take charge and grow up too soon. Keep in mind that this also happens in families where the parent in charge has a long-term illness or a major mental health problem.

Regardless of the situation, teenagers should never have to be in charge of their families. Too often in these families, the oldest children have to sacrifice their teen years. Society may praise them for being so responsible, but later in life, these kids experience profound unhappiness and anger. They tend to become very rigid and have little tolerance for weakness in others. They feel cheated out of their childhoods.

What needs to change in this situation? Simply put, Mom has to get help to be the mother again. She must resume her post as head of the family. Her son needs to be able to be a teenager and pursue his final high school dreams. The best-case scenario would be Mom getting into treatment and taking the reins from her son so he can have his own life back. The prognosis? Not likely.

Even if Mom does get off the booze, recovery is not easy, and stabilizing a family requires months and years of rebuilding trust and healing from old wounds. How is this young man — who has been running the family just fine without her help — going to trust her enough to hand her the baton in time for him to "just be a teenager" before he has to race off to college, a job, or other adult duties? And if Mom doesn't clean up her act, how can he leave his family knowing there's no one in the driver's seat? The situation is complicated. What's a real solution for this kid?

Whether or not Mom stops drinking and begins to take control of her life, someone needs to help this kid. Children in this situation desperately need support, and a support group based on Alcoholics Anonymous — like Alateen or Al-Anon — is probably the best choice. The group will not only emotionally lend a hand filled with understanding, but can also guide kids to the proper social service agency that can intervene. Most important, simply by attending Alateen or Al-Anon meetings regularly, teens can change the alcoholic family dynamics, which often can lead to a parent seeking treatment. Alcoholics and their family members are players in a wicked game with prescribed roles — which are very important in keeping the family functioning and keeping the addiction underground, where it can thrive. When a family member steps out of her designated role — say, by attending Alateen and refusing to play by the family's sick rules — the addicted family structure can implode, sometimes leading the addict into recovery.

In families where a long-term chronic problem has prevented the parent from taking care of his or her children, before the teenager can go off-duty at home, someone has to be willing to go back on-duty. This is never an easy task, especially in a situation like this one, where Mom insists on staying a drunk and other relatives have limited involvement. This is where any adult — like you, as a neighbor, the parent of a friend, etc. — can step in.

As we've seen with the previous question, there's often little you can do to intervene directly. Such efforts are at best meddlesome and at worst downright dangerous. If the parent has any tendency toward violence when under the influence, you will make the situation much, much worse for the teen you are hoping to help. A better solution is, first, to contact the necessary authorities and professionals (school guidance counselor, clergy, police, social service agency) and notify them of the situation. *They* will know how to intervene in a safe and effective manner.

Second — and this applies especially if the teen in question is a friend of your teen — open your home to him. Make it clear he's welcome anytime for dinner, sleepovers, and the like. Invite him to bring along any sibling in his charge, as well. Plan group activities from time to time, so you or other family members can occupy his siblings, relieving his responsibility to be their sole caretaker for at least a little while. And, much as you would with your own child, maintain an atmosphere of comfort and care, making it clear that if and when he needs an adult to talk to, he can approach you.

There is hope in situations like these. If the nonfunctioning parent gets or is forced to get treatment, things will improve. She will be assisted in understanding and facing her fears. She also will see how her alcoholism has affected her family. She will need support — from counseling, AA, and, if possible, friends and family. In the best of worlds, people who get support and are shown another way to deal with their problems generally are successful in making the changes that help themselves and their family.

Yet even if the addict never frees him- or herself of the habit, the family must and can get back to their lives. It is very important to remember that invariably another opportunity, meaning a crisis, will arise. While each new crisis presents a new danger, it also is a new opportunity to recover. Sometimes it takes getting to the end of the rope before you let go. With counseling and support groups to back them up, families will be better prepared and more confident the next time trouble comes knocking at their door.

"My boyfriend every so often gets drunk. When he is drinking, he gets mean. He hasn't hit me, but he has come close. He has smashed stuff, hit the wall, and threatened me. After it is all over, he tells me he is sorry and that he didn't mean to do it. He says it was the drinking. I love him and want to help him, but sometimes he really scares me. What should I tell him?"

I think any parent will recognize that the teen asking this question is right on the edge of serious trouble. When kids or anyone gets involved in a relationship where violence is fueled with drugs or alcohol, there is danger ahead. This kind of disturbing behavior does not magically go away. If your child comes to you with this question, or if you notice this kind of behavior taking place in her relationship, you need to step in and lend her a hand. As a parent of such a teen, you must try to get your child to break off the relationship. If that fails, see to it that she gets into counseling.

As with so many of the questions in this book, this one has multiple layers, each one revealing a complicated issue when pulled back. In addition to issues of alcohol abuse, anger, violence, and power in relationships, the whole subject of forgiveness needs to be explored. Forgiveness is so misunderstood that people — especially well-meaning kids who, rightly, have been raised to believe that forgiveness is noble — easily get trapped in nasty relationships. While forgiveness *is* noble, in this case, in spite of what is being reported here, no real forgiveness has ever been sought by the boyfriend. We'll discuss forgiveness a little later in this question.

First, let me go over some of the basic things you need to tell your child if he is involved in a violent or manipulative relationship. If, at the end of the discussion, your child still wants to stay in the relationship, I strongly suggest you seek professional help. It is no easy task getting a teenager into therapy. If that fails, and it often will, then seek out an able family therapist for yourself. Often the therapist will be able to come up with an intervention that will get your child to come in and talk.

Begin your discussion by saying something like this: "I am very worried about what is going on in your relationship. In fact, what you tell me scares me." Repeat back to her the exact points she has raised that clearly point to danger. In this case, the boyfriend (1) drinks too much on occasion, (2) gets angry and violent when he is drunk, (3) has gone so far as to throw objects and hit walls — and hitting your teen could be next, (4) is threatening her and frightening her, and (5) is not sincere about changing his behavior — even when he says he's sorry and promises it won't happen again, it still does. State your concern: primarily that your child will get hurt, and secondly that even if she never does, she is being trapped in a cycle of abusive behavior, and her devotion — fueled by his empty promises — will never let her out and into other, healthier relationships.

Then, state your recommendation that she break off the relationship. Make it clear that she has your full support on this, no matter what the fallout. It's quite likely that your teen will not be open to this. "But I love him," she may say. "I believe he will change. He needs my support." The truth is, she can support him the rest of her life and nothing will ever change. Many, many people are trapped in marriages or partnerships with alcoholic people because of this very belief. What he needs is professional help, maybe even treatment, and the best way to facilitate that kind of change is often through crisis. The loss of a loved one, like your teen, could precipitate exactly the crisis that is needed.

If your teen expresses resistance to breaking off the relationship, first of all, rest assured that a seed has been planted. She now has confirmation that she is in danger, she knows your opinion on the matter, and she knows she has your support. With each incident with her boyfriend, your suggestion will work away at her conscience, and she may — sooner than you think — follow through with your advice. However, before she does, you can reinforce your point by saying, "Since you don't seem willing to break this off yet, please do me a favor: Spend some time talking with someone else about this." Suggest she speak with the school guidance counselor, a family therapist, or a clergyperson. Tell her, "You can even bring your boyfriend to some of your sessions, if you want. I am worried and don't want anything bad to happen to you. Please do me a favor and see someone."

Situations like these can be very perplexing for parents. "Where is my child's common sense?" you may wonder. "Why doesn't she just leave him? Why isn't she looking out for herself? What seems to be the problem?" Part of the problem may be one we've touched on earlier. If (happily) she has not been exposed to abuse in her life, and if (not so happily) no one has sat her down and talked to her about abuse, it's quite likely that normally positive qualities — like good-heartedness, a forgiving nature, and a desire to support friends going through hard times — are getting in the way. She is willing to accept his apology and try to help him instead of looking out for her own best interests. Doesn't that seem like something a good friend or partner would do? This is a confusing issue for teens and adults alike. What really passes for an apology? What does it really mean to say to someone, "I forgive you?"

Most people think that any of the following declarations constitute an apology:

> *"I'm sorry."*
> *"I didn't mean to."*
> *"It was the drinking that did it."*
> *"I really need you to help me."*
> Or worse yet, *"Without you I am lost."*

None of the above statements, however, are true apologies. Saying "I'm sorry" doesn't mean the other person must simply accept and forgive. "I didn't mean to" never means all is forgiven. Forgiveness is only granted when the person who hurts the other goes over in detail what he did, what went wrong, and what he is going to do to make sure it doesn't happen again. Furthermore, accepting a true apology does not mean a relationship ought to continue. One is not necessarily connected to the other. For a more thorough discussion on what constitutes a true request for forgiveness, see chapter 2.

There is an even more dangerous issue lurking in this question. In any relationship haunted by the spectre of violence, accepting an "I didn't mean to" or an "I need you" takes everything a step further toward danger. Instead of placing the blame and the trouble where it belongs, on the shoulders of the boyfriend, the partner thinks *she* needs to help him to get better.

Victims often think it is their job to rehabilitate the person who abused them. Nothing, of course, could be further from the truth. In fact, what this means is that the person in danger thinks she is either responsible for the abuser's action or compelled to help him stop his violent actions. None of this is logical, but logic has nothing to do with it. Victims are so confused — by a partner's sweet words that don't match his actions, by society's enduring assumption that women will be caretakers, by their own hopes and dreams for the relationship — that denial is the knee-jerk response. The facts are too painful to face. They are willing to believe that what they witness isn't really true.

The sad truth is that this kind of thinking not only produces victims, it also produces the next generation of victims — this is how that cycle of abuse gets started. And no matter how good a parent you are, your child could easily fall into this kind of trouble. What does a parent say to a child caught in this web? You must get straight to the point and give her the facts: Her boyfriend owes her a *true* apology. He has to stop drinking. And finally, it is *his* responsibility to get the help he needs. It is not *her* job to rehabilitate him. He has to straighten himself out. She doesn't have the problem; he does.

Don't be surprised if she has trouble believing you. Get some material from your local battered women's shelter. Or better yet, take her there for a visit and a talk, if possible. This is not overkill. This is taking carefully measured steps to protect your child. Often it will take more than one beating or more than one threat to change a person's mind. Information about what can happen in dangerous relationships is very powerful. In the middle of the next crisis, your words and advice may indeed carry more weight.

As a parent, it is important to remember that advice given in the moment is often not heeded. But in the next inevitable crisis, your advice can mobilize your child to spring into action. No conversation is ever truly forgotten. That's why you need to have them.

"I am pretty certain I was raped. What do I do and what do I tell my parents?"

There are a handful of phrases that make a parent's heart stop — and this, rightfully so, is one of them. As shocked and as terrified as you might feel when hearing something like this come out of your own child's mouth, remember that it is nothing compared to what she must be feeling. *Right now,* your child needs your love, support, and strength above all else. She also needs you to take some action — and different kinds of action depending upon how recently the rape took place. Let's address urgent matters first.

If the rape has just occurred — if she's calling you in tears in the middle of the night or spilling her heart out the morning after — here's what you need to do, and quickly:

1. If your teen is not entirely forthcoming or sounds confused (which is, of course, entirely understandable), listen carefully and use your intuition. Lend her a hand by asking questions. Say, "Honey, am I hearing you correctly? Do you think you were raped?" She wouldn't be hemming and hawing about something that important if she did not want to spill the beans. Err on the side of your child.
2. From the start, try to remain calm and be reassuring. If you are present with your child as she tells you what happened, take her hand in a gesture of love and support. Say: "No wonder you are so upset. Rape is never your fault. I am so sorry this happened, but I am proud of you for telling me right away. I love you, and I will not let you down."
3. Next, start asking questions. Ask who did this, and what happened. Find out where, how, and when, getting the details of what took place as completely as possible. As difficult as it may be for your teen to remember these details, they will be necessary for a police

report and medical examination, and being asked to recount them now will help her remember the events as accurately as possible.
4. Call the police and follow instructions. Usually, an immediate step is getting your teen to a medical facility, where the police will get a report from your daughter.
5. Get your teen to a medical facility. If possible, make sure she does not clean up or use the bathroom before you get her there.
6. When these immediate steps have been taken, contact your lawyer in case charges need to be made.
7. Also make arrangements for your teen to see a counselor. You, as parents, may want to be involved in her therapy, too.

Now, let's step back and take a breath. Remember, this checklist deals with the immediate fallout of the worst-case scenario. But you don't have to wait for your teen to come to you in tears to discuss rape. A conversation about rape — how to protect yourself against it and what to do if it happens — is good ammunition for a teenager today. Better yet, make sure this conversation includes the debunking of some myths about the obligations and expectations surrounding dating, which can empower your daughter to avoid relationships and situations in which rape is likely to occur. By the way, every parent sending a child off to college should make some mention of the following points. Here, I'll get you started:

If you are discussing rape in general, say something like the following. If it makes it easier for you, you can read directly from this book:

"I know you might not have given this much thought yet, but now that you're dating (or spending more time out at night with friends), I want you to know I'm concerned about issues like rape. I think it happens far more often than people realize, and I also think most girls believe it will never happen to them. But it does happen, and I want us both to be prepared in case it ever does. I have this checklist that covers what we are supposed to do if you or a friend ever are raped. Let's go over it together. I love you, and I want you to know not only what to do, but how to get back in control of the situation."

1. If you are raped, get help immediately. This means going to a friend, a family member, a medical center, a rape crisis center, or the police. Let's get the phone book now, and we'll program these

numbers into your cell phone or write them on a card for your wallet.
2. Call home or come home right away. If you feel better having me call the police and drive you to a medical center, I will do that for you. If a friend or police officer can take you to a medical center right away, by all means go, but call me immediately, and I will meet you there.
3. Don't shower or clean up. Don't go to the bathroom. Get to the police, emergency room, or rape crisis center and follow their directions.
4. Don't blame yourself. It's not your fault. You did not ask to be hurt. It is not a crime to be trusting or naive or even irresponsible. It *is* a crime to rape another person.

If your child tells you that she thinks she was raped, go through this checklist, just to be safe. If you are wondering how someone could "think" they were raped, read the question in this chapter about date rape drugs. Rape can and does come with confusion.

Of course, if your child has been raped, there is no guarantee she will come and tell you immediately — or ever. Rape often goes unreported, especially among teens (who, by the way, are the victims of half the rapes in our country). Even when kids have a good relationship and fairly open communication with their parents, they are often so ashamed of what happened that they fear speaking to their parents. They don't want to let them down. You, as a parent reading this information, may find yourself wondering, "How can I tell if something like that might have happened? If my child is raped and doesn't tell me, what signs should I look for? If I suspect my child was raped, what do I do?"

Parents are not psychic. If you teen does not tell you, it is not going to be easy to find out what happened. However, if your teen went to a party and came back depressed, angry, or anxious, I suggest you talk to her immediately. You should not assume she was raped, but don't put it out of your mind, either. Gently ask, "I see you are really upset. Did something happen last night?"

As a final step in any discussion on rape — whether preventive or after the fact — you must review and break down the myths and stereotypes surrounding rape. Even if you are in the middle of a crisis, debunking some of the following assumptions will help tremendously. I know that the hours and days after a rape — at the doctor's office or at the police station — don't seem like the right time to discuss sexual misinformation, but trust me on this one. When the word gets out that your child was raped, she will need to be armed with information. Knowing the facts can help protect her from some of the hurtful rumors that inevitably will start up, and she'll be able to set the story straight. If you're just sitting down with your teen for that preventive talk about rape, knowing the truth about the following myths will help her be stronger and make better decisions as she dates. And this discussion is not limited to girls. Teenage boys, too, need to be aware of common sexual myths like these:

1. Guys should be aggressive — it's okay to push for sex.
2. Girls should be passive about sex. When they say "no," they really mean "yes."
3. Girls who *do* say "yes" are sluts who are "asking for it" — they deserve what they get.
4. Guys should pay for everything on dates. They should make all decisions about where to go and what to do. A girl then owes a guy something in return.
5. Girls secretly want to be pushed around. They actually like to be shown who's boss, especially when it comes to sex.

    Most teens, like most adults, are filled with sexual misinformation. Sadly, society hasn't changed very much when it comes to rape — it's up to you to make sure your teen knows what the real deal is with guys and girls. Your input is always far more powerful in crisis situations than anything your teen may have heard from his peers.

    Last — but by far, most important — in any traumatic event, it is essential that parents give their love and support. Hugs are in order. "I love you's" are essential, and your teen needs them often. All the information in the world, while helpful, can never really take the place of a parent's unconditional love. No matter how tough the crisis, lift up your child. Help him find meaning in the narrow places and dark events of his life. Let her know that in a world at times rocked by depression, aggression, and addiction, hope is always the pathway she can walk. The only way out sometimes really is up.

    For more than twenty-five years, I have collected potent quotes from friends and from events that have touched my life. I have been referring to them for decades. I'd like to share a few good ones to lift your teen's heart. You can write one of them on an index card and leave it on his pillow at night. Prop one of them on her computer screen every so often as a greeting when she gets home from school. Leave a comment in one of his schoolbooks. Tape one or two to the steering wheel of her car. Use your imagination. The point of all this is that your love and support are everywhere, all the time.

- *You can start your day (or your life) over at any time.*
- *The past is history. The future is a mystery. This moment is a gift.*
- *Take action and turn over the results.*
- *No one floats into recovery on the wings of victory.*
- *The things and people we love tell us what we are.*
- *Always pray for willingness.*
- *Live in the solution, not the problem.*
- *God looks beyond our faults to see our needs.*

Recovering from a rape is a long, involved process. It will require hours of counseling, support groups, and sometimes tearful, late-night talks. Toss every piece of goodness you have into your teen's ring. Use this terrible event to build hope and integrity. You really can help your child rebuild not only her life, but a better life. Let inspiration, love, optimism, and support be her building blocks.

"I've kept this a secret. But now I think I ought to tell my parents I was sexually assaulted."

At first glance, this question seems identical to the previous one. But there really are two issues being raised in this question: keeping secrets and sexual assault. While I'll recap some points about dealing with sexual assault here, I'll focus more on the topic of secrets. Traumatic events are often deeply tied to secrets.

Let me start with the criminal act. Sadly, sexual assaults are not uncommon. It is estimated that one-third of all girls in high school and college will be victims of some type of sexual assault in one of their dating relationships. This is not a rare event. Make that known to your teenager.

How do you know if something has happened to your child? The good news is you don't have to be clairvoyant. There is a high correlation between sexual assault and depression. If you notice a dramatic change in your child's behavior or an abrupt downturn in her mood over a short period of time, find out why she is depressed. Refer to the checklist on depression in chapter 7. Follow those recommendations and get your child help. Be loving and firm. Teens *do* want their parents to know what has happened to them. It is your job to break the ice.

If your child tells you she was sexually assaulted, you need to think carefully about what you are going to do. Definitely consult a lawyer who is an expert in this area. You often can get a good referral at a rape crisis center. Never rationalize not taking action because it might embarrass your family. The damage done by not responding is far worse than what you perceive to be embarrassing. However, don't get talked into to doing something based on someone else's emotions — or yours — alone. This has to be carefully thought through. Do not hesitate to talk this out with a counselor and/or clergy and, yes, the police. Make arrangements to get proper help. Victims are empowered by taking action.

Now, let's move on to the other serious matter in this question: secrets. As we've seen in the previous chapter on family problems, keeping certain secrets can cause a lot of trouble. Why? Because if a serious, traumatic event is kept secret, how can you get help? Many teens do keep serious secrets, and date rape and sexual assault are high on that list.

Teens tell me that they cannot tell their parents dangerous secrets because "They will get mad at me," or "I will let them down," or "They think I am so good, and this will really disappoint them." I even hear, "If I tell them, I will get punished, and that will make things even worse than they already are." True, many families live by old adages like "silence is golden" or "some things are better left unsaid." Make no mistake, unraveling secrets is a sticky, messy process for everyone. But that's no excuse for not heeding your instincts and rooting out a problem in your teen's life if you believe he needs help.

Let me give you some general rules about secrets. If you suspect that something bad has happened to your kid, there is no room to be blown off with "It's not your concern," or "Stay out of my life." You must find out what happened. This, as you might imagine, is easier said than done. How do you get your child to open up to you, especially if sharing of secrets has not been the norm in your family? Obviously, it doesn't work to put your kid on the spot by saying, "I know you keep secrets from me. Maybe we should talk about them now." It also does not help to simply say, "I was a teenager once, and I know what it is like to keep a secret. You can share anything important with me," or "If you are in trouble, talk to me." These kinds of statements do not work. What does?

Dr. Evan Imber-Black, in her groundbreaking book *The Secret Life of Families* (New York: Bantam Books, 1998), writes that sharing your own "teen secret" life with your teenager is the ultimate icebreaker. If your teen knows how you kept secrets, she is sent a clear signal that she can speak with you. Trust is built and open communication is created bit by bit, with the sharing of confidences. When your teen sees that your secret life might not have been all that different from his, he may sense that it is okay to share pieces of his secret life with you.

To create a more open family atmosphere, then, parents need to divulge some of their secrets to their teenager. Secrets that parents have kept from their adolescent, in most cases, need to come out in the open during the teen years. However, proceed with caution. Consult a therapist before spilling out a devastating secret — telling certain dark secrets will serve no purpose and can even make matters worse. However, as a general rule, teenagers are old enough to know — and need to know — the family secrets.

How do you go about telling your teen your secrets? It is not easy. Don't expect your teen to say much of anything the first time you discuss your secrets. You are just beginning to change the context of your relationship by doing so. The very fact that you are now giving your teen important, secret information will leave room later for her to come to you and talk. Keeping big secrets from your teen, or having your teen keep them from you, puts stumbling blocks in your relationship. Set a policy not to keep things from your teenager. Everything is either a step toward a better relationship or a step away.

When your teen opens up and does share that secret with you, how do you respond? In her book, Dr. Imber-Black addresses some of the key issues of concern for parents of teens. Here are two points she makes that you must remember if your teen tells you a significant secret. Use these two points as guideposts.

1. When your teen tells you a secret, ask yourself, "Does keeping this secret put my child in any danger?" Secrets such as bulimia, drug use, suicide or sexual assault, you cannot promise to keep without

jeopardizing your child's safety and cutting you and your family off from needed resources.

2. And at the same time, "Think back to when you were an adolescent. What were your parents' responses when you shared your secrets? Do you want to act similarly or differently?" (230).

As you make your way through all the questions in this book, you will be more than prepared to deal with these tough and often secret issues. No matter what trouble happens to your kid — or one of his friends — he can face any fearful event and more than survive. I am here to tell you that your teen is much more resilient than you imagine. Even if raped, teens can and will recover. I have spent more than thirty years working with teens who have faced every imaginable horror and test. I am witness to their triumph.

If your daughter comes to you and tells you she was raped, keep your fear down and your faith up. The biggest obstacle to recovering and reclaiming anyone's life is lack of attention. Asking questions, sharing secrets, and making that effort toward more open communication shows your teen you are committed to attending to her. What your teen will discover is that her recovery actually is the process of recovering who she is.

"My best friend told me a secret. She was raped at summer camp. What should I do to help her?"

This question, too, falls under the category of "dangerous secrets." Again, it takes a slightly different focus. The teen asking this question, like the one in the previous question, is harboring a secret. The difference is, it is not her own. What does a teenager do when handed a secret that is too big to carry alone?

Teens tell their friends deep secrets, often in strict confidence. Their content runs the gamut from sex to abuse to thoughts of suicide. What do you tell a kid whose friend has told her a secret that cannot be kept? How do you help him decide when it is important to break his friend's confidence?

Teens often are very confused about what they should keep in confidence and what they should not. At every seminar I give, I am asked a question similar to this one. Most teens take secret keeping seriously — they think that no secret should ever be divulged. At the same time, teenagers want to know what to do if they are stuck in the middle of one of these secrets. They need your help to sort it all out. I recommend you address it in the following manner.

If your child hints to you that she's keeping a secret she's not comfortable with, approach the issue by laying out scenarios that challenge her to sort out her values. The scenarios listed below are examples of situations that will make your teenager think about her obligation to keep — or not to keep — a dangerous secret. Introduce the topic along the following lines: "I know you were sworn to secrecy. But sometimes keeping secrets hurts the friend you're trying to protect. For example, how do you think you would respond to these situations?"

1. A friend swears you to secrecy and then tells you that he is seriously thinking about committing suicide.
2. Your best friend was raped at a party and only wants you to know. She is falling apart, but she has sworn you to secrecy.
3. Your best friend's boyfriend got drunk and beat her. You are told to keep it a secret, yet you know the guy, and you know your friend is in danger.

Continue by asking, "Are these situations similar to or different than yours? Tell me what you would do." Raising examples likes these gets the discussion rolling.

The goal here is to get your child to understand that a good friend is someone who gets help for a friend in need. Intuitively, teens know that to be true. Your job is to remind him about the power of being a true friend. And in this case, breaking a friend's confidence to get help is the right thing to do. Teens must also be told that a friend is not a psychiatrist or social worker. A friend is a friend.

Now, let's deal with the other issues in this question — namely rape, and how your teen can provide her friend support while remaining healthy herself. What do you need to do?

By now, you probably know most of the basics: Anyone who has been raped needs strong support. Counseling at a rape crisis center or with a seasoned professional is essential. The police must be notified. A lawyer should be consulted to see if legal action is recommended. Beyond these critical issues, this is a time to assist your child in understanding her role in supporting her friend through this crisis.

Sit down with your teen and ask, "What do you think your friend needs from you right now? Why do you think she told you what happened? Do you feel okay talking to her about what happened?"

Why do I bring up these questions? Parents need to teach their kids that in every friendship there are limits and boundaries. Each person has only so much to give. It is best to know right from the beginning how much effort your teen will devote to lending a hand. It is important that he is clear on his limits. Giving too much and then pulling back, especially in a situation like this, can make matters worse. The friend could then feel rejected and even further victimized.

The goal is to let your child know how she can be there for her friend, without ultimately letting her friend down by getting in over her head. Giving what she can will, in the end, be the biggest help. The friend will not feel abandoned when your child cannot respond to a particular need. There will not be rejection because, from the beginning, the extent of support was made clear.

There is one more issue you have to go over with your teen. It, too, is a big one. How do you help your teen deal with someone else's trauma? It is important you explain that there is no good way to become friends with trauma and pain. It *is* possible to make peace with the past, however. Friendship through the storms of trauma is extremely important in assisting someone to reclaim their life.

What can you say to your teen that will help her understand what her friend is going through? I suggest saying something like this:

"I want to talk with you about something very important. A lot of kids who have been abused or raped think, deep down, that they are freaks. They end up blaming themselves for the bad things that happened to them. After all, what happened was so bizarre that they suspect weird things happen only to weird people. If they were 'normal,' this rape wouldn't have happened. Do you understand what I'm saying? Keep your eyes and ears open when talking with your friend. Reassure her that what she is feeling is normal and what happened was horrible — and it was certainly not her fault."

It is critical to talk about these kinds of issues with your child. The message you want to give is that, often, kids who are abused see themselves as victims and have trouble seeing the way out. A good discussion around this very issue will open the door for your teen to really lend a helping hand to her friend. Friends play a huge role in turning traumatic life events around. The ancient axiom "If a person has a worry in their heart, let them relate it to their trusted friend" (Yoma 75a) definitely applies here.

If your teen understands, through all of this, that friends have the power to help friends heal, then you have given her a message that will last a lifetime. One of the unspoken pacts of friendship is that friends give unconditional acceptance. Love and trust is built through learning and knowing that you can share with and be respected by people who love you. It is as simple as that. Being a trusted friend will, in time, allow your teen's friend to rebuild her trust. Rape is, at a core level, a deep violation of trust. Rebuilding trust is the key to healing.

"If you are drunk and someone has sex with you, is that rape?"

I often wish that some of the questions I get asked were nothing more than quotes from the latest script of TV's *Law & Order*. However, tough questions, like these about date rape, at least point to the fact that bringing up and discussing the "hot topics" with your teens will get thinking and asking about really important things.

There is a lot of drinking among teens today — we'll talk about that more in the next chapter. It is inevitable that sex that goes with it. When alcohol is involved, judgment is obscured, inhibitions are down, and a slippery slope is stepped upon — one thing leads to another, and another. Even teens raised in supportive families fall into this trap. Then, they feel pressure from their peers to keep the door — and their mouths — shut on issues involving drugs and sexuality. We must open that door wider. Too many cases of date rape go unreported because of teens' confusion over issues like these. The bottom line is this: Any sex that isn't consensual is rape. It doesn't matter if the victim was drinking; if she said no, and sex was forced upon her anyway, that tips into the domain of rape.

At the core of this question is a basic understanding that when you get drunk, you lose control. Sex with someone who is not in control is not consensual sex. As a parent, you must support your teen if sex, alcohol, and the word *no* have all been present in a situation. Even if your teen is not sure that sex occurred, you must get involved.

If your teen comes to you with this question, begin a discussion with her or him by asking one or more of the following:

- "Did this happen to you or a friend?"
- "Did you hear that this happened to someone?"
- "What do you think the answer to your question is? Why?"

As I've said, it's always best to ask first: "Why are you asking me this now? Did something happen to you? Did something happen to your friend?" This puts the question in context and will give you further information that may be important. Your teen may have observed this behavior at a party, or have overheard someone else talking about it, and may be curious. Your teen also may have been the victim of a rape. The two situations require very different responses (if your child has indeed been raped, refer to earlier questions in this chapter for advice on handling the matter).

Regardless of the context, this is an appropriate time to have a conversation around the theme of what *no* really means when it comes to sex — and it's a conversation that's just as important to have with sons as with daughters. Simply put, *no* means *no* — it means stop; don't go any further. If your teen says *no* in the middle of a sexual situation, *no* must be honored, or there can be legal repercussions. If your teen is the one who is told *no* in the middle of such a scenario, it's time to *stop*. Period. Drunk or not.

Let me go a bit deeper into some of the issues raised in this question. Too many times, teenage girls report to me situations in which they have had too much to drink and then had sex. Often, they don't remember what happened or even how they ended up in bed. They remember a bit about the sex, but they are foggy on how the seduction went down. They may even start the conversation out in front of friends and make a joke about it. I assure you though, if you cut right to the core issues of having sex, particularly "drunk sex" and what that can do to someone's dignity and self-respect, the conversation changes. It is not a funny issue.

Unfortunately, I am also often told by teens who've had drunk sex and are confused about it, "I wish I could talk to my mom about this." They also say, "If my parents weren't so into the 'you disappointed me' thing, I would talk to them."

It is precisely at the time of crisis that children need their parents the most. It is at these moments when kids finally understand many of the things their parents have told them, yet they most fear approaching their parents for support or advice. Something is very wrong with that picture.

I am not blind to the fact that teens often keep their sexual activities hidden. I don't expect that to change. But what does need to change is this: When a teen is in trouble, she ought to be able to talk to a parent. Please remember that if your teen is in crisis and turns to you for help, if you punish her, get hysterical, or act totally out to lunch, it may be years before she gives you another chance. Teenagers need adult confidants, pure and simple. They want to know how to handle tough issues. It is your job as a parent to lend a hand and be there for them.

No matter how shocking a question your teen asks you, remember to listen to your child first and then respond thoughtfully. This is a time to talk again about what it means to keep your values intact. Your teen also needs to know how to reclaim her dignity. I recommend you spend some time discussing what it takes to forgive yourself for making a mistake. If you utilize these moments to explain how you integrate your values into your actions, and how you respond to life's challenges, your teen will remember your words for a lifetime.

"All of us are afraid of date rape and date rape drugs. We know 'roofies' and other drugs are around, and some guys use them on girls. So how can we keep partying, have fun, and stay safe?"

Once most commonly found in the "club scene," date rape drugs have made their debut among American high school students. These drugs are not just "out there" in exclusive urban nightclubs; they are available to your children, no matter where you live. In my day, kids whispered about "Spanish fly" (whatever that was in reality), but today "roofies" (Rohypnol), Special K, or GHB (gamma hydroxybutyrate, or "liquid ecstasy") are the rage. All are street terms for potent date rape drugs. All have a achieved a certain mythological status, at least among some boys. But the use of any of chemical that incapacitates someone must be filed under the letter *R*, for *rape*. And rape is rape no matter what urban legend gets attached to it.

Every parent needs to discuss date rape and date rape drugs with their teen, and the earlier in high school, the better. Naturally, this is not a discussion to be limited to daughters. Your sons need to know about this, too. Unlike many questions answered in this book, questions regarding date rape drugs will require you to do a little research — this is one time when you need to give your teen facts and information in addition to support and advice. WebMD is a good source for drug facts.

Date rape is a serious crime. It's not uncommon to read about some kind of sexual assault in which the victim was drugged and raped. Ask college deans all over the country, and they will tell you that this is a very underreported crime. Nearly every college guidance office offers information on date rape drugs and conducts informational seminars warning students about the dangers of date rape.

Rape is a violent crime, and when it's committed by someone the victim knows — even trusts — it creates all kinds of confusion, pain, and problems. Things worsen when the victim also was drugged. She will be confused, will have trouble recalling details, and may have no clue as to who assaulted her. It's a double whammy — the invasion of the rape and the stripping away of power, control, and often memory.

Date rape drugs leave in their wake huge issues for the victim. Trust and fear join hands to make the victim's life miserable. Often, the victim never knows who assaulted her, and is haunted by questions like "Who can I trust? Who should I be afraid of?" Years later, victims still wonder, even on innocent dates, "Is this the person who took advantage of me?" As irrational as that may seem, being drugged and raped is demeaning and vicious. The terrible loss of control leaves in its wake fear, self-doubt, and loss of confidence — a tough load to live with the rest of life.

It is not easy getting over any violent trauma. It is very difficult to prosecute these crimes. However, that does not mean date rape should not be reported. And it absolutely means that you must do all you can to help your teenager prevent it from happening in the first place. Even if the question is never asked, this is a topic you need to discuss with your teen once she is old enough to go out unsupervised with friends — let alone on dates.

Rape is not a pleasant topic to discuss with your teen. Just acknowledging the possibility that it could happen fuels anxiety. But since this is a mandatory discussion, I suggest you rely on the tried and true Parenting Principle that says, in effect: "If you are nervous discussing any hot topic, tell your child so." Tell him that this makes you very uncomfortable, but because you love him and this is so important, you have to talk about it anyway. Set a strong example. Important issues should never be ignored.

Before you sit down to have this discussion with your teen, arm yourself with some solid information on date rape drugs — what they are, what they do, and what your teen can do to reduce the likelihood that one will be slipped in her drink at a party. There is a tremendous amount of information available on date rape and date rape drugs. I often use the following Web sites as information resources: the Higher Education Center, Medline Plus, and Andrew Vachss, There are many other reliable sources — online and otherwise — that you can consult as well.

Where do you begin your discussion? Right out of the box, make it clear to your teen that rape is never the fault of the victim. It doesn't matter how the rape occurred or under what circumstances. It is still rape, and no one deserves it. Use an extreme illustration: "Even if you are passed out in a guy's room with your clothes off, no one has the right to rape you. Rape is a crime and a violent act. If you are raped, it is not your fault!"

What advice can you give your teen to stay safe? Following are some essential points. Introduce them by telling your teen: "I am really concerned about date rape drugs and rape. I want to share with you what I know. Let me go over some of this. Please ask me any questions you have on any of the points I bring up. And let me know if I leave anything out." Make certain your teen really understands each point mentioned here. After you explain each one, ask your child to repeat back to you what you just said. Ask her if she has any questions before you go on to the next point.

1. Alcohol and drugs are major culprits in date rape. They make people vulnerable, dull instincts, and can make some guys really aggressive. The first thing you can do to avoid date rape and date rape drugs is to stay away from places and situations where alcohol and other drugs might be available. Stay away from people who are obviously under the influence of them.
2. Never accept open drinks from people you don't know really well. Even taking a Coke or a 7-Up from a so-called friend can put you at risk. They could be spiked with any one of a variety of date rape drugs, like Rohypnol (roofies), Special K, or GHB. (It's a good idea to familiarize your teen with the names of the drugs; it gives you credibility and gives her buzzwords to watch out for if she hears them at parties.)

3. Watch out for your friends and have them watch out for you. Go out to clubs or parties in a group and give each other rides home. Always make sure someone knows where you are. If you're out with a guy on a date, let him know that people are aware of where you are, who you are with, and when you need to be home. Make a habit of checking in with someone when you get home (a friend, a parent, or a sibling).
4. Tell girls in particular that they don't need to be passive to be attractive. Suggest that they practice being assertive on dates in small ways: Picking movies you want to see, choosing the restaurant you want to go to, and setting limits about "fooling around" will give you practice for setting limits and making choices in future situations. Guys will know that you're not spineless and that you don't expect them to make all the decisions.
5. Talk to your teen about sex. See the other questions in this book, but by all means bring it into the discussion here. Never hide sex under a moral coat of denial. If your child is sexually active and you are not aware of it, it can spell trouble for her. Make sure you tell you teen that, when she feels pressure to have unwanted sex, she says "No" clearly and directly. Tell her, "Never give anyone a chance to mistake your 'No' for a 'Maybe' or an 'I don't know.'" This applies to whether your teen is sexually active or not. There is a difference between welcome and unwelcome sex. No means no.
6. Tell your teen to trust her instincts. Say: "It's not a good idea to go up to a guy's room or a secluded place. Watch out for guys who drink too much or use a lot of drugs. This can impair their judgment and lower their inhibitions. Drinking and drugs can also make them aggressive in a way that they can't control and sometimes don't feel responsible for. If something feels wrong, get out of there. Ask questions later. Don't worry about seeming rude or antisocial. Just listen to your gut. Get out."

It's all commonsense advice, but it's powerful stuff. Giving your child this kind of information can guard her against a dangerous situation and, best of all, it puts power and control into her court. Teach your child to be aware and assertive, and you'll give her tools that will serve her well her entire life.

* * *

While not every life crisis or traumatic event can be prevented, it's good to know that you, as a parent, can take some important steps that can have a serious, positive impact on your child's future happiness. As always, the main ingredient is constant, open communication. If abuse thrives in secrecy, then the key to dealing with — or even preventing — abuse and violent relationships lies with talking to your teen and creating an atmosphere in which your teen knows he can come to you for help and support, no matter what the situation. Likewise, you are teaching your teen — through your words and by your example — that she can be a source of support for her own friends in trouble. Being a teenager is risky business. It's at this age that kids begin to get a taste for the difficulties that lie ahead in adulthood. It's also the prime time to learn that however overwhelming or traumatic, problems can be dealt with, and lives can be reclaimed.

Chapter 6:
Drugs and Alcohol

"People come in a lot of varieties, but perfect isn't one of them."

Sarah is the president of her church youth group. She gets good grades, organizes major events for her high school, and is even the senior class president. She spends countless hours instant-messaging her friends about upcoming weekend plans. She dreams of becoming a lawyer. Meet her, and you come away saying, "That kid is full of smiles." You'd never guess she has a secret eating her alive, one she is determined to keep. I certainly didn't — at least not until one day when, after one of my seminars, she broke rank, pulled me aside, and told me about it.

Despite the cheery façade she greeted me with, I could tell something was coming. Behind her smile, she was welling up with tears. Once we sat down, away from the crowd, she looked right past me and out of nowhere quietly said, "I have a secret that haunts my life. It makes me feel like crap inside. I feel most of the time like something has bent my heart sideways. Like I have been 'Dracula-ed,' and I can't get the bloodsucker out of me."

I've learned that in situations like this, it's best to take it easy. If I let her take her time, she would release whatever was haunting her when she was ready. There was no need to push what was ready to spill. I took her hand. "It's okay, Sarah. You can share it or not. I am still with you. But I am curious. How do you cope with carrying the load?"

"Easy," she said. "Who notices anyway? I smoke dope to chill myself out. Most of my friends do, so it's no problem. I'm covered. Staying in disguise is easy." She paused and twisted her head toward the back of the room. A small shudder worked its way over her shoulder blades. I heard her quietly say, "Until now."

Sarah smokes dope like a lot of kids do, not for the experience, but to ease some great pain. What can she do? Her high school has a zero-tolerance policy toward dope. She would lose everything if she came clean. Beyond that, if she confessed her habit, then the secret she was smoking dope to quiet her anxiety would come out. Until she ran into to me, she felt too invested in her life — her charade — to tell anyone what really was happening. The risk was too high, the shame too deep.

Slowly, she turned back to the table, and our eyes made contact. I let out a long breath and said, "So who hurt you? Was it family or friend?"

As soon as I popped the question, her pupils turned into laser darts. She spit it straight out: "Yehuda, in my world, who is going understand what it means to be raped by an old boyfriend? Everyone will either think it's no big deal, or that I asked for it somehow. I do the best I can. Doping helps. I don't like hiding it. I don't like living a lie. But if I tell my mom, or someone at school, or even certain friends, I'm screwed."

That is how it goes for a lot of our kids today. They hurt so badly that even when the nightmare has ended, the memory of it lingers. They think they can make the pain go away with a few drinks or a few puffs on a joint. But, of course, it doesn't. My job — the job of any parent — is to be there when they wake up, find out that the nightmare hasn't stopped, and to ask real questions. It's our job to pay attention to their habits — including their drug and alcohol habits — ask questions, and act upon what we find. If we are lucky, we can show these kids that there is a way to get rid of the Beast, the one that still stalks the heart.

* * *

Before we begin any discussion of teenagers and drug use, I'd like to make a very important distinction: There is a huge difference between experimenting with drugs, which is fairly common, and self-medicating, which means trouble. Experimenting arises from a teen's natural curiosity, and while it's not something any parent should approve of, it's something to be expected. The good news about experimentation is that it very rarely leads to addiction. Kids who smoke pot once or twice — even those kids who try something stronger just once — are actually pretty normal, and while any drug use at all should cause the parent-radar to go off, limited experimentation is more an excellent opportunity to engage your kid in heart-to-heart conversation about drug use than it is proof that your child is destined for life as a junkie.

It's the kids who use drugs and alcohol to self-medicate — to put a stop to their anxiety or dull a deep-seated pain — that you should worry about the most. These are the kids who *do* develop long-term problems with drugs and alcohol. If our legal and educational systems separated out these two types of use, and treated them for what they are — curiosity and addiction — it might be possible to win the so-called war on drugs. Lumping everyone together and punishing them in the same manner solves nothing. Kids know the difference between someone who has tried dope and someone in trouble. Kids in trouble need help, whereas kids who experiment need talk.

Of the more than 24,000 teenagers I have surveyed, almost 100 percent know someone who smokes dope. Furthermore, nearly 100 percent also know someone who they perceive is in trouble with drugs. Not only that, but 75 to 80 percent of teens who attend schools in Drug Free Zones guarantee me that if I came to their school, they would be able to direct me to a student who at the very least would connect me up to a dealer. Better yet, they could direct me to someone on campus who will actually sell drugs to me.

Now, I realize this kind of information paints a bleak picture. It will continue to as long as we do not separate drug use from abuse. Experimenters or occasional users require drug education; the others require drug treatment. Unfortunately, parents have been led down a road of fear and trouble regarding drugs. Drug usage and abuse has been lumped together, resulting in little help to those who need it most. The message not only has failed — it has failed families and children in real need.

Key Points to Remember When Discussing Drugs and Alcohol

Let's not kid ourselves — teens have easy access to drugs and booze, and they use them for a variety of reasons. At my presentations, every teen I survey knows someone who has a drug or alcohol problem. Drug Free School Zones may effectively punish adults caught carrying (or driving with) illegal drugs within their boundaries, but teens at these schools know, just as well at teens at any other school — whom to talk to and how to score drugs. On any given weekend, a group of teens somewhere is getting blazing drunk at a party — with or without their parents' knowledge. However, all this does not mean an entire generation is growing up drug or alcohol dependent. There are critical points every parent needs to understand surrounding the issue of alcohol and drugs, and they need to be prepared to discuss them with their kids. The operant word here, as always, is *discuss,* not *lecture.* Before you begin, here are some points to keep in mind:

- Never be surprised that your teen experiments with drugs or alcohol. While I am not saying that abstinence is not possible, it is unlikely. Assume that, at some point, your teen will get either drunk or stoned. While this is cause for concern, it is not cause for alarm — unless the behavior becomes chronic.

- Remember that experimenting with drugs or alcohol does not necessarily lead to dependency. Most of the time, kids are simply experimenting. There is no scientific evidence that suggests that trying one drug will lead to trying another drug, or that getting drunk once or twice leads to alcoholism.

- Adopt a realistic attitude toward drugs and alcohol. Tell your teen that, while you prefer abstinence, you want to know if they get drunk or stoned. If they slip up, you want to them to come to you. It is important for you to know what happens as well as what your child thinks about getting stoned or drunk. There is a huge difference between social drinkers and binge drinkers. Similarly, there is a big difference between those who experiment and those who become drug dependent. Dependency identified and dealt with in its early stages is critical to success in treatment. This is why you need to have an open line of communication with your child. Tell your teen that it is always okay to talk to you if he ever finds himself in trouble with drugs or alcohol. There is a difference between being "dumb" with drugs and being in trouble. While one might be a costly mistake, the other can lead to a life of dependency. As a parent, you need to keep a finger on the pulse of your kid's alcohol and drug involvement.

- Reframe the definitions of *addict* and *alcoholic.* Take time to explain that kids who get into trouble with drugs and booze are often self-medicating against anxiety. You want to tell your teen that no matter what the circumstance, if she finds that taking a drug or getting drunk makes her feel better or makes her anxiety go away, that is a trouble sign. Explain that there are better ways to treat anxiety, and you are there to help her find them.

- Discuss the ethical and legal consequences of drug and alcohol abuse. Do some quick research on your own to get some basic facts. An excellent starting point will be the literature and statistics provided by MADD, or Mothers Against Drunk Driving (you can also visit them on the Internet at). Make clear all the consequences that can result from drinking and driving or getting stoned and driving. People die. People lose their driver's licenses and go to jail. People are scarred for life, physically and emotionally. Drinking and driving is not something that happens somewhere else and in someone else's headlines. If you have ever lost a friend to drinking and driving — or to a drug or alcohol overdose — tell your teen so. As with any other topic, having personalized discussions on drugs and alcohol in which you share your experiences are most effective.

Questions and Answers

"What's wrong with doping or drinking at a party?"

As with the last chapter, let's address the most blatant questions up front. I expect this question will send a few ripples up and down your spine if you hear it coming from your teen. What parent who hears this will not wonder, "Does this mean my kid is getting high?" Being worried is okay. And for the record, just because your teenager asked you about getting high doesn't mean he has already tried drugs or even wants to try them. He simply wants to know, what's the big deal? What's wrong with doping and drinking?

Remember that, often, the best responses to tough questions like these are more questions, especially ones that get your teen thinking about his own beliefs and opinions about such issues. Straight away, you can ask

"Well, what's okay about it?"

"Why do you think someone might want to get high?"

"Do your friends think getting drunk or stoned is a good idea? What have they told you about it?"

"What have you seen already, and what do you think about it?"

Be curious. Don't be afraid to ask your teen whether she's thought about getting high. Ask her straight out if she's tried drugs. Then, take a deep breath. If she has, do your best to stay calm. Ask what her personal experience was like. This is absolutely essential. The message you are giving your teen by doing so is that she can be honest with you, and you won't be judgmental or get "all freaked out." The comment I repeatedly hear from teens at my talks is, "My parents never ask me directly about anything. They don't want to know about what is going on. I don't like to bring anything up with them because most of the time they lecture me." Now is your chance to break this stereotype.

As difficult as it may be to ask these questions and hear the answers, when you fail to ask about drug or alcohol experiences, you fail to get across the most important message of all — that your child can come to you and discuss anything. Remember, experimentation is normal, and most kids do *not* get hooked on drugs if they try them a handful of times. Kids *do* get into trouble, however, when drug use is kept secret and becomes habitual. Your awareness of your teen's drug habits is essential if you are to step in the instant experimentation slips into something more serious. The only way to find out if your child is experimenting or potentially in trouble with drugs or alcohol is to ask. Most likely, you will discover that things aren't as bad as you feared, but not as good as you hoped.

Of course, all parents hope that their child has not tried drugs. The odds, however, are not in their favor. Nearly every teen in America knows someone who has tried them. Your kid goes to school with drug users and likely socializes with them. Given this scenario, how can you arm your child with real information and sound values?

Straight talk. You bet — go for maximum impact. Make sure your teen understands that "what's wrong" with drinking and doping at parties is this: Drugs and alcohol at parties can lead to arrests, car accidents, and serious legal trouble. It can lead to date rape and sexually transmitted diseases. It can lead to fights and violence. It can lead to suspension from school sports and other activities. At worst, it can lead to death. At best, it can lead to embarrassment and loss of self-respect and dignity. Parents must discuss real-time consequences like these with their teens. Straight talk and real talk is the order of the day. Ask questions and have your discussion always stem from a genuine desire to know what's going on in your teen's life.

When I present these consequences to the thousands of teens I speak to at my seminars, they're often surprised. "Nobody has ever brought up these kind of questions," they say. "Like what would happen if a doper friend shoved his stash under my seat and I got stopped by the police. I never even thought about that." Often, they add, "I never thought about whether it might not be cool to go to a party where there's a keg. My parents never said anything to me about that. They say, 'Don't drink,' and that's it. They don't talk about why." In my seminars, I make a point to.

Does this mean my kids never went to a party and saw their friends smoking dope? Of course not. Does it mean they never had a beer in high school? Nope. Does it mean they never got drunk? Ridiculous. But I'd like to think that our talks helped to put the brakes on potentially dangerous situations. A parent's job is to help his or her child think — *before* going into a situation that could involve drugs or alcohol

— about what might happen, what could go wrong, and whether taking a risk is worth it.

Every teen wants to be in the driver's seat of her life. It's a top priority to be in the know. When teens are truly able to think through situations and examine the underlying consequences for themselves, they are far more equipped to deal with the ethical dilemmas in their lives. Teenagers are looking for meaningful input. Discussing consequences — as well as putting them in the context of your family's value system — is a potent way to directly impact your teenager.

"There's a big party I really want to go to this weekend. My parents are freaked out that there will be drugs and beer there. What should I tell them that will make them calm down?"

If you are the parent who "freaked out" when your kid told you about this party, don't feel bad. Parents often freak out. It's our job to worry. There have definitely been times I "freaked" and could not calm down. It's okay to lose it once in a while. But after you do, get right back down to the business of parenting.

When my kids started going to high school parties, my wife and I laid out some ground rules. (Note that the best time to establish such rules is *before* your kid goes to that first party.) We told them that we knew they were going to be around people who were drinking and drugging, an inevitable fact today. Even if the party is held at someone's house, even if the parents are home, even if it will supposedly be dry, it's likely that someone will still bring booze and drugs to consume in their cars or down the street if not at the party itself. The ground rules we set for party going revolved around that fact:

1. Our kids were allowed to stay at a party as long as no drinking or drugging was clearly going on inside the host's house.

2. If drugs and alcohol were openly present in the house, they had to leave. *In the house* and *openly present* were the key words. They did not have to leave if some kids wandered in stoned or drunk. With our youngest son, we had some added leverage. He was a student athlete, thus being around drugs could get him kicked off the team. Of course, I am aware that varsity athletes do get stoned and drunk, but abstinence is in the rulebook. We went with that and

this general rule: "Use your best judgment. Open usage is the no-no."

There's another way to make certain your teen does not end up at a party that turns into a full "blow-out," particularly if your teen is younger, say, fourteen or fifteen. Call one of the parents who is hosting the party. Often, parents will not be at the party, or, worse, they will be there supplying the alcohol. Sadly, in some circles, it is even common for parents to score kegs for teens at parties. To them, "don't drink and drive" means "get stoned or drunk at our house, and we will make sure you don't drive home."

Make certain your teen knows you are going to call. Yes, your calling will most likely upset him. That's okay. Use his anger to have a good discussion about what goes on at parties and why you've set the guidelines you have. If your teen does encounter trouble, you are more likely to hear about it if you have discussed it with him first. An ounce of prevention here is worth more than a pound of cure.

Then, get on the phone and give those folks a call. Even if you know them and are certain they're going to do everything possible to keep drugs or alcohol from making the rounds in their house, that doesn't mean that kids won't show up at the party stoned or high. Even if there is nothing going on inside the house where they can see it, that doesn't mean kids won't be smoking weed down the street or drinking in their cars. By making the call and telling the host parents that you are worried there might be drinking or doping at the party, you are doing them a favor and showing them your support. In most cases, especially if the party is indeed legitimate, your phone call will be welcomed. Once you've checked the party out, lay down your guidelines, then let your child go.

Bear in mind that I don't recommend this tactic for older teens, say seventeen or eighteen. At that age, it is time to respect their maturity. Still, remind them about your concerns about drugs and alcohol at parties and maintain your ground rules.

I know that the whole notion of making phone calls and checking after your kids seems odd or downright distrustful. Be realistic; not every teen is a model citizen, and whether or not you trust your own teen, you can't trust all the others in attendance.

I am not suggesting that you interrogate your kid every time she heads out the door. The simple fact is that every teen needs and wants some guidelines. A good deal of the time, she will not listen to you or follow your advice. Often, he still will break the rules. He still needs to know your values and what you're thinking. Keep at it. The real effect of doing this will be putting some brakes on your teen's activities. It gets him to think twice, and thinking twice can save a life — quite literally, when it comes to drinking and driving or doing drugs.

"How come we have these D.A.R.E. programs at our school? We do get some information, but it's also a joke. Does the school really think this works?"

D.A.R.E. stands for Drug Abuse Resistance Education, and it's the biggest drug education program in America. It partners a community's law enforcement officers and schools together to educate students (usually in the fifth grade) about the dangers of substance use. The arguments in favor of this program — and others like it — are many: It familiarizes kids with local police officers, sends a strong "no-use" message, and purportedly teaches students how to "just say no" to drugs. Even so, this student is right: Like most school-based drug education programs, it does not work.

Study after study points out that drug education programs like D.A.R.E. have no long-term effects on preventing or reducing adolescent drug use; significantly, they are no more effective than no program at all. An exhaustive study by the Research Triangle Institute of North Carolina concluded that D.A.R.E. had a limited effect on adolescent drug use, and a scholarly article entitled "Truth and D.A.R.E.: Tracking Drug Education to Graduation and as Symbolic Politics" (E. Wysong, R. Aniskiewicz, and D. Wright, *Social Problems* 41 (3): 488-492, 1994) reported that the program had no lasting influence on students' drug-related attitudes or behaviors, and no long-term effects in preventing or reducing adolescent drug use. It actually can have the opposite of the intended effect with certain students, alienating those who already use or have experimented with drugs.

Additionally, the presence of such programs reassures parents that someone is talking to their kids about drugs — and therefore they are off the hook. But guess what? You're not. The idea that teens will "just say no" to drugs is a nice slogan that never worked. Parents must look at the real world of teen drug use and not dream about what they would like to see or what they hope is happening. Parents also cannot assume that their kids are getting all the information they need from a school program — in short, they cannot underestimate the impact that a one-on-one discussion, complete with their own stories and experiences, will have with their kids.

Part of the reason programs like D.A.R.E. fail to prevent or reduce teen drug use is because students don't take them seriously. Why? The programs simply don't take their opinions and life experiences into account. The most common comment I hear from teens regarding D.A.R.E. and other programs like it is this:

"The teachers or the police officers just come in and talk at us. There's never any follow-up discussion. It's just the same old deal. They give us all kinds of information and try to scare us. No one takes the time to talk with us, ask us our questions. It seems like the only thing they care about is that as long as they don't see kids stoned under their noses on campus, everything is okay."

Let me explain what is truly missing in drug education programs. It sounds bold, but believe me, if you understand what I am about to tell you, the door will swing open to real drug education and awareness. Kids who try drugs generally report a pleasurable experience, which is a simple but obvious fact. Think about it for a moment. If drugs did not make someone feel good, then why would anyone ever take them? If drugs did not get people high, no one would use them. If you really want to make some headway and get your kid's attention, then it is essential not to avoid the fact that drugs *do* get you high, which for most people feels *good*. Feeling good is the trap that can lead to addiction.

Most drug education programs avoid any discussion of the physical pleasure that comes with drug taking. People are afraid of it — admitting that feels too much like encouraging or tempting your kid to take drugs. "How can anyone tell kids that drugs make you feel good?" you may think. "Isn't that promoting drug usage?" I say, "How can you not bring up that point?" Only telling students about the dangers of drugs sets up drug education programs for failure. Of course drugs are dangerous. But if that is the only message you are telling your teen, how can that possibly compare to what his friends are telling him? They are telling your teenager that drugs make you feel good. Who do you think wins the debate? Effective drug education has to connect all the dots. The danger begins with pleasure; leave out the fact that when someone gets high, he is fooled by his own body, and you lose the rest of the message. Kids simply do not believe it.

I know that for a lot of you, talking about the pleasures experienced when getting high is scary. It feels like walking on thin ice. You are afraid you might really be giving the wrong message. Trust me, you are not. In fact, you will be connecting real-time with your kid. A parent's job is never to avoid issues with your children. Your teen is counting on you to tell her the truth, even if the truth is hard for you to discuss.

Where is the best place to start your discussion? Try some version of the following questions.

- Why do your friends think drugs are such a great experience?
- Why do you think experts are always saying drugs are dangerous?
- How can something so dangerous feel so good?

These questions will lead you to a frank discussion about the dangers of taking drugs. In the course of your conversation, discussion will lead from pleasure to the dangers of self-medication.

Let me let you in on a secret: If your child knows right out of the box that the drug experience starts with pleasure, she will not be so impressed with the experience. Nor will she think that her drug educators lied to her about the real experience. She will now have a simple and profound connection between pleasure and danger. She might experiment, but she will talk to you about it. She will be far less likely ever to get into trouble. Real information is powerful.

Parents cannot simply assume that a school or any other educational program will provide enough good information for their child, get them thinking about why taking drugs is or is not a good idea, and help them make responsible choices based on what they learn. Count on taking care of things yourself. You, as the parent, have to pick up the ball yourself and talk with your teen. The message consistently must be this: "We discuss everything in our home — drugs, relationships, sex, love, anything." You have real information in your hand. Give it to your teen.

"Didn't you use drugs in college?"

Ah, the moment of truth. What do you do when, in your discussions with your teen on the dangers of using drugs and the benefits of staying clean, you are asked this awkward question of your own youth? If drugs *are* so bad, why did *you* give them a shot? And at your own child's age, more or less? This is one of the most common questions that kids want to ask their parents. They can see through this little piece of hypocrisy, and they need it settled — or they at least need to make sense of it — before they'll believe much more that you have to say about drug use. You may think that your past has risen up to haunt you, but before you panic, relax and remember that your teen will learn his most profound lessons from the stories of your own experience. Don't hesitate to share your mistakes and what you learned from. When you admit the truth and discuss your failures, you will form a closer connection with your teenager.

Here is how to approach this touchy question. I'll divide it into two categories.

1. *If You Used Drugs*

I certainly fall into this category. I used drugs when I was in college, and I have been clear and open about this with my own kids. (I also never avoid discussing my experiences with students, if asked.) I've explained to them what I did and what happened to friends of mine. I've told them stories, some of them funny, others tragic. All of this helps to demystify the topic. The reason pure educational information is so often ineffective is because it keeps the subject impersonal. The key to drug prevention and education is providing useful and personal information. For parents, that includes telling your personal stories. It is, after all, part of your family's history.

I've told my kids what "smoking weed" was like, who gave it to me, what the environment was like back then, what information I had about drugs (which wasn't much and wasn't accurate), and why I chose to stop doing drugs. All of this kind of information is relevant and appropriate to share with your teen. Talk to him about the drugs you used. Explain to him what motivated you to experiment with drugs. If it took you a long time to come to grips with your drug usage, tell your teen that, too. Compare information. And, of course, remind him how the same kind of information that was hard to find back then is accessible today.

Don't avoid dealing with this question and above all, don't lie. You don't have to share every detail, but don't fake it, either. Your teen can read your emotions like an open book, so you might as well be honest.

I suggest you also refer to other questions listed in this book about drug usage and ask your teenager about his experiences. This way, you will cover most of the topic and bring a level of closure. (By the way, in case this crossed your mind, there is no correlation or study that ties casual drug use by parents to habitual drug use by their children. There *are* studies that point to children of drug addicts and alcoholics being predisposed to addiction and alcoholism, but that is not the issue being discussed here.)

2. *If You Did Not Use Drugs*

Be straightforward with your teen and tell her, "I want to let you know why I never used drugs." Explain why you *didn't* succumb to pressure in the sixties (or seventies or eighties) to do drugs. Explain why you made a decision *not* to. You also might want to tell her about times, at parties or in college, when drugs were offered to you, and what you did or said in response. Be specific, but do not preach. Here, you are doing more than merely relating your history, you are communicating your values and demonstrating your ethics. This does not mean your own teen will not experiment, but it will give her pause before she does.

Please do not start giving a sermon about how righteous you were not trying drugs. Who among us has lived an exemplary life? Your goal is to explain how you went about making an important decision and how your hope is that your teen, too, will make the same choice. Even if he doesn't, the core message you must communicate is that if he gets into trouble, you want him to speak to you about it.

Education, in order to make an impact, has to be intimate and personal. In your conversation, it is important for you also to talk about friends who experimented with drugs and what happened to them. Ask your teen, "Do you see why I never got stoned?" "Do you know kids who have similar experiences?" "Has what I said made you think more about why your friends use drugs, or why not?"

You'll be amazed at how much you and your teenager are going to enjoy talking about both of your experiences. Supply your teen with "real dope" on her family history. Remember, no classroom can ever provide something that unique and personal.

"I am pretty sure my parents tried drugs in college. I am also quite sure they lied to me about it. Should I even bring it up?"

When I survey students at my seminars, I ask, "How many of your parents have admitted that they tried marijuana?" About 30 to 40 percent of them raise their hands. Then I ask, "How many of you think your parents have just flat-out lied to you about it?" With a loud burst of laughter, sometimes up to 40 percent more of the kids raise their hands. When I tell parents about this, they laugh, too. But the truth is, it isn't funny at all.

When you lie, it sends a signal to your teenager that sometimes it is okay for her to lie, too. If you expect honesty from your teen most of the time, you have to model honesty. Of course, I am not speaking about coming clean on every secret (see chapter 4 for more information on what secrets should and should not be shared).

There's no guarantee that, by admitting to your teen that you lied about using drugs, you will then keep him from experimenting. But it is true that lying about your drug usage can drive a wedge between you and your teen; it can literally keep him from coming to you if he gets into trouble. Lying conveys a message that it is okay to keep things like using drugs underground and below the radar. It's just not the example you want to set.

In addition, holding onto a lie creates a lot of anxiety. It is not easy living with the tension that comes from lying to children. Living with anxiety is like paying interest all the time on a loan you really don't owe.

I know that those of you who have lied to your teen about your drug usage are going to have a tough time digesting what I am about to ask you to do. I know it is not easy to come clean, but let me show why you need to have "that talk" with your teen and how it will teach him some very important lessons. Look at it this way: You are about to set a new and powerful example for your child.

How do you go about doing this? What do you need to say? It is not as hard as you might think. Tell your teen something along the following lines: "Do you remember when you asked me if I ever tried drugs? Well, I suspect you picked up that I was a bit evasive when I answered. Not telling you the truth has really been bothering me, so I have to set the record straight."

Go on to explain that out of fear and misplaced judgment, you lied about an important issue in your life. Do that, and you will set a new standard about how important it is to come forward with an embarrassing lie. What will this accomplish? Your teen now will know that, in the case she has gotten into trouble and lied about it, mistakes can be corrected with dignity. Facing the music takes on real and important meaning. It will also give you the opportunity to share your own drug experiences with your teen, passing along more important stories and information as you do.

Come clean and tell your teen the truth. Turn the fact that you lied into a life-learning experience. Your truth telling will create respect for you as a parent, and it will build more confidence in your teen.

"All my friends get drunk all the time. They get really wasted — pass out and puke all over the place. They think it's funny. What can I say to them?"

Binge drinking — technically, consuming five or more drinks in a row — among teens and college students has become a favorite party pastime. It doesn't take a mathematician to know that we're in trouble when 44 percent of college-age students binge regularly on college campuses. It used to be that teens would go through several trial runs at getting roaring drunk until they figured out how *not* to poison themselves on alcohol, and that was the end of the it. Yes, back then, there was the risk of wrecking cars, passing out, lying in bed or on the front lawn vomiting your guts out, or even getting arrested or being dropped off at the emergency room to get your stomach pumped. All of this was and is dangerous, and parents of these children were terrified their kids were turning into alcoholics. Now, kids regularly die.

The drinking culture of teens has changed. Binge drinking *does* kill a certain number of kids every year, through fights, accidents, and alcohol poisoning. According to the National Institute on Alcohol Abuse and Alcoholism (NIAAA), on college campuses alone, binge drinking claims the lives of 1,400 students aged eighteen to twenty-four each year. Whatever the message we are trying to give to our children about drinking, it does not seem to be getting through.

Our society clearly has helped set up the conditions for binge drinking. The legal age for drinking is twenty-one. Ponder that in light of the fact that an eighteen-year-old can get married, have children, vote, and join the army, but cannot have a drink. In addition, many families have parents who come home every night and have a few drinks to loosen up or drink themselves under. Most directly, in my opinion, the upsurge in binge drinking on college campuses is tied to new zero-tolerance policies and a return to prohibition on many college campuses. As a result, drinking has become one of the new secret rites among young people in our society today. And binge drinking is weekend entertainment for both boys and girls.

Considering all this, it's highly likely that your teen, at some point, is going to get drunk. Don't be at all surprised if this type of question about drinking is, in fact, your child asking about his own drinking habits. That may be the only way he feels he can discuss the issue. And not discussing getting drunk and drinking with your teen is a big mistake.

What do you need to bring up with your teen when you discuss binge drinking? Make her know you are aware of what is happening in her world. Certainly tell her that you are aware that binge drinking is not going to disappear overnight. And the concerns about it are real: Death easily can be around the corner with a drunk driver, and anyone can choke to death in his own vomit right out of the gate on the first episode of binge drinking.

Obviously, most parents will deliver the message that if you get drunk you do not drive. Be sure to remind your teen to call home at any hour if he is drunk, and you will get him. Any piece of M.A.D.D. literature will give you a good list of things to say and to do. Yet while communicating this information is important, it does not address the deeper issue of *why* someone binges.

Kids binge because their friends binge. They binge because they are socially awkward, and this is a way of getting attention. They binge because they are literally trying to drown their problems in a bath of alcohol. They binge because no one has ever discussed the perils of binge drinking with them. As a parent, you have to remember that *you* are the ethical brakes on you teen's desire to do something wrong. Talking with him applies those brakes. And please don't think that a general warning about the obvious consequences will stop the drinking. Get personal. Get your teen to think about the impact of such drinking in his own life. Ask him:

- "How dangerous do you think it really is to get flat-out drunk?"

- "What do you think life would be like for someone who drank, drove, and then killed someone? Besides having to do jail time, how do you think someone puts their life together after something like that?"

- "What do you think life would be like for someone who encouraged his friend to binge drink, then had that friend die of alcohol poisoning? How would it feel to watch that happen?"

- "Let's suppose you or one of your friends got drunk, and ended up in bed with a girl. How are you or he going to feel about yourself the next morning?"

- "Let's say you or one of your friends got drunk and made an ass out of yourselves. One of you took off your clothes in front of everyone. The next day you find out what you did. How do you feel? Was that cool?"

- "One of your friends passed out and lay on the floor vomiting. Did you do anything about it? The next day, how do you feel about what happened? Do you think you will say anything to your friend?"

You can generate a list like this and talk about it. I am sure some of you reading this even have memories of a few of the scenes described. I know I do.

Other consequences are more subtle, but still significant. Getting drunk can easily take away a teen's dignity. Kids are very aware of that specific point. They get embarrassed after a drunk, then seldom have someone to talk to about it. Never avoid discussing the ethical impact of drinking, or how drinking affects one's self-respect.

There are other questions that should follow the first round of discussion. Building a meaningful discussion with your teen means building a good base around a particular topic. Onetime conversations seldom work. Here are some questions to get your teen thinking further about friends and what they are doing:

- "If your friends are getting drunk and that bothers you, why are you hanging out with them? Are they really your friends?"

- "Why are you watching them get smashed, anyway? Where's the entertainment in that? If you don't enjoy it, why do you stay and watch?"

- "Have you ever seen anyone take advantage of someone else when they were drunk? How did that make you feel, and what did you do about it?"

If, in response to the above question, your teen tells you something like, "So and so had sex with this girl" or "cursed out another friend," or "got in a fight," then ask,

- "What did you do about it? Is this person still your friend?"

- "How do you think that girl felt about it? Did you talk to her about it?"

- "Did you talk to your friend about how this behavior made you feel? What was the response?"

The whole point of this discussion is to frankly talk about the consequences of drinking. It is not just entertainment on the weekend. Bad things can happen.

Finally, I also think that parents have to teach their children how to drink. I am serious about that last statement. Talk is not enough. Now, I am not suggesting that you sit your kid down and get him drunk. I am suggesting that, at an appropriate age, he has a drink with you in your home. Talk to him about alcohol. Talk about the dangers of getting drunk. Treat him as an adult. Tell him what you expect from him. I know this will sound outrageous to some, but talking to your teen in this way will put booze in perspective in his life. Drinking *can* be done responsibly. It can be an enjoyable activity, with its dangers kept to a minimum. Your teen has plenty of people in his life teaching him to drink irresponsibly. You can teach him how to do it safely and sensibly — and remember, this is not done by words alone, but by the behavior you model as well.

Part of the mystique of drinking is that society has made it taboo. Anytime a parent can demystify a youthful taboo, its power will be diminished. If kids see alcohol as mysterious, they will use it in mysterious and dangerous ways. Explain to your child that alcohol is a poison when used in excess. "When the brain is poisoned," tell her, "then you see the drunk. How cool is that?"

Most importantly, though, if and when your teen gets drunk for the first time, talk to him the next day and find out immediately what he learned from the experience. This is crucial. If he feels remorseful, give him room to get out all his feelings of stupidity and shame. If he hurt someone, help him talk about making amends. If he sullied his dignity, teach him ways to reclaim it. Treat that first big drunk as a learning experience that will help your teen mature.

Ironically, the best learning about booze comes after the first drunk. I wish it wasn't true, but it is the case. When my youngest son came home and told me what had happened when he got really blitzed, he was remorseful and ashamed of himself. We had one of the best talks of our life. I was able to tell him about my first stupid drunk and share with him how I survived it. Now, it was his turn to learn from his mistakes.

Take advantage of these situations. They do not mean the worst has happened. They mean you are now on the same page with your teen and can have an important conversation. And no, it does not mean your teen will never drink again. It will, though, bring some awareness and hopefully put the brakes on alcohol use.

Remember that kids who have a binge-drinking problem often don't see the problem. They see another party as another drinking opportunity. You must ask tough questions. Alcoholism and the attitude toward binge drinking is not in the bottle, it is in the person. The bottle is just the symptom. Your job is to have a significant conversation that wakes your kid up and gets her to think.

> ***"Is there something wrong with having a drink or two in the morning before school? My friends and I drive to school and pass a bottle around in the parking lot before hitting class. School is a total bore, and at least I get through the day without any trouble. I am not flunking or anything."***

Yes, there are alcoholic children. They drink a bit in the morning and sip their way through the day. If you speak to these kids privately, they will report they also have a drink or two before going to sleep. What is going on here? This is not binge drinking. They are not getting smashed on the weekends.

The classic drunk is not the binge drinker, or the drunk who goes wild and beats family members, or the one that disappears for days at a time on a spree. While binge drinking is a huge problem today, it is not the issue in this question.

The student writing me this question is the classic alcoholic; he is the common drunk. "Ah," you ask, "but how is it possible for a teenager to become an alcoholic? Doesn't it take years to develop the habit? This kid is only in high school." The answer is that, most often, this kid has been sipping for years. This teen is using alcohol to numb himself daily. This is what I call using booze to self-medicate against anxiety.

It is clear that this teenager is in denial about his problem. Addiction is the only disease that tries to convince you that you don't have it. In the question, the teen comments that he is getting through the day just fine. Drunks' logic often goes something like this: "I am not falling-down drunk; therefore, I am not an alcoholic." It is very hard for them to admit that while they are asleep, their disease is doing push-ups.

Denial, though, is really never total denial. If you examine the question a bit closer, you can read that, between the lines, the student is in fact asking, "Do I have a problem?" Otherwise, why ask the question? And the answer is, of course, "Yes, you have a problem."

Frankly, I have never met a teenage alcoholic who was not aware that she had a drinking problem. Don't think for a moment these kids enjoy taking a few swigs every morning in the bathroom, in their bedroom, out in the garage, or in the parking lot before school. They don't. Here is the major problem facing drunks and druggies: Kids who are, in my opinion, forced to self-medicate in order to relieve anxiety usually don't have easy access to treatment. They also know that in general, talking to others about a drug or alcohol problem will only get them in more trouble. The penalty for being caught drinking doesn't help identify kids who need help; rather, it drives them underground.

You might wonder, "What kind of anxiety could a teenager possibly have?" From my survey alone, it's apparent that teens today are under all kinds of pressure. Add into the mix a 50 percent divorce rate, the terrorist attack at the World Trade Center and Pentagon, escalating violence around the world as wars erupt, and increased pressure to succeed. Kids today are also often overscheduled. There's little time left for kids to be kids. Add in the absence of meaningful adults in kids' lives today, and you've got a recipe for anxiety. Often, relief for this anxiety is spelled V-O-D-K-A, the booze of choice for teens — colorless, odorless, and tasteless. The first-period teacher is never gonna smell a thing.

I am deeply concerned that we ignore and neglect children in our society. Most kids in trouble are given the message that few care about their personal problems. A noncaring environment drives teens into secrecy. Worse yet, when kids turn to "unacceptable" means of relieving their anxiety, by self-medicating with drugs and alcohol, for example, society often responds with jail terms, school expulsion, or long-term suspension. Thankfully, nationwide there is a new trend — the growth of Family Drug and Alcohol Courts, which are extremely effective. These courts provide access to treatment and rehabilitation, with family involvement, for juvenile offenders, their goal being behavior modification (rather than punishment) through ending the cycle of drug abuse.

And remember, kids in trouble don't necessarily go on to become adult alcoholics. Yet the first step in arresting potential trouble is learning to become aware of the warning signs. According to the National Council on Alcoholism and Drug Dependence (NCADD), the following may be signs that your teen is in trouble with addiction:

- Smell of alcohol on the breath, or sudden, frequent use of breath mints.
- Abrupt changes in mood or attitude.
- Sudden decline in attendance or performance at school.
- Loss of interest in school, sports, or other activities that used to be important.
- Sudden resistance to discipline at school.
- Uncharacteristic withdrawal from family, friends, or interests.
- Heightened secrecy about actions or possessions.
- Associating with a new group of friends whom your child refuses to discuss.

What do you do if you discover or suspect that your child is drinking regularly? You think you smell liquor on his breath in the morning or evening. Vodka or other kinds of alcohol are missing from the liquor cabinet. Or your booze has been watered down, the oldest trick in the book.

If you suspect trouble, sit down and talk to your teen right away. Some people move when they see the light; alcoholics move when they feel the heat. In other words, take action; the earlier you intervene, the better. But when you do, spare the drama. Please don't pull out the watered-down scotch and vodka bottles, stick them on the coffee table, and then call your teen downstairs for a talk. Having a problem with alcohol does not mean your child is bad or a criminal. It means your teenager is having some kind of emotional trouble. She is using liquor to get some relief.

This is the time for understanding, not for yelling or lecturing. Say something along the following lines: "I am quite certain you have been having a real hard time these past few months. So hard that you have tried, it seems, to keep things in balance by drinking. I love you and am concerned about you. Is what I am saying pretty close to the truth?"

Follow up with more questions and comments, such as these: "I know you need some help. I think we all do. I want us all to get that help." Make certain you also say: "I am not ashamed or disappointed in you. I am upset with myself for not being there for you when all this started. This has to change. I love you, and all of us are going to do better. It is time to get help." If you want to learn more about alcoholism quickly, rent the movie *Stuart Saves His Family*, starring Al Franken, as well as *28 Days*. I recommend seeing them before you talk to your child. Better yet, watch them *with* your child, then talk about what you've seen. The antidote for stopping trouble with drugs and alcohol, as it is for so many other problems, is putting in quality time with your teen.

There is no formula for dealing with issues of addiction. In spite of what you might read or see on TV, you cannot draw up some nondrinking contract or pledge and assume that doing so will end the problem. Once you've confronted your teen's alcohol use, you and your teen need to seek professional help. Call your local social service agency. There you will find professionals who deal with teen alcohol abuse. You also need to contact AA (Alcoholics Anonymous), who has programs for teens and for you, the parent. Attend their meetings. Work with a substance abuse counselor and after-school programs. Detox and inpatient treatment may be necessary in extreme cases, but not necessarily in your teen's situation. All of this will provide help.

Having spent a lifetime with ex-junkies and AA members, I have met more saints in those circles than anywhere else. There are rewards on the other side of crisis. There will be ups and downs; there may be times when your teen falls off the wagon. This is not a failure. It is all part of the process of recovery. The real payoff is that all recovery roads lead to the ability to love and be loved. A pretty nice outcome, if you ask me.

"I smoke dope once in a while. I gotta tell you, I don't see anything wrong with it."

There is a tremendous amount of confusion associated with marijuana usage. Like many teens and adults who smoke marijuana, this teen sees nothing wrong with getting high every so often. Because the drug use isn't an everyday occurrence, it must be harmless, right? That's not necessarily true. If this is your teen, you still must find out whether he has a drug problem. Generally speaking, if we as a nation wish to make headway on the drug issue, we must separate the kids who experiment drugs from the kids who are abusing drugs. If we never make that distinction, we never will make any progress in lending a hand to kids who have real drug problems. As long as the medical profession is held at arm's length and the drug problem is viewed as only a legal issue, many lives will continue to be lost.

The main question to ask your teen is, "How often do you smoke and why?" If the answer is "seldom" or "it depends, but at the most once a month," your child is an occasional user and falls into the category of those who experiment with marijuana. Your teen is not drug dependent. However, if your teen indicates she is smoking regularly — say, once a week — an evaluation of her drug usage is in order. Refer to the other questions as a guide to seeking professional help.

If you child is smoking only occasionally, what can you hope to accomplish by talking with him? I wish I could tell you that a simple talk with a parent about smoking marijuana would stop drug experimentation, but that would be a lie. A more realistic goal is to raise your teen's awareness about all the consequences surrounding drug use. Indeed, that may change his attitude.

Let me supply you with some more important information about dope smoking. As a parent, you need to understand some of the myths about marijuana usage. Keep in mind that the so-called drug education your child has received in school probably hasn't made a big impression. As I've mentioned previously, drug education programs like D.A.R.E. have not been successful. Teens definitely experiment with drugs. They try all kinds of drugs even after completing even years of drug education (SAMSHA, Office of Applied Studies, National Household Survey on Drug Abuse: Main Findings 1998, Washington D.C.: National Clearinghouse for Alcohol and Drug Information (1999)]. With this in mind, let's look not at the politics of drug education, but at the facts:

1. Few teens use drugs regularly. In 1998, 90 percent of twelve- to seventeen-year-olds refrained from regular drug use (SAMSHA, Office of Applied Studies, National Household Survey on Drug Abuse: Main Findings 1998, Washington D.C.: National Clearinghouse for Alcohol and Drug Information (1999)]. Even if that statistic is underreported, the truth is that while most kids may experiment with drugs (bear in mind that nearly one-third of our population has tried marijuana at some time in their lives), they do not use them on a regular basis. We are not creating a nation of drug addicts. Still, we have a sizable population of teenagers who do have drug and alcohol problems.

2. The use of one drug does not necessarily lead to the use of others. In fact, "...the majority of drug use (with the possible exception of nicotine and cocaine) does not lead to addiction or abuse" (Marcia Rosenbaum, Ph.D., *Safety First: A Reality Based Approach to Teens, Drugs and Drug Education,* Lindesmith Center, 1999).

So where does this leave you with your child? The odds are that your teen might experiment occasionally, but does not have a dependency problem. Still, this is not a matter to brush off as trivial — any drug use carries with it serious consequences, which must be discussed with your teen. Approach the issues surrounding drug experimentation in the following order:

1. Legal Issues

There are lots of ways to talk about legal issues and consequences. I recommend asking reality-based questions that make the issues personal for your teen, open the door to much discussion, and let you play out many different scenarios. For example, ask your teen to consider the following: "Let's say one of your friends stashes dope in your car one night during a party. On your way home, you are pulled over by the police. What happens if the cop finds the dope in your car?"

Your teen may reply, "The dope is my friend's, not mine. I'm okay."

You can then respond, "But it's in *your* car. *You* are busted for possession. What comes next? Are you going to jail? Who has to pay for the lawyer? Is your car going to be confiscated? Will you lose your license? If you are convicted and even just given probation and community service, are you aware that you are not eligible for a college scholarship?"

Raise as many consequences as you can think of as the discussion rolls along. Turn those consequences into questions. In effect, you are coaching your teen to become self-reflective. Bringing up real-life situations will help speed up your teen's understanding of legal consequences. For many teens, this will not repeat what has been covered in school. Often, this will be their first discussion on these issues.

2. Risk Taking and Health Issues

The health issues surrounding drug use of any level are extremely important to discuss with teens of all ages. The main focus question in this section is "how do you know if you are getting in trouble?" With younger teens, the use of marijuana can have profound effects on brain function if used regularly. If your child is young and a regular user, you need to gather together some health facts from the Internet (such as WebMD or Hazelden, to name just two) or your local library before going further. And of course, seek professional help. Start at WebMD.com and seek more resources.

With older teens, your discussion should center on the following kinds of questions. Begin by asking

"Why do you smoke marijuana?"
"Why do you think it's okay to do so?"
"How would you know if you are getting yourself in trouble with a drug?"

"How would you know if you were becoming dependent on a drug?"

Listen carefully to their answers. Remember, telling your teen that you simply disapprove or, worse yet, panicking, yelling, or lecturing will only drive your child underground and put him at risk. Conversation is key. As Ward Cleaver once said in an episode of *Leave It to Beaver,* "We yell at [our kids] trying to make an impression. All we do is confuse them, and they don't understand a word we say." As tough as these issues are, parents do have to try to control their tempers. In the end, it can make a huge difference.

The more you discuss drug usage openly, the more likely it will be that if your teen gets into trouble, you will know about it. Knowing that is a comfort. Early intervention is the greatest indicator of success.

3. *Ethical Issues*

Potent ethical issues that impact teens should never be ignored. Too often they are — dope miraculously appears, and no one thinks about its consequences. When you discuss the ethical issues surrounding drug use with your teen, personalize the issue with questions and scenarios like the following:

If there are younger siblings in your home, ask your teen, "Do you think it's okay to turn your little brother or sister on to drugs? If not, why?"

Point out the fact that research suggests some people (perhaps up to 5 percent of the population) might be genetically predisposed to addiction — their physiology is wired so that when they drink or use drugs, they respond differently than others do. Outline a scenario like the following: "Say you are at a party where people are smoking dope. Although you not aware of this, one of your friends, who has never smoked dope, is genetically predisposed to drug addiction. Do you think it is okay to turn that friend on to dope? How would you feel knowing you were the first person to get that friend high, triggering a life of addiction? Knowing that, do you think it is okay to turn on friends to dope? Or is it a bit like Russian roulette?"

Don't avoid discussing the drug trade. Buying dope means participating and supporting a criminal enterprise. Furthermore, we are now aware after September 11, 2001, of the connection between narco-traffickers and terrorism. Ask your teen:

"What do you know or think about all the crime that comes from narco-traffickers? Do you mind getting stoned with weed that came from the hands of someone who murders or is involved in a criminal enterprise or even terrorism? Is it cool to get high on weed that came from folks who carry guns and use them on other people?"

When discussing this particular issue, you might want to rent the movie *Traffic* and watch it with your teen. *Traffic* is a brilliant film that takes on the complex business of drugs and drug usage in families. You might also want to read with your teen articles that link terrorism, slavery, and the drug trade. Such articles include the Drugs and Terror page of Parents: The Anti-Drug:

http://www.theantidrug.com/drugs_terror/events.html

Also see "Narco-Terror: The Worldwide Connection Between Drugs and Terror" on the U.S. Department of State's Web site, and the MSNBC article "Sex, Drugs and Guns in the Balkans." Arnold S. Trebach has written several controversial books about drug policy reform, including a new one titled *Fatal Distraction: The War on Drugs in the Age of Islamic Terrorism*. All the references above are very interesting and potent reads that will add fuel to your discussion.

At then end of these discussions, be very careful not to lay down ultimatums, especially with older teenagers. I do assume you will tell your teen what you expect of her. You most likely will make it clear that you do not want her to smoke marijuana. You do not, though, want to close the door on her. Make sure you mention how you value her opinions. And finally, be certain to say to her, "Please remember, you can come to me if you get into trouble, twenty-four/seven. In the real world, mistakes do happen. If at any time you think you are becoming even a little dependent on dope, please come and speak with me." The message you must repeat regularly is that you are always there for your teen. Always thank her for raising questions honestly and having an in-depth discussion with you.

A final word: Always keep your focus on what is happening right now in your teen's life. Do that, and odds are you will know if real trouble arises.

"Weed is my best friend. I smoke every day and I see nothing wrong with it. Why does everyone hassle me about it? I am doing okay."

This question, unlike the previous one, is not written by a teen who experiments with marijuana. It is more likely this teen is abusing the drug. However, even if your teen tells you that he is using drugs regularly, that does not mean he is destined to become a drug addict. In fact, I do not even like to use the term *drug addicts* for teens who are regular users. I prefer to view these teens as kids who are self-medicating against their anxiety and problems.

There is a recurring story that I hear from teens across America. At nearly every seminar I give, I spend time talking with students about what I like to call the myth of the "stoner." A stoner is a kid who smokes dope regularly, talks about the joys of partying and getting wasted, and regales anyone who will listen to his amazing dope tales.

Most teens today know someone who is a stoner. Teens who regularly go to parties know that part of the entertainment will be the antics of a stoned or drunk classmate. Often, movies and cultural myths lead us to believe that stoners are joyful party animals. In fact, nothing could be farther from the truth. We all might have loved Cheech and Chong flicks, but the real-life stories of the Robert Downeys and the tragic deaths of Kurt Cobain, Jimi Hendrix, Jim Morrison, and Janis Joplin are all too real to be ignored.

The truth is that stoners do not use drugs to be the life of the party. They use drugs to numb their anxiety and pain.

Every time I discuss the issue of self-medication with students, a few so-called stoners come up afterward and speak with me. Often, they are in tears and deeply bothered by their dependency. They explain to me that they *need* to smoke marijuana or use other drugs. Why? They report they need to take something to relieve their gnawing anxiety. Marijuana gives them symptom relief. Smoking dope is not a joy. They describe it as their defensive strategy against pain.

Once you get past that adolescent bravado, you find a kid struggling to find some kind of balance to make it through the day. They know why they have gone from experimenting or occasionally getting high to becoming regular users. Every parent needs to reframe this question and break through the protective barrier. What you need to find out is, "Is my child anxious all the time? Is that why she is smoking dope?"

If the answer to those questions is yes, you need to seek professional help for your child. Consult your local social service agency, clergy, or family doctor for a good referral.

"My doping has really gotten out of control. My friends and I are wasted way too much of the time. They might not admit it, but I know I am in trouble. I need to get some help. What should I do?"

Let me recommend an approach that can help your child and your family. It also applies to anyone seeking professional help to deal with any drug dependency problem. First of all, do not panic if your teen comes to you and tells you she has a drug problem that is out of control. I know that is easier said than done. I confess I, too, would most likely panic. However, as soon as you calm down, here is what you must do:

Sit down and talk with your child. Have your teen tell you why he thinks he needs to smoke so much weed. Ask him,

"How long has this been going on?"
"When did you suspect you were getting into trouble?"
"What happens when you don't smoke?"
"What are the main things that make you anxious?"

This is definitely not the time for lectures. Clearly, if this is your teen's problem, you must get her into drug treatment. Let me clarify for you what drug treatment is all about. It is important to know that not every child who is abusing drugs needs to be packed up and sent off to drug rehab. Often, an after-school program along with therapy will work just fine. The first step I recommend is to seek out a clinic or social service agency in your area that specializes in adolescent drug problems. Make certain they have a veteran psychiatrist on their staff. An experienced psychiatrist can evaluate whether your child might need antianxiety or antidepression medication. A trained psychiatrist may discover that your teen is actually not dependent, but in fact clinically depressed or suffering from anxiety. Often, if you go to a drug treatment facility or clinic, your teen will have all the professionals on staff to assist with a complete evaluation. All of this is necessary in formulating a treatment plan for your child.

Second, make sure part of the treatment plan includes you. I recommend that the plan also include the family seeing a trained family therapist. A clinician experienced in working with teens who are struggling with drugs — and their families — is invaluable. Again, the best setting to find these people is a clinic or treatment center.

Why am I recommending this? The answer is simple. Too often teens are shipped off to a rehabilitation program somewhere without a proper evaluation. Or, they are placed in a treatment program that does not involve the family. Given the fact that drug rehabs, when used as the only modality of treatment, have failure rates up to 80 percent for drugs such as cocaine or heroin, it is critical for families to be involved in a treatment plan that includes the whole family. I don't want to paint too rosy a picture of the world of drug treatment. Relapse is common. But it is important for parents to be armed with the proper information as they seek to find and establish a treatment plan for their child.

Where do you start your search for help? Begin with your local social service agencies. They often serve entire communities and are neighborhood based. Used as a starting point, they can also give you the best referrals. Furthermore, if you are not a family of means, local social service agencies can give you high-quality professional help and can easily be found in your phone book. Jewish Family Services, Catholic Family Services, and the local Council of Churches, as well as other nonprofit agencies, can provide high-quality care and often have fees that operate on a sliding scale. And of course, in any community, support can be provided by NA (Narcotics Anonymous) or AA (Alcoholics Anonymous). Participate in them. Do your homework. Ask a lot of questions. Find out who provides treatment in your community. Not everyone needs to go out of town to get what they need for their teen.

Make certain you are involved every step of the way. All too often, I have seen teens come out of treatment clean only to return to a tumultuous family, where no one has changed or understands that a drug problem is also a family problem. In fact, rehab is the easy part. The hard work of successful treatment — but also the rewards — takes place *after* the drug problem is cleaned up. Recovery is a lifetime process.

"*Some of my friends use ecstasy regularly. If they are going to a dance club, they always use it. I haven't tried it, but everyone tells me it is safe as long as you don't get a bad batch. I gotta tell you, they love it. It makes them feel great. Is it really a problem if I take it?*"

The alternative ecstasy question I am regularly asked is:

"I use ecstasy a couple of times of month. I've been taking it for years, every time I go out to a dance club or hit a hot rave. It never has caused me any problems. I make sure I drink enough water. I just love it. It makes me feel so much closer to everyone. What could really be wrong with it?"

Ecstasy has been around since the late 1960s. The first time I ever heard about it was in San Francisco, where some Hell's Angels were giving it away free on the street. It wasn't known as ecstasy then. The Angels called it "hog," after their Harleys. It wasn't until the early '80s that it became popular in the emerging dance club scene. Its use exploded in the '90s, and its popularity doesn't seem to be slowing down. Today, it is called X, Adam, and XTC. Some researchers argue that there is not sufficient evidence to justify making the drug illegal. Believe me, that definitely contributes to the urban legends surrounding the drug. Ecstasy has taken the place of cocaine as the "in" drug.

Ecstasy is one of many "club drugs" — drugs that are used at dance clubs. The club phenomenon has been hot for nearly two decades. These are cutting-edge, upscale, all-night dance clubs. They feature truly avant-garde electronic music and extraordinary light shows. The music is hypnotic and extremely creative, and the dancing is very hot. It is not easy to get into many of these clubs. There is a pecking order of admission. How you dress and who you know moves you up the list. Often, they open after midnight. Dancing goes on until dawn.

The club scene is not some sideshow. Fashion models, high rollers, and celebrities hang out at the most upscale clubs. They are the subjects of travelogues on cable television. But these clubs also have a dark side. Drugs like ecstasy are so readily available that many dance clubs ought to have as their motto "Better Living through Chemistry."

The companions to dance clubs are raves. They used to be truly underground all-night dance gatherings held at secret locations. Only on the day of the rave could you get a map or a series of directions to find it. They were often held in hidden parts of industrial parks and other out-of-the-way places. It was from the rave scene that ecstasy emerged.

Now, I don't want to totally put down this scene. Sans drugs, dance clubs are pretty amazing places. They're fun, and definitely the best place to hear some of the most creative music being played today. There are clubs where drugs are not allowed, and many kids who love clubs and raves push hard to not let drugs into their scene. But let's not kid ourselves: They are also underground drug supermarkets. Any police department will second this opinion.

Collectively, club drugs include ecstasy, officially known as MDMA (methylenedioxymethamphetamine), Rohypnol (flunitrazepam), GHB (gamma-hydroxybutyrate), and ketamine (ketamine hydrochloride). The last three drugs are also date rape drugs. All have various and changing street names. (For a discussion of those drugs, see the questions dealing with date rape in chapter 5.) Periodically, chemists dream up other drugs and experiment with them at various clubs. Most of them came right out from your local veterinarian's drug supply. Yep, some of these are animal tranquilizers. If it will put down a horse, imagine what it will do to your teen.

The parent drug of ecstasy is MDA. Both are amphetamine-like drugs. Their effect is a psychedelic high mixed with a speed rush. Because it lacks the frightening roller-coaster, ego-dissolving effects found in other psychedelics like LSD, it has become popular. For many years it was legal, and its long run of legality contributed to the underground cultural lore of the drug. Raves, dance clubs, and the techno-music scene also contributed to its spread.

I am aware that most parents are not familiar with this drug. It wasn't around or that popular when you were in high school and college. In the following paragraphs, I'll cover a few of the basics of ecstasy for you. Keep in mind that if your teen's behavior matches the items on this list, it does not necessarily mean he is using this drug. Use the following only as leads for information and potential discussion:

Ecstasy users do leave a trail. According to the Teen Focus Web site, teens who use ecstasy will:

- Stay out very late at night. Raves and the dance club scene often do not start until after midnight, and they go until dawn.
- Become very irritable the day after using ecstasy due to the depletion of serotonin in the brain. (Of course, your regular, everyday teen has radical mood swings anyway.)

- Use a baby pacifier. No, I am not kidding. The drug causes the user to clench her teeth tightly and, just as with a baby's teething, the pacifier eases the discomfort. Pacifier sales have spiked because of ecstasy. Now you know what you've been seeing when kids walk down the street with pacifiers tied around their necks. It's not just a fad.
- Use fluorescent light sticks. Ecstasy heightens visual perception. Light sticks are easy to obtain and have become the "in" thing to use while dancing at clubs.

How do you tackle your teen's questions about ecstasy? The same way you talk to your teen about any drug. Your goal is to get into a real discussion about this drug with your teen. Take a look at the other questions in this chapter. They will serve as your guide to what kind of questions you need to ask. As with other drugs, the consequences — physical, ethical, and legal — have to be brought into the conversation.

Many teens do think this drug is safe. It is not. The high on ecstasy is very intoxicating and extremely sensual. It is a feel-good drug, but it is not addictive, like heroin. Most kids really do enjoy taking it. Your job is to get your teen thinking about what is true about the drug and what is myth. Since ecstasy has such an upbeat and positive reputation on the street, you need to have a clearer sense of the problems associated with this drug so you can communicate the truth to your teen. Facts like these can be found on the Teen Focus Web site:

1. Ecstasy can put you in the hospital. Emergency rooms in twenty-one metropolitan areas tracked by the Drug Abuse Warning Network reported 4,511 emergency-room visits involving ecstasy in 2000, a 58 percent increase over the 2,850 cases in 1999. It was found that people twenty-five years old and under make up 80 percent of ecstasy emergencies, and 60 percent of those involving GHB, the major date-rape drug.

2. There is direct evidence that chronic use of ecstasy causes brain damage.

3. The longer that ecstasy is used and the higher the dosages, the worse the memory impairment, according to a Dutch study. Regular users of the drug frequently forget simple tasks and routinely lose their train of thought.

4. The drug trade raises big ethical issues. The primary buyers — and many of the low-level dealers — are teenagers and college kids from middle- and upper-income families. As a result, America's suburbs are being hit with ecstasy-related drive-by shootings, executions, and assaults as violent international crime groups stake claims to the ecstasy market.

5. An article from *Scientific American* reveals that ecstasy causes a severe depletion in the brain of serotonin — the very same neurotransmitter that many antidepressant medications aim to augment.

6. Ecstasy can cause long-term brain injury. Research by Johns Hopkins University showed that people who had taken MDMA scored lower on memory tests.

If you want up-to-date information on ecstasy or any other drug, I suggest you call the National Institute on Drug Abuse at 1-888-NIH-NIDA or visit Teen Focus at http://www.focusas.com/Ecstasy.html. You can call them at 1-877-362-8727.

As I have pointed out already, never deny the "high" of the drug in your discussions about ecstasy with your teen. Getting high, for most people, is a wonderful physical experience. It also is the ultimate trickster. The brain reports, "If this drug can make me feel so good, then how can it be bad?" Drug education has to connect all the dots, including this one. Leaving out the discussion of what happens and what you feel like when you get high means, in the end, all the real information about the dangers of drugs will be discounted. Of course, it is a good idea to discuss other natural ways to get high without drugs, but the thrust here is to not deny the fact.

The main myth around ecstasy is that is not harmful and the high is truly wonderful. It has the power to make people feel not only at peace, but deeply connected emotionally. However, it *is* harmful, and while the high may seem wonderful, it is like all other chemicals: It has consequences.

I suggest when you discuss the more detailed aspects of this drug, you go online with your teen to a reliable Web site that discusses ecstasy. Teen Focus is one that is filled with information for parents and teens. Use that as a basis for your discussion. If you are not certain how you should suggest doing this, you can say to your teen something like the following: "I am concerned that you are thinking about using (or are using) ecstasy. I am not an expert, and I don't know much about this drug. I don't know what your friends have told you, either, or whether what they know is true. Let's go on the Internet and find out what is true and not true about this drug."

Naturally, if your teen still insists on using the drug, you need to contact a drug counselor. Kids can become dependent on drugs for all kinds of reasons. Often the allure of drugs is masking other problems. Drug treatment programs that are effective deal with all the issues involved.

On the other hand, if your teen is still not certain whether to use the drug or not, get a commitment to keep discussing the issue with him. Talk has the power to dispel myth. The more your teen knows about drugs, the less likely he will be to become dependent.

* * *

There's no doubt about it: Questions about drugs and drug use are some of the toughest ones you'll ever have to field, and they will yield some of the toughest discussions you'll ever have with your teen. You might find out information that breaks your heart. You also might discover that your teen is more insightful, mature, and responsible than you ever imagined. Whatever the result of the conversations you have with your teen about drugs, as long as you are able to suspend judgment and manage your fear enough to truly listen (remember — discuss, not lecture), you can be assured that you will at least have opened the door of communication between you and your teen a little bit farther. You will have increased that crucial level of trust and honesty. In the most extreme of circumstances, you will help to save her life. The best antidote for any trouble that may befall your teen is you — your willingness to listen and also to share, your openness to discussion, and your support in any situation. Don't leave it up to schools and drug-prevention programs, no matter how well-intentioned they may be. The one who knows your child best and who can make the biggest impact in his life is none other than you.

Chapter 7:
Depression, Suicide, and Self-Harm

*"When one door closes, another one opens —
but it's hell in the hallway."*

I call David "The Anonymous One." I met this quiet young man one afternoon after one of my seminars. He wore an empty, weary look that seemed to say, "No one understands — why keep trying?" As we sat alone in the corner of an empty classroom, he ran through the details of his upbringing. His life path, it seemed, had been pretty well mapped out for him at birth. Its beginning and middle, so far, were ugly, filled with family violence and general senselessness. From where I sat, I could see that his life could easily end there as well — and soon — if someone didn't step in and offer this guy a hand up.

"Yeah, so what that I get beat at home?" he said with a resigned, apathetic tone that frightens me more than the most intense anger. "I mean, maybe I got it coming, or maybe that's just the way it is. You think no one else lives like me?" David is a victim. Someday, he may even create victims — if his own propensity toward self-destruction doesn't claim him first. Drugs, overdoses, and, most disturbing of all, dreams of suicide are part of his routine.

"So how do you survive?" I asked him gently. "You know, get up in the morning? Go to school? What keeps you carrying on? And what made you take the risk of coming here to talk to me?"

"I don't know," he replied. "I think, sometimes, it would be better to talk. And you seem to listen. As far as survival goes," he said, glancing sideways at the wall of the classroom, "easy. I just learned to escape as soon as my brain woke up. What I mean is my mind is my safe harbor. I pretend I'm just walking through this life, or watching it like a movie, not really living it. I don't plan too far ahead. Who knows how long I'll be here anyway?" His voice trailed off, and he gave a little laugh, as if making a joke that only he understood.

Since David was quiet and never caught much attention from teachers, school staff, and other adults, no one had ever bothered to speak with him, look into his eyes, and see his pain. As he slipped his way through school and through life, no one could see that he was always thinking short.

Even at seventeen, David believed his life would be short — in fact, he was planning it that way. His friends and teachers would talk about their hopes and dreams, about going on to college and about fulfilling goals. When David hit high school and woke up to the realities of his life, he knew for sure none of those dreams were for him. His dreams were blank. His pain rendered him hopeless. The only way through life was to numb himself and entertain thoughts of escape. And of all the likely ways to escape his life, one stood out as the easiest, the most certain, and the most permanent: suicide.

I talked to David a good long time that afternoon, for while his life may have seemed hopeless to himself and to anyone else on the outside, I found one small spark of hope to hang on to. I don't know what made him do something he'd never done before and confide to an adult — albeit a stranger — his thoughts about suicide, but I do know this: If he hadn't, in some small way, wanted to keep on living, he would have kept those plans secret. He would have plotted silently and eventually carried them out. By choosing to reveal them, however, he was sending up a cry for help. It's a cry for life, for a second chance, and it's one we, as adults and parents, must learn to hear.

* * *

Teenage depression — and with it, suicide and other forms of self-harm — is perhaps the most silent and deadly of secrets harbored among young people today. One part of the reason it's kept so quiet is because of the stigma it carries; a more significant part is the fact that, until relatively recently, depression was seen as an adult-only disease. Things have changed in the last ten years. Maybe it's because more teens are becoming depressed; maybe it's because the awareness of teen depression — and with it, suicide — has increased significantly in recent years.

Today, nearly three million adolescents suffer from depression — about 8 percent of all adolescents as well as 2 percent of children, according to the National Institutes of Mental Health. And according to a recent report from the Centers for Disease Control, 19 percent of high school students have had suicidal thoughts, and more than 2 million of them have plans. In fact, suicide has become the third-leading cause of death among ten- to twenty-four-year-olds. Yes, you read that right: It's the third-leading cause of death among *ten-year-olds*. The impact of depression among kids *cannot* be underestimated — and its deadly clutches are reaching toward ever-younger victims.

Yet sadly, of all those adolescents struggling with depression, most suffer for years before they are diagnosed, and less than one-fifth ever get the help they need. Often, the symptoms of depression are written off as ordinary teenage moodiness. Often, the only kids who are noticed are those who act out or cause trouble (unlike my friend David). And once depressed teens are identified, finding them the appropriate help — psychiatrists and physicians who specialize in adolescent mental health issues — is often difficult (Pat Wingert and Barbara Kantrowitz, "Young and Depressed," *Newsweek,* October 7, 2002).

Still, help is out there — in the form of talk therapy, interpersonal therapy, and even medication — and the symptoms of depression can be identified before the disease debilitates a teen or even claims his life. What does that require? Simply this: Getting to know your teen, inside and out.

Key Points to Remember When Discussing Suicide and Depression

I get more questions about depression and suicide than any other category of questions. The students' queries range from extremely disturbing requests — some ask me about the best ways to commit suicide — to poignant cries for help. You'll find that there are fewer questions in this chapter than in others. That's because the same questions tend to be asked over and over again. More than questions in any other category, these are primal, straightforward, and urgent.

Regularly, teens report to me that they feel helpless when facing the issues surrounding depression and suicide. They report that when friends mention depressed feelings or suicidal thoughts, they have no idea how they should respond or what their responsibility is. If they are experiencing these feelings and thoughts themselves, they often can't identify or articulate what is wrong, let alone know how to talk about it, or to whom. Most alarming, these kids tell me that suicide and depression has not been discussed in school. Or if it has, the message was delivered as a lecture with little time for in-depth discussion. The only way to discuss these issues is to boldly bring them up. The best person to do that, as always, is you.

What are some of the basics you need to know? First of all, know how to recognize if your teen is suicidal or clinically depressed. The following is an important checklist of potentially depressive behavior. If your teen reports, or if you observe, that he or she is

1. not eating regularly or has lost his appetite
2. experiencing insomnia
3. neglecting her schoolwork
4. radically curtailing his social life, including online computer time
5. neglecting personal hygiene and wardrobe
6. continually obsessing over her problems

You may have reason to be concerned. If this behavior has been going on for more than a few weeks, your child needs to speak with someone. She truly might be suffering from depression. Consult with a local mental health agency, speak to your family doctor or clergy, and secure help. Board-certified child psychologists can be found by contacting the American Academy of Child and Adolescent Psychiatry (www.aacap.org) or visit the American Psychological Association (www.apa.org).

As always, there are preventive measures you can take to keep your finger on the pulse of your teenager's mental health. And as always, the best place to start is by cultivating a close relationship and open communication with your teen. As Dr. Harold Koplewicz, founder and director of the New York University Child Study Center and author of *More than Moody: Recognizing and Treating Adolescent Depression,* told *Newsweek* magazine, "Parents have to know their children. Adolescence is not a good time to introduce yourself. Money should have been put in the bank earlier. Then, during adolescence, it's a continuation of a close relationship. You understand what your child's sleep habits are like, what his energy level is like, what her concentration is like, so you can observe when changes in usual behavior last for a month. Then I would get an evaluation."

By this point in this book, you have received countless tips for doing just that — putting money in the bank and developing a closer relationship with your teen. Here are a few more that pertain specifically to depression and suicide:

Be a good listener. Yes, it is tough to hear your teen describe his sadness and sorrows. It is not uncommon for kids to have thoughts of suicide and depression. Most of the time it is nothing more than just having thoughts and feeling down. As common as depression is, most of the time, all your child needs is for you to be his sounding board. Teens do need to vent, moan, and groan.

If you notice behavior changes tied to the moaning and groaning, pay closer attention. Use the general checklist for depression I've just given you. If you check none of these items as you observe your teen, your child most likely needs the good old comfort of love as he rides out the blues.

On the other hand, you must take action if your child is suffering from depression or thinking about suicide. Parents must set the standard of involvement, as silence only increases tension and insecurity. Depression in general does not last long. Medical help and counseling have revolutionized its treatment. Most kids respond well to this treatment if they have someone there for them, lending support. Trouble develops when no one pays any attention to kids' needs. Left unattended, kids feel powerless. Left untreated, depression can become very dangerous.

The word *suicide* naturally frightens any parent. What do you do if your teen mentions suicide or hurting herself? What should you look for? Are there warning signs? The technical term for this is *suicidal ideation*. Kids who are suicidal, most of the time, will say they are suicidal. If you ever hear the word *suicide* or hear your child say she thinks of killing herself, there are two questions you need to ask immediately:

- "Are you thinking of committing suicide?"
- "Are you trying to tell me that you are going to hurt yourself?"

Mere mention of the word or act of suicide does not cause someone to commit suicide. In fact, the opposite is true. Bringing up the issue will most likely relieve your child, and your questions nearly always will be answered truthfully. So don't hold back. Ask.

If the answer to these either of these questions is yes, ask your child, "Why do you want to kill/hurt yourself?" This answer, too, will be hard to hear, but even before counseling happens, you must find out what is going on in your kid's life. When you get professional help, what your child has told you will be very significant. Even if the episode and ideation has passed, you will be able to provide valuable assistance to your child in therapy. It also strongly signals to your teen that you care for her deeply and are going to stick it out with her. It is a signal that you love your child.

Finally, ask your teenager, "Do you have a plan?" The more serious your teen's thoughts are, the more detailed his plan will be. If he has a plan, spend some time discussing this. Again this is critical. If the answer to this question is yes, ask further:

- "How are you going to kill yourself?"
- "Where are you going to do it?"
- "If you have a weapon, where will you get it?"
- "What do you think everyone will be thinking when they find out you killed yourself?"
- "Who do you want to find your body? Why?"
- "Can you see your own funeral?"
- "Who do you think will be there?"
- "What will they say about you?"
- "Who do you think will cry the most?"

Now, I know just reading what I have written is very upsetting, but suicide is a desperate, dangerous, angry, and often planned act. If your teen tests positive to the questions on this checklist or has mentioned suicide, get immediate help. If you do not know where to turn, call 911 or look up a suicide hot line. By all means, during this period, until it passes, never leave your child alone. He must be kept on suicide watch until this passes.

Depression, and with it, the desire to commit suicide, is very real. Many people view depression as some kind of core ethical weakness. It is not. It is the body's physiology out of whack. It is not going to be cured simply by a lot of love and attention. Of course that helps, but ignoring a desperate cry only leaves your teen in major-league risk. Turning a blind eye will not make this go away. Your teen just can't toughen up and make it better. Trying to stop depression or suicidal thoughts on your own is like going to the ocean and trying to hold back the waves. Depression can, however, be treated. In the case of your teen, it will be up to you to make sure that her depression is acknowledged, diagnosed, and given the medical and psychological attention needed.

Your love does matter greatly, but only in the context of getting professional help. Suicide is a cry for help. The tough and sad situations are those that happen without any warning or those that were ignored.

Questions and Answers

"I feel really sad all the time, but how can I talk to my parents about it? I don't even understand it."

Depression among teenagers is very real, which is not something that many people would have said even ten years ago, when depression was — or at least was perceived to be — for adults only. Today, even kids who seem to "have it all" suffer from persistent discontent and anxiety at one end of the range, to debilitating clinical depression — often accompanied by suicidal ideation — at the other. We'll talk about the reasons for this in future questions, but here, let's focus on the part of the question that lays the groundwork for all following questions: "How can I talk to my parents about this when I don't understand it myself?"

Unless you've got an awful lot of so-called money in the bank, it's not really likely that your teen will approach you when he is experiencing mysterious, hard-to-pinpoint feelings of melancholy and distress. For most people, such vague, uncertain feelings *are* difficult to talk about. Are they something to be ashamed of? Are they something that will pass? If nothing is going wrong in my life right now, and still I feel this way, is it all just in my head? If I tell someone, will they think I'm crazy, or just feeling sorry for myself? If it *is* just in my head, why can't I shake it? Why won't it go away?

Teens, as any parent knows, are moody creatures — and who wouldn't be, with the hormonal trapeze act taking place in their bodies? But teenage depression is something deeper and all-encompassing than day-to-day mood swings, and it takes a keen parental eye to note when one shifts into the other. It's probably normal for your teen's mood to be up one day and down the next; she may be livid at breakfast time and vivacious by dinner. Take note of these swings. If something seems to change — particularly, if she seems down more than up, or is down for longer and longer periods of time, or if anger and self-righteousness seem to be replaced by sadness and resignation, or if she seems more tired or withdrawn than usual, take note of that, too.

At that point, it's time to sit down with your teen and have a talk. The more you deal openly with your teen's concerns, the more likely they will be short-lived. Ignoring them and keeping silent will only make matters worse. Take the time to find out what is bothering your child by asking questions such as the following:

- "I've noticed you seem down more than usual. Has something been bothering you lately?"
- "Do you feel down off and on, or all the time?"
- "Why do you think that might be?"
- "How long has this been going on?"
- "Do you feel physically okay?"
- "Do you have trouble sleeping?"
- "How's your appetite? Do you still enjoy your favorite foods?"
- "Are you keeping up with your schoolwork?"
- "Do your friends notice you're having problems?"
- "Can you talk to them about what you're feeling? Do you find yourself spending a lot of time talking about this?"

These questions provide a gentle exploration into the symptoms of depression. I am not asking you to make a diagnosis — that is a job left up to a professional. What I am suggesting is that you explore the possibility. If, from your talk, it is clear that your teen's behavior has significantly changed, then he just might be depressed. If things do not change, then get your teen professional help. Counseling — and medication, if that's required — can be a lifesaver for a depressed teen.

However, remember: Not every teen who asks a question like this is depressed. He simply may be, as he says, feeling "down." Often we get down when we get overwhelmed or isolated. Isolation from feelings is often the cause a good case of the blues. Left in isolation, the seeds of depression can grow. As a parent, it's your job to keep "checking in" on your teen's moods, concerns, feelings, and questions.

And teenagers have all kinds of questions, including existential and spiritual ones. Don't be surprised if your teen replies with questions about the meaning of life, about God, about suffering, and more when you ask her what is bothering her. All those kinds of questions and thoughts are extremely important. And again, it's not up to you to know the answers to these deep, all-encompassing questions. Sharing your own questions, thoughts, and ideas about such matters is exactly the right thing to do.

Never be afraid to step into the middle of your child's confusion and questions. Take that step. Give him a hug. Share your concern. Acknowledge his feelings. And top it all off with intimate discussion in which you, too, share your struggles in life.

Still, keep that parent-radar turned up high. If your teen's sadness persists, seek professional guidance.

"Does it mean anything if you don't care whether you live or die?"

This is not a question any parent wants to hear from a child. No one wants to think that someone so young, so full of life and promise, especially someone we love so much, can be so enveloped in hopelessness that he can't believe in the potential he possesses, the possibilities that lie ahead. But increasingly, teens are feeling this way. They are facing enormous pressure from every direction — school, family, peers, sports or other activities, boyfriends and girlfriends, even their own changing chemical makeup — topped with mounting fears of terrorism and unrest in the world, especially since 9/11. If your child asks you this question, take a deep breath. There's a lot you will need to find out. It's quite possible that your child is experiencing normal teenage mood swings, being overwhelmed by the expectations and demands heaped upon him, or feeling the weight of uneasy times. But he also could be suffering from something much more serious, and it's up to you to find out. If suicidal thoughts do come up or if you suspect your child is facing serious depression, you have to marshal your resources and get help. Let me give you a little context for evaluating your teen's question.

If this comment came during a knock-down, drag-out fight with you or a friend, or after, say, an incident at school for which your child was blamed or punished, it does not necessarily reflect suicidal thoughts, but may merely be a reaction to the fight or incident. Nevertheless, it is important for you to find out more about what is going on with your teen's emotional state.

Before you begin to ask questions, spend some time thinking about what is currently going on in your kid's life.

Is she still leading a normal social life?

Have his sleeping or eating habits changed in the last few weeks?

Has your child recently experienced a crisis or major disappointment?

Did your child break up with a boyfriend or girlfriend recently, and is feeling depressed over that?

Can you pinpoint a starting point for any unusual behavior, say, a party or date during which something distressing might have happened?

Is your child involved with alcohol or drugs? (Drugs and alcohol can heighten negative emotional thinking, and they are often used to numb unbearable pain. If they are a symptom of or are at the core of your teen's problems, they must be addressed immediately.)

If the answers from this observation reveal that your teen is struggling more than usual, the chances that she is clinically depressed or suicidal go up, and counseling is in order. While "yes" responses to the above questions do not *necessarily* mean your teen is suicidal or depressed, you must entertain that possibility. Depression and suicidal thoughts are serious matters. You must not ignore what is happening.

After making the observations described above and giving some thought to what may be going on in your teen's life, it's time to sit down and have a discussion with your child. This will not be an easy conversation, so don't expect it to be. Right out of the box, ask the following:

- "Why are you asking this question?"
- "What is going on in your life that makes you think it has no meaning?"
- "Are you telling me that you are thinking about suicide?"

If your teen says, "I don't know what's going on, but I'm really bummed out," or "Yes, I do think about suicide," before going any further, tell her if you have ever had depressive feelings or suicidal thoughts. Many of us, at some time or other, have been "really bummed out" without knowing why, or have felt it didn't matter whether we were alive. For many of us, it passes, or we find a way to work through these feelings and cross over to a brighter side. If you have an experience of such feelings you can share with your teen, briefly go over what was going on in your life then, and how you resolved the issue.

There is an important reason I am suggesting this to you. It is always best, even in tough circumstances, to "normalize" issues.

Challenges and situations filled with high emotional content are even harder to deal with when the panic button is pushed. Since problems are part of our lives, and finding a way through them is how we move forward, normalize them as best you can. It will make discussions saner and more helpful, it can help your child feel less alone, and, if counseling is needed, it can help him feel more comfortable with that, too.

Having said that, if your teen admits to having serious suicidal thoughts, it won't do to brush them off with, "Oh, I felt that way once, honey, but it didn't last long." Suicide talk must be taken seriously. Your child needs attention *now*. Suicide is the angriest and most desperate act anyone can do. It is a very mean sword thrust into family's lives. If successful, it is complete rejection of family. It shuts forever all doors to resolving problems. If, in your conversation, it becomes clear that your child is actually suicidal and not simply pondering the meaning of life, then you must immediately seek professional help. I mean *immediately*. The admission of suicidal thoughts is a cry for help that must be responded to. Again, call a suicide hot line or 911. They will be able to direct you to the most immediate and appropriate assistance. And do not leave your child alone — a suicide watch is in order until a physician or mental health expert gives the all clear.

"Why is life so difficult?"

This little question can be unsettling to any parent. Why is my kid asking this? What is going on that is so hard right now? Is my teen really having such a hard time? Relax, this is a question that's frequently asked, and is as normal as apple pie.

Kids today are subject to all kinds of pressure and confusion that did not exist even ten years ago — let alone back when you were a teenager. And new pressure points are added all the time: the possibility of terrorism, the upsurge of school shootings, and more. And this is not to mention the huge social and technological changes that also did not exist ten years ago. We are smack-dab in the middle of an information revolution, and as a result, everything is happening faster, and there seems to be more of it. Keeping up with e-mail alone adds hours to the day.

I think you understand how magnified everything appears to teenagers today. Teens today feel pressured to pack more than ever into their lives. And no doubt, 9/11 added even more uncertainty and a sense of urgency.

Study after study points out that teens are very stressed. At the core of these studies is a clarion call challenging parents to simplify and not overbudget teens' schedules. Studies have recently pointed out that the school day should start later, for example — children are not getting enough sleep. They are coming to class and sleeping there.

Add into the mix the push for standardized testing. Toss in on top of that preparation for SAT exams and the college admissions pressure that begins second semester of the junior year, if not sooner. And finally, add to the database fractured and overworked families. Is it any wonder that kids see life as difficult? When do kids find real time to be kids today?

Teens who do not have nurturing home environments are going to wrestle even more with life's difficulties. There is a partial antidote, however. A home that has love, concern, and caring will lessen the tension and make life easier to face. If your teen's home environment is lacking — if it harbors neglect or even violence — then you, as the parent, need to address that, for the sake of your child. See chapter 4, Family Problems, and chapter 5, Violence and Abusive Relationships, for more information.

Despite all this, however, remember that life's difficulties can't be avoided. The world is becoming a more complicated place, and odds are your teen's life in it is only going to become more complex than it already is. What do you need to communicate to your teen about life's difficulties? How can you prepare your teen for what lies ahead? Let your teen know that life is difficult, and that this difficulty is reaching people earlier and earlier in their lives. Let her know that you understand she is under stress. At the same time, put it into context. Jesse Owens, the great Olympian and statesman, said it best: "Find the good. It is all around you. Find it, showcase it, and you'll start believing in it. Life doesn't give you all the practice races you need. The battles that count aren't the ones for gold medals. The struggles within yourself — the invisible, inevitable battles inside all of us — that's where it's at."

Clearly then, do not ignore the difficulties. Try to put them into some kind of meaningful context. At the very least, you will teach your kid to endure. Some things do take time to change.

Make certain not to minimize your teen's difficulties and struggles, and stay open to discussing anything with him. That will make a great difference. Parents should never underestimate the power of the support they give their children simply by listening.

"How can I tell if my friend is serious when he talks about suicide?"

Suicide talk is not rare among teenagers. In my surveys, no less than 85 percent of teenagers, and often more, tell me that one of their friends has mentioned suicide. What is most confusing for teens is this: Precisely what should they do when they hear this kind of talk? Often they think that what is said between friends must be kept confidential, and the heavier the secret, the higher the confidence. They also carry with them the myth that talking to someone about suicide, especially asking someone if she is thinking of committing suicide, will be just the trigger that takes her over the edge.

Considering that suicide is the third-leading cause of death among adolescents today, it's very important for parents to shatter the myths surrounding it and assist their children in helping their friends get help.

First of all, you might be wondering, "Why would my child even bring up such a question with me? We barely talk about anything, let alone his friends, and let alone anything that heavy." It's time for that to change. When it comes to topics like suicide, everyday contact and conversation with your teen can literally save a life — his or another's. (Follow the Parenting Principles in chapter 1, particularly those listed under Conscious Communication, and you will begin to have substantive conversations with your teen.) Touching base with your teen every day does make a difference. And if you also follow the Parenting Principle of making your home a place for your teen's friends to hang out, it will become natural for you to ask your child about his friends.

As we've seen in other questions on other topics, it's very important for your teen to know what being a good friend means. Teens often think that a good friend is a confidante, psychiatrist, and counselor all rolled into one. But no one, and certainly not a teenage person, can be all these things rolled into one, especially when a friend's needs become desperate and her secrets too great for any young person to bear alone. Your child needs to know, from you, that a good friend is someone who gets help for her friend in a time of need.

When the discussion turns to suicide, as it does with this question, I recommend that you, the parent, step in and make the phone calls to get your child's friend help. That may mean calling the school counselor, the friend's family, a clergyperson, or even a suicide hot line. This is not a time to sit back and not take action. Involve your teenager in the process. If he feels comfortable speaking directly to these resources to provide more information about his friend's situation, encourage him to do so, but be present, if possible, when he does. If he wants to take his friend to the school guidance office or help the friend talk to his parents, that's fine. Just make certain that you follow up, and make sure that someone truly responsible is notified and takes appropriate action.

This is a wonderful way to show your child the power of your family's values and love. The impact of your action and support will last your child a lifetime and mirror for her not just your caring and concern, but how that caring and concern translates into a personal rite of passage into her own adult life.

"My friend is really depressed but wants me to keep it a secret and not do anything. What should I do?"

The point I always emphasize with teens is how important it is to be "in the know" with their close friends when they are in trouble, and also when to break a confidence. As with the previous question, any secret that threatens the life or health of a friend — especially one dealing with depression, abuse, substance abuse, or suicide — is not a secret to be kept. While personal confidences, of course, must be honored, cries for help demand a response.

There are things your teen needs to know, in particular, about friends who are depressed. First of all, depression is very common among teens and adults. The biochemistry of depression is very real. Announced depression is, indeed, a cry for help. While obviously neither you nor your child is a therapist, it is a good idea to find out the extent of his friend's depression. Remember that checklist that appeared in the introduction to this chapter? This is a good place to use it. There is a difference between feeling down and being clinically depressed, and that checklist, while nowhere near a diagnostic tool, can help alert you to warning signs that indicate your child's friend has something more than the blues. For your reference, here it is again:

Ask your child if he notices any of the following happening with his friend:

1. He is not eating regularly or has lost his appetite.
2. She is experiencing insomnia.
3. He is neglecting his schoolwork.
4. She has radically curtailing her social life, including on-line computer time.
5. He is neglecting personal hygiene and wardrobe.
6. She is continually obsessing over her problems.

If none of these checklist items show up, your child can assume her friend is probably just "feeling down" and needs a shoulder to lean on, a good ear, and a good dose of love and friendship to help her ride out the blues. However, if some of the above do show up, intervention is necessary. The other key question to ask is "How long has this been going on?" If the answer is more than a few weeks, tell your child that her friend needs to speak with a counselor. Assure her that her friend's confidence will be kept. This friend really might be suffering from depression, and if so, she will need help. Where can this help be found? Here are some suggestions that can help you and your teen direct her friend in the right direction:

1. Have the friend speak with the school counselor, his parents, his family doctor, or a clergyperson. If your child is comfortable doing so, he may offer to go with his friend as he does this.
2. If that fails — say the friend is resistant, unwilling, or even angry about this intervention — then your teenager herself ought to go to the school counselor, clergyperson, etc. about her friend. If your teenager is uneasy about doing this, then you can make the phone call and arrange for your teen to meet with whomever you contacted, accompany your teen as she speaks with these people, or even take matters into your own hands and speak with them yourself.
3. If you know your child's friend well, sit down and talk to him yourself. It then will be your job to get him help.
4. If you know the family of the friend in trouble, a phone call may be in order — but only if you are certain the response will be positive.

Nearly 100 percent of all of the teens that I have surveyed mentioned that they had a friend who at one time or another was seriously depressed. Depression, especially among teenagers, has been too long ignored in our society. By keeping an eye out for the welfare of others, in particular your close friends, you impart important family values to your teen. The gift of a true friend is stepping in and lending a hand when real help is needed. This is particularly important in the case of depression, where one's perception of what's happening and what's really happening can be very different, and someone on the outside — someone close enough to recognize when behavior isn't normal — is needed to step in and speak up.

In situations like this, always be sure not only to praise your teen for being a solid friend, but also thank him for coming to consult with you. Tell him that you are proud of him for recognizing when to take action on behalf of someone is in need.

"I broke up with my girlfriend. Now she says she can't live without me. She even said she might kill herself. I feel bad and scared. She keeps calling me all the time and following me around. What am I supposed to do?"

Most parents know, from experience, that desperation, even depression, can often follow breaking up. Given the fact that so many young people grow up as victims of abuse and experience deep and troubling relationships at home, dysfunction is bound to carry over into their relationships outside of home. If a teenager's daily life is filled with desperation, it's no surprise that this desperation will spill over into relationships with girlfriends or boyfriends. When a kettle boils over, the water runs all over the place.

As I mentioned before, anyone threatening suicide should be taken seriously. Even if the threat is nothing more than an attempt at manipulation, and a nasty one at that, it has to be attended to. It is vital to make it abundantly clear to your child that he is *not* the cause or source of this problem. Furthermore, he does not have to get reinvolved in the relationship to help his ex.

I have been very blunt with my own children on this issue. More than once they have come to me, telling me about a friend whose ex-boyfriend or ex-girlfriend threatened suicide after they broke up. Each time, I have made certain that they told their friends that even if,

God forbid, the ex-partner did commit suicide, in no way is or was that the fault of their friend. My kids report back that this assurance helped their friends, and even managed to some real help for the teen in trouble.

Suicide is a very personal, desperate, and angry act. Threats of suicide also can be cries for help. Parents need to explain this very point to their child. Whenever a breakup takes a dark and potentially deadly turn, we often hear that nobody ever thought anything was wrong. People say, "It seemed like he was fine. Maybe a little sad, but I never suspected suicide."

If your teen comes to you and reports that her former boyfriend has mentioned or threatened suicide, then it is your responsibility, along with your teenager's, to make sure that this is reported. This does not mean your child has to contact her former boyfriend. Trusted friends of the ex-boyfriend (or ex-girlfriend) can be mobilized to reach out and lend support. The school guidance counselor, a suicide hot line, the police, the family, and a clergyperson are all appropriate people to notify when a suicide threat has been mentioned. Threats should never be ignored. Follow-up must be made to ensure someone has contacted the threat-maker and taken appropriate action.

Please emphasize to your teen that it is dangerous to gossip about or mention the suicide threat to anyone other than proper authorities, particularly loose-lipped friends. Not only is that disrespectful and unethical, but it will only worsen matters by embarrassing, putting down, and hurting his former partner further. Never give anyone more reasons to be down on herself — particularly someone who's made a suicide threat.

Once the proper authorities have been notified of the threat, and you are certain they have followed up on the report, you must make it abundantly clear to your teen that her involvement stops at that point and goes no further. Suicide threats are not opportunities to start talking or dating again. In fact, sometimes they are veiled attempts to emotionally entwine your teen and hold her hostage in the relationship again. As a parent, you have to be very firm and make certain that your child does not get back in communication with her ex after the threat is reported. Leave any further contact to the professionals.

"One of my good friends cuts herself. It really scares me. She tells me it makes her feel good. That makes me more scared. Her

parents know about it, and she sees some counselor, but why does she do it?"

I do not get many questions about cutting and other types of self-mutilation. However, this is a question that comes up with some regularity, and it certainly is a serious one that merits discussion.

There are a lot of reasons why kids cut themselves, burn themselves, pull out their hair, or otherwise hurt themselves. Many are victims of abuse or some other traumatic incident. Survivors of child abuse, particularly sexual abuse, often hurt themselves as a way of further punishment for whatever they believe they did to deserve the abuse in the first place. Some of these kids think that this is a way to cut, burn, or pull out the part of themselves that was abused. If you can find it, I recommend reading "The Thin Red Line" by J. Eagan (*New York Times Magazine,* July 1997) for a detailed and graphic discussion of this serious problem.

Kids who have been abused, as a defense, go numb to their feelings. They block out their emotions to escape the pain. As time passes and none of their issues are resolved, they get tired of not feeling. Nearly every teenager I have spoken to who is a victim of abuse and now self-injures tells me they do so because they are tired of feeling nothing. They hurt themselves to feel. Hurting themselves makes them feel alive. They are trying to take action against their deeper, inner pain. Teens who do this have a hatred of the way things are in their life.

Kids who engage in self-injurious behavior do feel better after they hurt themselves. It actually reduces their anxiety. The first time a teenager explained that to me, I was horrified. It's hard enough to imagine someone regularly slashing her wrists, let alone to hear that it brings on relief. Self-injury happens when something is too painful or overwhelming for an individual to handle alone. Cutting or any other form of mutilation breaks the anxiety cycle, floods endorphins — the body's natural painkillers — into the body, and gives temporary relief.

Various visible signs indicate that a teen has this problem. The following list includes a lot of different behaviors; teens who exhibit any of them must get professional help. These behaviors can include

- Burning oneself
- Cutting oneself

- Excessively scratching oneself
- Hitting oneself
- Pulling out one's hair
- Puncturing one's skin with objects
- Excessive body piercing or tattooing (as distinguished from the popular fad of body piercing and tattooing, which is not necessarily self-mutilation — see the question on body piercing in chapter 4)
- Swallowing cleaning fluids or other toxic liquids that burn or scar the digestive tract
- Sexually acting out
- Being involved in abusive relationships
- Engaging in extremely risky behavior

Any child who is locked in a desperate struggle of self-inflicted violence is crying out for help. Only a professional familiar with the actions and methods of self-mutilators should work with these children. If you see or hear about someone hurting himself, please help him get to someone who can help — contacting a counselor or family doctor is probably the best place to begin.

If your child is suffering from this affliction, the following five points, adapted from the Web site www.kidssafe.com, can help you respond to your teen in ways that will help her while she is in therapy.

1. Respond to your child medically, not emotionally.
2. Empathize with your child. Try to see the situation from his perspective, not your own. Self-mutilators' actions are not horrible to them; they actually, in the moment, are helping them cope. Remember this is not about you, but about your child's inability to handle something that happened to him. (Of course, if you abused your child, the situation is different.)
3. Never tell your child she should be ashamed of herself. She already feels bad enough.
4. Never think this is an attention-getting stunt. If your teen knew a healthy way to get help himself, he would.
5. Never ask your teen to stop because it upsets you. She can't stop until she learns, in therapy, how to handle her feelings and understand what happened to her.

And finally, don't hesitate to seek out therapy for yourself and your entire family as well as your teen. This will help you all understand your teen's situation, learn how to deal with it, and give him the support and love he needs as he heals.

"People tell me I am wrong because I think I am not thin enough. Is there anything so wrong about wanting to get down another size? What is wrong with being super thin?"

Most of the time, if this question is even asked at all, it is asked by a girl. If your daughter is obsessing about food, engaging in bizarre eating habits, or has undergone a significant weight loss (of more than a few pounds), the alarm bells should be going off. Eating disorders like anorexia and bulimia are dangerous and all too common among young women today. Often, they are not noticed until it is too late. Young people who starve themselves become very skilled at hiding the fact that they are not eating. Furthermore, who is going to follow a kid into the bathroom to see whether she is vomiting or taking laxatives to produce rapid weight loss?

Let me be blunt: Any teen with this problem is at tremendous risk, one that can be life-threatening. Eating disorders are not something that can be simply talked out with your teen. If your child has this disorder, you need to seek professional help. Ask your family doctor or therapist for a referral, or do your own research. It is critical to find someone whose practice specializes in eating disorders.

There are countless theories floating around that try to unravel the mystery of self-starvation and skewed body perception, as well as why someone would develop this disorder in the first place. In general with eating disorders, there is a big disconnect between society's image of the perfect body and how a teenager views herself. Furthermore, underneath the need not to eat can be enormous anger, a desperate need for control (in this case, over one's body), self-loathing, a desire to be "perfect," and a true inability to nourish oneself. The very secretive nature of the problem compounds treatment.

When seeking help for a teen with an eating disorder, try to find a therapist who is also skillfully trained in family systems theory. Better yet, work with someone who is part of a clinical or hospital team. Eating disorders go well beyond the refrigerator — they can indicate a deep-seated psychological issue. As you seek help and try to understand your child's disorder, keep the following in mind:

1. Your child does not see her skinniness.
2. Body fat is disgusting to her.
3. In her mind, she is never truly satisfied unless she gorges and/or vomits.
4. She may have a lot of energy.
5. She may refuse to recognize that there is a problem and see no need to make a "nonexistent" problem go away.
6. She may feel totally helpless, so she controls her helplessness by starving or vomiting.
7. She may see herself as inadequate, average, plain, or lacking distinction, and a way to be better — i.e., thin — is not to eat. She may also be angry, and not eating becomes a way of acting out.
8. Once she starts seriously losing weight, the loss may become almost impossible to contain. Anorexics often get caught up in being a waif and having everyone want to take care of them.
9. Anorexics also may get obnoxious and push people away. They need love, but see food as the only way to this emptiness. They purge the food, and the vicious cycle goes around and around.

As a parent of a child with an eating disorder, be aware that logic is not going to prevail. It is, though, important to understand that the seemingly irrational response of your child to the problem is to be expected. They are starving to death and cannot see it. This is why reading up and understanding the disorder is very helpful. Understanding its secretive nature eliminates being surprised. Getting involved with an on-line or local support group also will strengthen you. Most of all, you must stay the course in therapy. I cannot underscore that enough.

* * *

It's hard enough to imagine anyone wanting to harm a child, but there's almost nothing as heartbreaking as a child wanting to harm himself, as unfathomable as a child wanting to kill herself. But it happens, and more often than any of us care to think about. But think about it we must, if we care for our kids, their mental health, and their happiness. We must act upon the depressive symptoms we see in our kids. We must watch them and talk to them and love them persistently, no matter how challenging their "ordinary" teen behavior becomes, no matter how pesky or embarrassing they think we are. We, as parents, must be the safety nets they can fall into when life seems to pull the rug out from under them.

Depression can be treated and young lives turned around. And the sooner depression — and the suicidal desperation that sometimes accompanies it — is arrested, the sooner teens can get back on the road toward a healthy, functioning adulthood.

Chapter 8:
Spirituality and Social Consciousness

*"We didn't all arrive on the same ship.
But we are all in the same boat."*

Mike lives in Staten Island. He attends high school and is fairly active in various clubs. He plans to attend college somewhere near his home next year. A couple of years ago, he showed up on one of my live conferences online, and we have been writing regularly ever since. In 2001, Mike's best friend lost his father in the World Trade Center attack. Since then, his life has changed.

Shortly after 9/11, Mike wrote to me. "Yehuda," he began, "you know I went to Israel last summer and thought I understood about terrorism. I mean, our group had lectures about Hamas and Islamic Jihad. We lived through suicide bombings. We talked to a lot of Israeli kids about what it is like living in the middle of all that hatred and violence. Then Danny loses his father. I feel like I am falling apart inside and angry at the same time. I'm out of control because I don't know what to do."

"Hey, Mike," I replied, "let me ask you this, not just as some guidance counselor, but in general: Is 9/11 being talked about in school or at home? Where's the forum? Are your friends hanging out with Danny?"

I asked because I vividly remember that even after the Columbine shooting and the Oklahoma City bombing, a lot of schools and families simply bypassed the discussion. Yes, they started it up, but it quickly disappeared. We have a nasty habit in some parts of America: A lot of parents do not talk to their kids, particularly about tough events like these. Most of us want to, but we don't know how. It is like some of us have forgotten that, at one time, we were teenagers, too. When we do talk, we often simply give a one-way lecture. It is as if we fear contact. And it became obvious, in my correspondence with Mike, that this avoidance isn't just limited to parents.

Mike jumped right back and wrote, "Y, not nearly enuff. I asked my history teacher, 'Why aren't we talking and studying this more?' She said, 'Too much talk will only frighten and depress some of the students. Besides we have to move on. All of you have to prepare for the State

Regents exams. I wish I could spend more time studying this in class, but we have to follow the state curriculum. And you have to pass the exam to move on. So, that doesn't leave us much time, does it?' All I could say to her was, 'Just please make sure the most relevant thing ever to happen in our lives is discussed. I mean, this is our history.'"

Mike and I are still talking. I constantly tell him and all the kids who write me that life is all about finding meaning and the defining moments of our lives, *especially* in the midst of crisis and unanswerable questions. The important questions in life should never be swept away. They deserve our attention and our respect. I think Mike finally is getting it right. If only his parents would sit down and talk with him some more.

* * *

So often, others in society — maybe even us as parents — sell our teenagers short. Granted, when you're a parent of a teen, it's hard to focus on little more than urgent matters at any one time: How is my child doing in school? Why are her grades slipping? How am I going to tell him he can't go to that big party this weekend? Why haven't we heard back from the university? Why can't she do her own laundry? Is he hiding something in that sty of a bedroom? The truth is, with all these petty — and not-so-petty — concerns clouding our vision of our teens, it's easy to forget that deep below the surface, beneath the grades and boyfriends and parties and peers, there is a singular individual who is carefully crafting his own thoughts about the world and his place in it. This is an inevitable part of growing up — in fact, it's a milestone of growing up — but still, somehow we as parents are surprised when our teen comes to us with questions not of curfews, but of God, of the mysterious workings of the world, and whether her presence in it makes any difference at all.

Such questions don't raise the alarm that some of the other questions in this book might, but they are deeply serious and often, especially to us parents, deeply perplexing. How do we respond to questions on matters we don't really understand ourselves? Pointing to Sunday-school teachings or passages from our holy text of choice are pat solutions — teens have heard this stuff before; what they need now is practical understanding, an idea of how these teachings, values, and beliefs actually work in their lives and in the world around them. They need this understanding especially now, when tragedies are rocking the circles they live in — from the world to their country to their very schools.

As a parent, you may also wish you had this understanding. Having many of these same questions yourself, you may feel particularly unequipped to supply answers. Always remember, though, as you read this chapter and as you have subsequent conversations with your teen, who you are is enough. Your presence, your attention, your thoughts, and your stories — *that* is what is important here, more than any definitive answer, for no one of us has those. Believe that your teen is insightful enough to know this. Her mind is a complex, caring, sophisticated place.

Key Points to Remember When Discussing Spirituality and Social Consciousness

Questions about spirituality, social consciousness, pain, and suffering can overwhelm parents. I'm often asked, "I really have never given much thought to my own spiritual issues. How am I going to tackle my kid's?" Or "What do I know about questions of social consciousness and activism? I have enough trouble just keeping the family together. Where am I to begin talking about things like that?" Ah, but remember: You don't have to have all the answers. In fact, there *are* no "answers" to many of the questions that fall into this realm. There are only ideas and theories and deep feelings and instincts — and of course, more questions.

Where are you to begin talking about issues like these? Start by taking some time and exploring your own feelings, beliefs, and questions about these subjects. Then, simply be prepared to share them with your teen. The potential here for deep, heart-to-heart talks with your teen is vast and great. You'll find yourself sharing not facts and checklists, but values, family stories, life lessons, and your own wonderment about how things work in the world. Not only will you have the opportunity to pass family treasures along to your child, but you'll also get some fresh perspectives on these topics from someone with a different experience. Just because your teen hasn't been on Earth as long as you doesn't mean you can't gain from his insight, face questions that poke holes in or illuminate your theories, or share a wonderful conversation on philosophical topics that have boggled the brightest minds since the beginning of time.

The questions you will encounter here are not about rules, but about ethical action and attitudes — they are spiritual questions, in the broadest sense of the word. To answer their teens' spiritual questions, parents need to bring their life experiences and understandings to the table. Notice that, here, I'm using the word *spirituality,* not *religion.* The reason for that is quite simple. I chose the word *spiritual* to be as inclusive as possible, encompassing not only all faiths (or lack thereof), but all matters beyond human influence. By *spiritual,* I mean all those questions and experiences that focus on the difficulties and even despair that are bound within our human imperfections. Wrestling with God's world is very much part of my tradition. Spiritual struggle leads us to discover our core ethics and values, and to live them out day by day.

Naturally, that does not — nor should it — exclude or diminish your strong religious beliefs. As a rabbi, I certainly consider myself a religious man, and my faith is core to my family, its history, and the values I have sought to instill in my own children. Every family must pass on some kind of religious or spiritual tradition. Religion is bound in community and history. Kids who are raised with a set of beliefs are given a framework with which to live, to evaluate situations in their life, and to make decisions based on some idea of right and wrong. Kids who do not grow up with some sort of spiritual underpinning become adults who lack that as well.

Having said all that, let's move on to practical matters. How, then, do you prepare yourself to discuss these important issues and questions raised by your teen?

1. One of my Parenting Principles states, "You don't have to be an expert in anything. You simply have to share and care." Your personal inner experiences are very important to your teenager. Bring them to mind and use them when you discuss those big spiritual questions.

2. Teens often feel like life is hell. They have spiritual dilemmas. They often are confused by religion and spirituality, and they often have questions they feel they aren't supposed to ask. And who hasn't? Now is the time to share your own questions — even those personal, sticky ones about faith that still hound you — and the conclusions you have reached, if any. For you to lend a helpful hand, all you need to bring to the table is your life experiences. Explain what you think you have learned from facing your own spiritual challenges. Lessons learned along your road of life will be the cornerstone of these

discussions. They are fundamental in passing on your values to your child.

3. You do not have to have all the answers. Teens do not expect that from their parents, nor do they necessarily want that. What they want is to be engaged on the "big issues" and know they can talk to you about any quandary. Inscribe in your heart the Parenting Principle that says, "Share what has touched your life." Talk about what you believe in — God, love, compassion, truth, kindness, honesty — and share your uncertainties about these topics. Approach your teen's questions with love and respect, and you will successfully engage your teen's spiritual dilemmas.

4. When you are asked to deal with vast spiritual questions, bring the discussion down to the small things you know for sure, having learned them from direct experience. "I don't know why life seems harder for some people than others," you might say, "but I do know this: Lending a hand to people in need *always* makes you feel better, no matter how bad your circumstances may seem. I remember feeling really lost and depressed in college, but nothing made my life seem more meaningful than the Friday afternoons I spent reading books to kids at a homeless shelter." Your life experience and what you know is more than sufficient. Successful conversation comes from talking about what you know and what you think is possible in any situation. Use the small, important examples in your experience to bring ethics to the forefront in any conversation. This is not philosophy, this is life.

5. You can discuss any topic with your teen. You can discuss racism, hatred, anger, and forgiveness. You can discuss epoch-making issues like the Holocaust or the destruction of the World Trade Center. Draw on your personal experience and understanding to discuss these perplexing issues. Never shy away from expressing your deepest thoughts as well as admitting, "I don't know." If the topic is really beyond you, simply explain why you aren't certain how to respond. It is always all right to say, "I don't know what to say. I don't have an answer for that, but I struggle with it all the time, too." Your teen's respect for you will only grow larger.

The following questions cover several spiritual issues on teens' minds today. Certainly, by the publication of this book, more world events will have taken place that will raise more questions. And teens will always be pulled back to the age-old questions that philosophers have been grappling with for centuries. Use these questions to get you thinking about how to respond to queries of this type in general. I am absolutely certain that your teen will place before you her own unique questions, ones that will amaze you and awe you with their depth and originality.

Questions and Answers

"Since the terrorist attacks on September 11, 2001, a lot of my friends are really angry. They say stuff like, 'Let's kick every Muslim out of our country,' or 'We ought to go over and kill those guys,' and all kinds of other things. I want to talk to them about tolerance, but I feel weird about it. We have Muslim students at my school, and some of them are freaked out. I am just as angry as my friends and want to go after terrorists, but I see tolerance as important, too. What should I say or do?"

Every parent needs to spend some time talking with his or her teen about the effect terrorism has had on everyone's lives in America. The events of 9/11 must never be forgotten. If there was ever a time to talk about tolerance, then this is it. I often tell people that while bad things do happen, it's what we do when they happen that's key.

When times are easy, we overlook important issues, like fairness, what's happening in other parts of the world, and how what one country takes for granted can bring another to its knees. When times are hard, like they are now, there are important lessons to be learned and issues to be discussed. But I am not just talking about global politics. There are other things parents often take for granted that they need to be watchful of now. Before we get into the meat of this question, let me alert you to some of these.

In any crisis, it is important for parents to monitor their teenager's emotions. Naturally, those emotions are in a state of constant flux. However, parents have to keep an eye on their kids to see if major events are affecting them adversely. If you become aware that your child's fuse has become short or he seems angry or depressed, you need to sit down and talk with him about his feelings. Anger can be a sign of depression; so too is an ongoing sense of hopelessness and frustration. All of these feelings need to be discussed. If you suspect your teen is depressed over a specific event, go back to chapter 7, "Depression, Suicide, and Self-Harm," and revisit the checklist for depression. If your child's behavior matches warning signs on that list, seek professional help.

That aside, let's address the issue raised in this question: tolerance. How can you effectively approach that issue? If I were the parent of the teen asking this question, I would first commend her for her immediate concern about tolerance and the welfare of innocent people in her school. Already, she is setting aside her immediate reaction of anger to look beyond herself to others who may be suffering unjustly. That's a very mature position to take, and you should tell her so.

Tolerance is important. It is a building block not just of this country, but of every family in it. Think about it for a moment. What would families be like if there were no tolerance, if no one looked out for the welfare of each other, if no one transcended their immediate impulses and made moves to sustain peace? Families would be in chaos (and no doubt, some are). Now take that image and impose it on a larger institution, say, a school, a community, even a country. Tolerance is what keeps us all living and working together. When it breaks down, as it does regarding certain groups in certain communities following certain events (look back in history to the advent of AIDS, the Holocaust, or even the Salem witch trials), fear and violence inevitably erupt.

As a parent of a child who needs to learn about tolerance, or who recognizes intolerance and wants to do something about it, spend some time talking to him about the kinds of comments he hears at school. Ask:

- "How does that talk make you feel?"
- "What do you think you can do about it?"
- "Does it bother you? Why?"

As you talk, it is important for you to comment and express your opinions. Praise your child for caring and being willing to take a stand to care for others. Encourage him to speak out. If possible, tell him to take a more active role at school to get these important issues discussed in the classroom.

Obviously, if your child expresses a concern that some students might really be going off the deep end, give the school a call and report it. Violent episodes like the Columbine shooting can erupt at any school, and almost every one could be prevented by intervention. Before nearly every school shooting in recent years, someone was aware that trouble was brewing. The problem was, no one called about it or took any of it seriously. As a parent, if you sense trouble, pick up the phone and take action. Trouble dealt with and discussed before it happens often brings about dramatic new understanding. Let me give you an example.

Years ago, I ran the migrant farmworker school for the Davis Unified School District in Davis, California. In any given year, the racial tension between the local students and the migrant farmworkers' kids ran extremely high. One year in particular, the threat of violence nearly exploded just as school started. Students started arriving at school armed with knives, bicycle wire, whips, box cutters, and more. The situation was getting out of control. Fortunately, almost right away, one of my students told me what was happening. I managed to get all the ringleaders on both sides together for a series of tough, face-to-face meetings.

What came of this? Good things. By the second meeting, all the students realized they had believed lies and rumors about each other. Not only did they not know each other, but not knowing each other only fueled more lies and more trouble. After four meetings, they began laughing and joking with each other over how they had just "followed the herd" and believed so many half-truths. I worked hard with those kids. I knew that no one, especially teenagers, likes to think they are not "in the know." And once the truth came out, big concepts like tolerance made sense. The trouble ended before it really got started and went out of control.

What is important in this story is that before the concept of tolerance was even mentioned, I got everyone together and talking. Tolerance could be understood only after everyone understood each other. This is a model to follow in educational programs. In every family, you must follow the same process. Talk about things first. Ask questions. Clear up the confusion. Finally, teach the concept.

Having the freedom and ability to say what is on her mind is very important to your teenager. Provide that opportunity in the middle of crisis, and your teenager will feel more empowered and less helpless when facing news that can shake an entire nation.

"Is religion important?
Does it make a difference in anyone's life?"

Many teens have religious and spiritual questions — even those who grow up in strong religious households or attend parochial schools. This should come as no surprise. Adults have these questions, too. Many teens tell me that their religious upbringing teaches them *what* to believe but not *why* they should believe it. Whether your family is religious or not, this is a very important question. It aims directly at the significance of one's values.

How are you to address this? What if you, as a parent, are confused about religion, too?

There is nothing wrong about being confused. I often tell people that confusion is a very high spiritual place to be. Teens are not looking to you for all the answers — they are looking to you for an example. Teens look to parents to see how they grapple with and engage difficult issues in their own lives. If that were not the case, then all a parent would have to do to answer a question like this is simply print out a sheet of beliefs, hand it to his child, and that would be it. Obviously that does not work. So what does?

This is a marvelous question because it opens the door to searching and exploring for meaning in life. I recommend you approach it by asking the following:

- "Why are you asking this question now?"
- "Is there something going on now or has something happened recently that has caused you to think more deeply about your life?"

It's important to include in your question a query about what is happening right now in your teen's life because, when this kind of question arises, there often *is* something going on. It doesn't have to be a crisis. It merely means something is going on. As a general rule, questions never arise in a vacuum. They are most likely linked to a new or current problem. Ask, and you will find out.

Now if you have, at some point in your life, thought about this same question, definitely relate what you discovered. Talk about how religion or spirituality fits into your life — or how you came to exchange old beliefs and values for ones that *did* fit your life, if that is the case. Remember, one of the Parenting Principles is to share what has touched your life. Talking about what you believe in and your uncertainties about religion, even God, is very important. The message to your teen is that there is meaning to be found in exploring and searching. Sometimes the exploration confirms long-held beliefs. Sometimes it leads to new ones. Sometimes it deepens faith. Sometimes it leads to more questions, more wondering. Share this with your teen. Your job is not necessarily to provide black-and-white answers, but to demonstrate that life, that spirituality, is a journey that never ends.

Someone once told me that one way to understand God is to think of G-O-D as Good Orderly Direction. I always liked that little aphorism, and it's one you might consider using to help explain the concept of a higher power to your teen. Add any other aphorism or image that has helped you concretize such abstract concepts along the way. I believe that deep, spiritual questions about life and its meaning ought to be discussed in a very personal way. How religious or spiritual matters make a difference in life is a very practical question. Never turn this kind of question into a philosophical or religious lecture. Address it personally. Here are some basic tips for you to consider for discussion:

- "How do you think religion or spirituality has made a difference, if any, in your life?"
- "Are there personal life events that have transformed your thinking? Can you share them with me?"
- "What ethical challenges have made you question or seek out your faith? How have you resolved them?"

Remember, you are not looking for "answers," but for deep, ongoing discussion. Mother Teresa once said, "We can do no great things, only small things with great love." I love that statement. I suspect every parent has some life experiences of doing those "small things with great love" that they can share with their kids. The answers to many of these big questions, as I've mentioned already, often revolve around the small but important things in life. Discussing big life issues in a profound practical context focuses and enriches your discussion. It brings it down to earth. A question like this is not a onetime event. It is an ongoing topic for life.

"Why is it that, so many times, when there is every chance for something bad not to happen, it does anyway? Is there something you can do to prevent such things, despite that fact?"

This question raises the topic of the classic book by Rabbi Harold Kushner, *When Bad Things Happen to Good People*. The simple truth is that, often, in spite of our best efforts, bad things *do* happen. If your teen asked a question similar to this one, I suggest you ask her, "What is happening in your life right now that made you want to ask me this?" As we've seen time and again, a general spiritual or philosophical question often is rooted in something very important and practical happening right now in your teen's life. Please don't avoid asking those personal questions. They are a key to generating good discussion.

So, how do you address this profound question? Probably spouting a lot of philosophy is not going to do the trick. Your teen is asking for advice on something very down-to-earth and, possibly, immediate. How does one relate to the unfortunate things that can happen in life? In particular, those times where everything was tried, and yet the situation turned out to be the opposite of what was hoped for?

I often discover that behind these questions there is a real situation that needs attention. For example, your teen is really asking about a friend who got off drugs, got his life going again, and then had it all fall apart. Or one of her friends had some kind of psychiatric problem, got help, then got severely depressed and had to be hospitalized again. This question has also been asked of me in the context of a family problem. After a teen had felt that real progress had been made in family counseling, one of his parents just up and left the marriage. And of course, I have been asked this question in regard to the death of a loved one or the suicide of a friend. This is a big question, and it is important to respond to it.

Core to helping your teen understand this question is teaching him that no one ever is in total control of his life. As much as anyone might wish to be able to control the outcome of an event — or thinks they can — that simply is not possible. However, we *do* have control over how we respond to a difficult event. The World Trade Center attack is a classic example of how something out of control can be responded to with great heroism and meaning. This is an extremely important lesson to discuss, but it is sometimes a very difficult one to teach. Teens expect immediate results. They understand cause and effect, and how a certain outcome can be expected from certain actions or decisions. They expect things to turn out okay if a situation plays out okay. Parents, with their lifetimes of perspective, know that is not always the case. Teens need not only your stories — illustrations and examples of times when things did not work out as planned or an unexpected crisis came up — but also your stories about how you dealt with these times, and your ideas of how to face such situations without falling into despair.

The Talmud states that each of us is obligated to bless both bad tidings and good tidings in life. Implicit in this teaching is that it is important to see, find, and accept the meaning that is to be found in every situation, good or bad.

What are some useful things you can say to your child to bring some understanding to this deep issue? For starters, tell them that they have asked a very profound question — a question that has been discussed by philosophers and theologians down through the ages. It will make their eyes pop out. Linking their thoughts to those of great historical thinkers will really get their attention.

Also, when I fall back on my own reservoir of life stories about what happened when something I thought was going well went south, the messages I impart always revolve around the notion that things aren't necessarily going wrong just because they're not going my way. I think that is a very important point to make. When, in spite of her best efforts, things go terribly wrong, remind your teen that life has to be worn like a loose garment — she must live it with a certain amount of ease, trying not to become too tied to any one outcome. It's quite all right to hope for the best in any situation, but not to expect it in every one. There will always be unforeseen obstacles, even in the best-laid plans.

Another important point is that, while life must be lived going forward, it can only be understood backward. Every parent has a story of a situation that seemed to have a very bad ending, yet, down the road, some unexpected good came out of it. In tough predicaments, tell your teen those stories, too. Say, "This might be the time to learn something from this lousy situation. What do you think you are discovering in the midst of all these problems?" Even if there's no "good" in sight, you can always turn these situations into lessons. Your teen is filling his own well of life experiences.

No parent wants their child to suffer, but parents can point the way to bringing greater meaning to their kid's struggles. It is a good idea to remind your child that who she is in any crisis has to be good enough. Remind her that in life, everyone must row with the oars they have. It is your job to make sure your teen has her oars, and that she knows how to use them. In other words, you can call on God, but also row away from the rocks. The best way for you to teach this lesson is to share the stories of your life. Let your teen in on how you found meaning in your dark hours. Then you might ask him:

- "What are you trying to handle right now in your life?"
- "How are you doing with it?"
- "Do you think you can find some meaning in your current difficulty?"
- "Would you like to spend some time with me — see if we can find not only some answers, but maybe some lessons that you are learning as you go through all of this?"

These kinds of questions do not resolve everything. Your attention will, however, lend support and build inner character in your child. It will give him permission to expect that his life has a deeper meaning, even if all things do not unfold as he plans. Life is not just a series of events, but a story of meaningful events.

Teens today need parental guidance, comment, and notation brought directly into their daily life. Great decisions lie ahead of them in the New World. Parents can assist untangling all those questions by discussing and letting their teens know that it is possible to face challenge with honor, inner strength, and ethics.

"I have so many questions about life. Who am I? Why don't I know who I am?"

Often teens are shocked when they discover that their fundamental questions about life are the questions philosophers have asked through the ages. Questions about self-identity, like these, are very age-appropriate. If you think back to your high school years, didn't you sometimes wonder who you were and why it seemed so difficult to find some kind of answer about the meaning of your life? Lots of high school students quest after life's meaning. Most parents, however, are not asked these questions simply because it never occurs to them to ask their child, "Who do you think you are?" or "What do you think you are meant to do in this lifetime?" While religious instruction can provide an important framework for these questions, family stories often can provide real grist for the mill in answering these self-reflective questions.

If you are a parent of a deep thinker, how do you approach a question of such magnitude?

The key to helping your teen through these questions is a discussion about what he perceives to be his core values. By values, I mean the inner forces that direct him to live his life authentically. This may seem like a weighty, intimidating conversation to initiate, but it's easier than you think. To do this, I like to tap into unusual stories from my life, and I suggest you look for the same stories in yours. Events that made you think deeply, or tales about when your life was on the line or really tested, bring to the surface your dedication to live by a deeper standard — a value. As is the case with so many other topics raised in this book, stories are often the best way to open philosophical discussions about life. ==Powerful personal tales often confront you with fate and destiny — fate being what happens to you, and destiny being what you do with it.==

Sometimes I really do think that the only things we are uniquely qualified to tell are our own stories. Use your life stores. Told with meaning, they will transmit your values, legacy and ethics. Stories reveal a lot about ourselves. I often tell the following story to get kids thinking about the meaning of their lives.

Years ago, when I was working the mean streets, I had an unusual and dangerous encounter. I was on the Upper East Side of Manhattan around 2 A.M., working with a street outreach team. On nights like these, we patrolled from 8 P.M. until 5 A.M., talking with the hundreds of runaways, teen prostitutes, and hustlers that populate the desperate netherworld of the city. We had just parked our van, and I was sitting in its open door, talking to a group of young hustlers who, after turning tricks, liked to have a cup of hot chocolate and a caring word. Suddenly, up the street on the corner, a young man appeared and began firing a pistol. He was screaming, spinning around, and firing into the air — very angry and very stoned.

Suddenly, two young men started running down the street, away from the shooter and toward the van. From my vantage point in the doorway of the van, I recognized them as hustlers who had stopped by for hot chocolate once or twice in the past. When they were about six feet from where I sat, they both leaped in the air and jumped right on top of me. They pummeled me to the floor of the van, and I banged my head hard. One of them screamed to the driver, "Get the hell out of here!"

Claude, who had the wheel that night, put the van into gear and we took off — six legs sticking out the side. After a moment, we pulled up around the corner and parked. By then, the sirens of the NYPD were wailing and the gunfire was gone. I immediately asked the two kids, "What was that for? What's going on?"

"Yehuda, that dude was screamin' your name," one of them said. "He was gonna cap you. We couldn't let that happen."

I said right back, "Look I'm flat-out grateful that you saved my life, but I want to know why you did it. You hardly know me. What made you jump in?" It's not every day someone saves your life, almost takes a bullet for you.

"It's like this," said the kid. "If you die, Yehuda, then caring would go off the streets here. We couldn't let caring die."

To this day, that kid's words still stun me. I didn't know either of those kids well, and I never saw them again after that night. I can only assume they did not survive. Yet they were willing to risk their life for a core value. I took that lesson to heart. I use it across the country to open discussions on core values and living authentically. I spend a couple of minutes telling the students what that incident meant to me. I then ask them to think about the following: "Imagine that, God forbid, someone would walk into this room right now with a gun and start shooting. (Not something far-fetched in kids' minds these days.) How many of you would just flat-out put your body in front of the person sitting next to you and take a bullet for her or him?"

Of course, as soon as I ask that, no matter where I am, everyone starts laughing nervously and the room buzzes. The whole purpose of this kind of discussion is to get teens to think about their core values. You too, as a parent, can do the same at the appropriate time.

I wrap up this part of the discussion by asking some telling questions. I suggest you use some version of the same questions after you tell your tale.

- "What are the most important values you think you live by?"
- "Are there values and situations for which you would die? If so, why is that the case?"
- "What do you think your values tell you about who you are and what your life is all about?"

Certainly, I recognize that not all of you have such dramatic tales to launch this kind of discussion, but each of you has experienced some kind of dramatic event that has challenged you to take a stand or think deeply about your life. Those experiences shaped you and need to be retold to your children.

There are other ways, too, to get answers to these kinds of questions. I believe this kind of discussion has become especially relevant after the events of 9/11. Terrorist acts and school shootings certainly are powerful events that need to be discussed, so please don't hesitate to discuss such life-impacting issues every time there is an opportunity. Ask your child questions that get her to think about the significance of her life. If, for example, you are discussing school violence, particularly the kids who cause it, you might consider asking the following:

- "What kind of values do you think those kids were raised with?"
- "How do you think they would answer the question, 'Who am I?'"

In other words, to help your child discover who she is, use the world around you to focus on her life and values. If you don't bring it up, who will?

"Why do so many kids put down other kids? What can I do about it?"

Putting down others is endemic to our culture. Turn on talk radio and you hear it. Put on any cable news channel and you will find it. The music industry thrives on it. What used to be the domain of Don Rickles and other comedians — back when comedy even had satire — it has now become the background music of family conversation at the local Wal-Mart. We have substituted thoughtfulness with quick ways to demean others.

Every student I have ever spoken to in any school setting in America hears offensive language that attacks others on a daily basis: "Oh, he's such a fag." "Your hair is so gay." Yo bitch, come over here." "That girl is a 'ho," "Shut up or I'm gonna stuff you." "Say that again and I'm gonna smoke you."

Just sit in any hallway in any high school in America, and I guarantee you will hear students use phrases similar to these and others more aggressive. It gives even me pause to see how the "F-word" has revolutionized grammar. Today it is used as a noun, verb, adjective, and adverb.

Why is demeaning and vulgar language so popular? How do you get kids to change their language? What can you do about it?

The hallmark of teen life today is not that teens are out of control, as many would suppose, but that they are not given any real guidelines. If there is no meaningful and thoughtful input in their lives, then it stands to reason that off-the-wall language can be expected. Now, don't jump to conclusions and make the mistake of blaming society at large for the preponderance of offensive language. Leave that for the politicians and focus instead on your family.

Parents who mix family matters and the current political rambling over the latest morality lecture will only turn off their kid in the end. Why waste time with issues and perspectives that are not helpful to your family? Spend time building your family. Spend time setting good examples for your kids and clear expectations for their behavior. Spend time empowering your teen with strong, clear values, and you will see results. I am still amazed at how many people somehow think being a "yea-sayer" to the latest highly opinionated talk show host will be a help to their children and family. Since when does a talk show host possess the gospel truth? Who gives someone else the right to hijack our own opinions and values, insisting that only his or hers are right? These people are not raising our children. We are.

Several years ago I treated a family that came to me with their teenager in tow. The problem? According to the parents, their child was disrespectful and abusive. They reported he "took his mouth and used it to put down everyone all the time."

As time went on, a curious picture emerged. The son did admit, "Maybe I do cross the line sometimes." But he also reported that his parents just could not stop complaining day in and day out about the ills of society. The boy said, "At the dinner table, my old man gets the grand prize for putting down others. He actually quotes stuff he hears on the radio. And my mom parrots her favorite radio therapist. Hell, I'm mild compared to them."

I found his remarks insightful. I asked the parents what they thought their son was trying to say to them. Instead of replying to me, they each turned to each other and began their own radio monologue about what was wrong with society and their kid today. Neither of them were talking to their son. After a few minutes of this blabber, I got up, went over to my desk, unplugged my radio, and handed it to them.

They looked a bit astonished. I told them: "Hey, I have a suggestion. The next time your son needs your wisdom and tries to understand what you are saying to him, I suggest the following. Since quoting your talk shows and the editorial page doesn't seem to hit the mark, hand him the radio and tell him to listen. That way you never have to worry about communicating. He will get it straight from the source. Since the source is not you, but the radio, I want you to underline that now in our session. Hand him the radio and smile and say, 'Son, it's all on this station. You just listen to it, and everything in our family will make sense.'"

Needless to say, they got it. In fact, they all burst out laughing, and things changed after that.

I don't want to belabor the point, but it is time for every parent to give their child permission to be decent kids when they speak to others. Not follow the crowd. Not live in a family where the F-word is used more than the word *love*.

On the practical level, encourage your teen to talk with their friends and make a pact with them not to allow "put-down language" in their circle. Everywhere I go in America, I tell kids to stand up and cut out the attacks. I embolden them to guard their mouth and watch out what is said to their friends. I challenge them to make it clear in their circle that put-downs are no longer tolerated. I also tell them to make it clear that from now that they will respect the person who responds to their request to stop the put-downs. Kids welcome this challenge. Surprise them and step in to lend them a hand.

A lot of trash talk comes from our lack of involvement with each other. Change the standard in your home and encourage your child to change it among her circle of friends, and the put-downs will cease. Yes, it's pretty much as simple as that.

Work toward a vision that is centered around your family and your friends. Begin from there, and real change becomes possible. If you really want to change the world, then change your family. Begin with those "small things" done "with great love."

"Why is life so hard? Why is it easier for some people and not for others?"

Who of us hasn't asked ourselves a question like this one? Who hasn't looked around after years of hard work and seen neighbors or friends having more success than us? And of course, this question doesn't just apply to adults. If you think back to high school, you might remember trying out for a team, auditioning for a play, or working hard for a spot on the honor roll — and someone else just coasted along and beat you out, seemingly without effort.

This is not an insignificant question. A lot of life happiness rests on making peace with these kinds of situations. Before you answer this question, as always, ask your teen, "Why are you asking this now?" Most likely, she has recently tried hard to accomplish something, only to fall short and watch the prize — whether it be a position on a team, admission into a college, or a high class ranking — go to someone else. As a result, this loss has given your child pause to ask deep questions like "Is life really fair?"

I think the sooner children understand that life is not necessarily "fair," the better. There *is* injustice in the world. Many things happen that are beyond anyone's control. The key is to communicate to your child that real success depends not on what happens, but on how you respond to what happens. A friend of mine once put it this way: "True self-esteem demands that I make the least of my unlucky circumstances and the most of my ability to overcome them."

At every one of my seminars, I give students two simple aphorisms. Taking them to heart can help anyone find personal meaning in their life challenges:

1. Never say, "Why is happening *to* me?" Always say, "Why is this happening *for* me?"

2. Never say, "Why me?" Always say, "Why *not* me?"

You can also help your child cope with life disappointment and stay optimistic by being a positive model. Don't be a parent who constantly complains about life. Avoid blaming others for your troubles. How you respond to adversity, as well as how you relate to others, is noted and taken to heart by your children. Often, it is not what you say that really makes an impression, but how you act. Your teenager will not follow what you teach nearly as much as he will follow how you practice that teaching.

The more you show your teen that happiness isn't about getting, but is about giving, the better off she will be. Every teen needs to understand and be nourished by her family's core values. Put simply, live with a measure of dignity. Honor that dignity with a positive attitude toward life, and that will bring happiness. At the end of the day, I suspect every parent wants his child to realize that the only way to get to the other side of life's problems is to face them. While there is a bit of good in the worst of us and a bit of bad in the best of us, that does not mean any parent cannot model for their child strong and abiding values.

Teens want to know what they are up against in life. Small doses of your life philosophy in action is what is called for here. How you relate to adversity and hard times will be the compass for your teen's life. The real winners in life are those who learn from every challenge.

"Does someone's beliefs really make a difference in their life? Can someone really make a difference in the world?"

Many teens today hold deep spiritual and religious beliefs. They think about God and grapple with questions that theologians have pondered throughout the ages. Few parents can quote the Bible, the Talmud, the Koran, or even the great Western or Eastern philosophers. Does that mean you have nothing potent to say to your children about these deep musings? Hardly. You have much to tell your teen.

Most teens today are not interested in political causes, but they *are* fiercely loyal to friends, sensitive to injustice, and concerned about the welfare of others. Making a difference in another person's life is a high priority. Most teens know that simply preaching words to a friend has no more effect than tossing a rock off the side of a building. At best it might make a dent, but not change anything. But when a teen asks a deep question like this one you can be sure they are wondering, "Does who I am, with my beliefs, make a difference in the world? Do my values make a difference?"

Now I suspect that every parent will answer yes to this question. Every parent knows at least one person who made a profound difference in his or her life. You have met someone who has touched your heart. You've known or had contact with someone who has changed your thinking. The question for you now is, how do you transmit those powerful personal experiences to your teen?

Let's leave the school, the library, history, and even good movies out of the picture for a moment and focus on the family. What your teen really wants to know is how your life has shown you that your beliefs have made an impact in your life.

Family history is incredibly important to children today. What does family history mean? It means knowing the family saints and sinners. It means being aware of the family legacy. Teenagers want to know both the serious and funny stories that have shaped the history of your family. Everyone has some tale, some incident that shaped your life, or some meeting with a remarkable person that carved out your way of thinking. It is one thing for a child to get a book education, but it is more remarkable when that child encounters pieces of those books in his own family's story. Kids today still love a good yarn.

How do you go about translating events in your life that shaped your beliefs and ethics into life lessons for your teen? The key is telling the compelling tales of your family — its triumphs and tragedies, its golden moments and dark valleys. Values become alive when the oral history of a family is passed down from one generation to another.

When asked, these kinds of questions give you an opportunity to tell the tales of your life. When you sit down to talk to your teen, tell her you are about to share some of the important stories and memories of your family's life. Encourage her to ask you any questions. I have done this over and over again with my own kids. I regale them with tales of my youth and their grandparents. Sometimes the questions they ask me are dead serious. Often, they are gut-splitting hilarious. One thing I know: They remember them all.

Sometimes, when I want to tell them a very serious tale, or when I particularly want them to remember a conversation, I say this up front: "The story I am about to tell you, I want you to carry with you the rest of your life. After I am gone, I want you to tell this tale. I am giving it to you just like it was given to me by your grandmother and grandfather (or whoever told it first). This story tells who we are as a family, and now I give it to you as part of your heritage." The setup may sound a little dramatic, but that's fine — it ensures your teen will remember it. Your family history is important — and, yes, often dramatic.

Too many kids tell me they do not know the story of their family. They might know their grandparent's name, recognize a face, but not know many stories. If you want your children to appreciate the historical grandeur of America, to love their heritage, to live with strong beliefs, then give them their heritage through your tales. History books are not enough. Your stories will give them a personal and profound knowledge of who they are and where they come from, and also that historical events do have an impact on personal lives.

Old letters are wonderful ways to bring all this to light. Most families have, tucked away in some closet, old letters written by relatives or grandparents. Some parents even have their old love letters. I suggest you gather up those letters and reread them. Pick out great passages and read them to your teen. I even recommend keeping the letters in a special place where your child can read them. I want my kids to remember, after I am gone, where they came from, who their family was, and what we have stood for. I think most parents feel the same way. Here is a very simple way to give that to your children: Get those letters, read them to your kids, and then keep them in a special place.

Here is an example of what I mean. This letter comes right out of the special letter box that sits in our living-room hutch. It was written by my father on December 22, 1945. He had just returned stateside from fighting in the Pacific Theatre in World War II. He fought in nearly every brutal island battle in the Pacific. Long before *The Thin Red Line* or *Victory at Sea* were hits, I knew the frontline stories of every beach head my father made. In this letter, he is writing to my first cousin Arnold on his eighteenth birthday. Both of them are gone now, but through this letter and countless other stories, their memorie endure in our family forever. The following is a powerful letter, written right at the end of the war. In it, my father writes to Arnold about making a difference.

> "Your birthday this year marks a great occasion for the world. The end of the greatest, cruelest, most devastating war, the world has ever seen... You fortunately have been spared its horrors, but you belong to that generation which will have to remember what it left in its wake, so that it will not occur again. A vow was made after the last one [World War I], but the people soon forgot. Wars are made, they do not just happen."

Well, enough of serious talk, but I thought I would inject a note of seriousness because most people do not think for themselves. They have others do that for them.

Every family has a powerful spiritual legacy to pass onto their children. The key to passing on that legacy rests in your telling the tales of the family at the dinner table, by a campfire, on a cold winter night beside the fireplace, after church or synagogue, or when taking a walk on a spring or fall morning. Whenever the opportunity occurs, take it. Even take it while waiting for the doctor or on a drive to the mall. The more your teen knows about the meaningful moments that made a difference in his family, the more he will make that a part of his life. He will be the better for it, and you, as his parent, will be the prouder.

"If God cares so much about the world, why is there so much suffering?"

or

"If God is supposed to protect us, why did he let [the Holocaust, 9/11, the Columbine shooting, Hurricane Katrina] occur?"

I always am asked several questions about God and suffering, many more since 9/11. Human suffering and tragic events are not far from any teenager's mind, particularly in this day and age, when they seem to be hitting closer and closer to home.

What does a question like this tell us about teens today? It tells us they are normal, need answers, are open, are questioning, are questing, and are not turning away from the deep, spiritual issues of the world. It is also a statement about their great hearts, their deep capacity for caring.

Does that surprise you? It's no wonder. Often, researchers limit their search into the hearts and minds of teens today, focusing on the negative — what teens are doing wrong or what terrible things are happening to them. Statistics highlight rates of drug abuse, alcohol-involved accidents, pregnancy and STDs, and depression. But no parent should fall into the trap of letting headlines shape the view they have of her unique child. Parents who are involved in their teen's lives know a lot about their teen's issues. I recommend that you trust what you already know about your child. And, of course, always ask questions.

Teens read about world suffering. They are aware that there is child slavery in the Sudan, they are keen to the reality of terrorism, and they are concerned about the millions infected with AIDS. They are aware that starvation is not limited to the Afghan people, but that people all over the world — including people in their city or town — have hunger and poverty knocking at their door. Your child also knows kids in his own school who are suffering. Teens today sit in church, synagogue, or mosque and think about these things. Teens, whether they are practicing a religion or not, grapple with this issue. Most teens do believe in God. Most teens do wonder why there is so much suffering. This is a normal question, and it is a question that spans the ages. While this may be a question all religions attempt to answer, it is your turn, as a parent, to give it a try.

Please, though, remember this basic Parenting Principle: *You don't have to be an expert in anything. You just have to share and care.* This is not the time to race off to your Bible or run to the Internet and do a Google search on *suffering*. It may fascinate you to do spiritual philosophical research, but your homespun answer and wisdom are often more important than anything your teen might have read. The power of parental wisdom is great. Your role as a parent is simply to discuss what you think about suffering. Think about answering these questions for yourself before having a talk with your teen:

- How have you experienced suffering?
- How have you wrestled with it?
- What it has taught you in your life?
- Have you ever found meaning in your suffering?
- What have others told you about suffering?
- Did what they say make sense?
- How do you understand big examples of suffering, such as the Holocaust or 9/11?

The most potent way to address profound questions like these is to talk about the toughest trauma you have had to face and how you dealt with it. The maxim that applies here is "Faith without works is dead." Your personal stories and actions are priceless.

The following series of questions can give you some ideas about where, in your treasure trove of memories and experiences, you might look to find such stories.

- What did you do when you lost a loved one?
- How and why do you keep that person's memory alive?
- What do you do, personally, to deal with suffering around you?

- How do you lend a hand to those in trouble?
- How do all of these questions relate, in your mind, to God, your spirituality, or your core values?

And certainly, if you are struggling with the same issue your teen brings to you, discuss this with her as well. If you tend to avoid thinking about profound issues, certainly explain to your child why this is the case. The important point is to engage and not avoid big issues. Your child does not expect you to be the wise philosopher or sage with all the answers. Your child simply wants you.

"I see so much going on in this world — so much pain, so much fear. I even see it among my friends and in my school. I want to do something, but I feel so small. What can I do that will make a difference?"

If your teen asks you this question, pull him close, and tell him you're honored to have a child with such a big heart. No matter what your family life has been like, no matter what your fears have been about guiding and misguiding this child as you have raised him, he has emerged with a sense of compassion and responsibility. Who isn't overwhelmed by the unrest, the poverty, the unfairness in the world? Even at that, it's all too easy to ignore as we find refuge and excuses in work, or denial, or our own feelings of futility. These problems are so huge. What *can* one person do?

At the risk of sounding like a broken record, the best any of us can do is "small things with great love." While few of us are in a position to take on worldly problems singlehandedly and make much of a dent, we can look around ourselves and find one place, one life, one small thing we can do to make a difference for someone. Maybe not the whole world, but someone.

Begin talking with your teen about this issue by giving her a chance to air her frustrations, her anger, her despair. Even if you can't explain much about the underlying causes of enormous maladies like poverty, injustice — even loneliness or abandonment — you can acknowledge that these are issues that tear at many people's hearts. If you feel your own futility keenly, admit that to her. Then, encourage her — and perhaps yourself — to find that small thing that will make a huge difference for someone. I assure you that it will not be hard to find.

Consider the rich opportunities that exist for making a difference in your very community. Does poverty or violence get your teen down? How about taking a step to combat such issues at the ground level by getting involved with kids growing up with them? Depending upon where you live, your teen can volunteer time with children in homeless shelters, transitional housing programs, or after-school or library programs designed to keep kids at risk occupied and to give them positive influences.

At the other end of the extreme, there is likely a retirement home in your community filled with lonely souls, many of whom feel forgotten at the end of their lives. An hour a week spent in the company of someone who hungers for conversation and a bright face can be nourishing for the visitor and the visited. Remind your teen that aged people have seen much in their lifetimes — war, unrest, depressions, and personal loss, all issues your teen may be worried about today — and have weathered them all. There is much to learn from the generations that have gone before. Reaching out to touch one life can create a lasting intergenerational relationship, one that benefits all involved.

If you're a member of a church or other religious group, encourage your teen to explore the opportunities for outreach or community service that are offered there. Learn about volunteer opportunities in town, or search the Internet for more far-reaching efforts. Chances are, an opportunity for making a difference exists for any topic your teen might be concerned about — from knitting hats to warm people in Afghanistan to cleaning up a public park.

The importance of taking action — however insignificant it may seem — is twofold: First, someone, somewhere will be the fortunate recipient of a good deed done by a caring stranger; second, your teen will see firsthand that small actions do add up, and at least some of her feelings of helplessness will be soothed by evidence that she, herself, can change things for the better.

* * *

As deep and complex as some of the issues raised in this chapter — and this entire book — have been, I want to underscore that all the questions raised here point to one inevitable fact: Your teen, despite the trials and travails, the mood changes and crises, is becoming an adult.

Better yet, your teen is becoming a thinking, questioning, caring adult, one who has a deep place in his heart for the welfare of friends and others, one who is thinking about and acting on her feelings of personal responsibility.

In short, your efforts at raising this child as best you can have been successful. And while your job is not quite finished — as a caring parent, will it ever be? — you can know that by opening the lines of communication with your teen, you are building with her a relationship that will reward you both as she joins you in adulthood.

It is my hope that as you have worked your way through this book, you have been less overwhelmed by the potential pitfalls that lay before teens than you have by the depth of their thoughts and the sincerity of their concerns. I've presented here some of the worst scenarios you can face with your teen, but also, I hope, some of the best and most hopeful. Stay close to your teen, and together you can face any scenario adolescence has in store.

Afterword:
The Greatest Gift

The greatest gift parents can give their teenagers is the gift of conversation. Today, that means focusing on your teen's questions. I truly believe that we now live in an age where responding to our children's questions is more important than in any other time in the history of our country.

The events of September 11, 2001 left deep impressions on all Americans. In particular, it had a stunning effect on teenagers. The sight of thousands of people running for their lives from the collapsing World Trade Center towers is etched deeply into the minds of this generation's children. Furthermore, witnessing thousands of New York City firemen, police and paramedics rushing *toward* the same towers sent another message to our kids. As they saw the fire spreading, the debris cascading down, the smoke billowing, they also saw people rushing toward the destruction as if their very lives depended on it. Seeing all those rescue workers run toward certain death to save others changed the way many kids think about their lives today. September 11 changed many teens, in particular. It raised many questions about their own lives: What would they die for? What would they live for?

Knowing this makes this book all the more important. Our children are now aware that life holds tragedy as well as heroism. But if any of the real lessons of heroism and caring for others are to take root, they must be planted and carefully nurtured in the garden of the family.

Everyone loves a picture of a parent holding the hand of a little child. It is comforting and speaks of love and family. But we don't often see pictures of parents and teens holding hands. How *do* parents hold the hands of their teenagers in this quickly changing world? To hold the hand of your teen, you need to hold fast to their questions.

That is the secret of this book. As parents, when we sense the worlds of our teens shaking, we can truly offer them hope and comfort — in the form of listening to them openly, empathizing with them deeply, and addressing their questions and issues with honest communication. I know that to be true. I believe it with all my heart. Ω

About the Book

"Here is a down-to-earth, sensible prescription for parents of teens. No one has spoken to and, more importantly, *listened to* more teens and pre-teens than Yehuda Fine. His lifetime of caring shines through the pages of *The Real Deal*, and it is a beacon for parents (and any adult who works with our youth). Parents and teens need not live in parallel universes. *The Real Deal* prescribes guidelines, point by point, that make conversing with youngsters as normal as breathing — and almost as easy."

— Dr. Pat Montgomery, considered by many to be the founder of the Homeschooling Movement, Founder and Director *Emeritus* of the Clonlara School Home Based Accredited Education Program headquartered in Ann Arbor, Michigan. The progam now serves families in all 50 states and 28 foreign countries.

About the Author

Yehuda Fine, rabbi, teacher, family therapist and author, spent 16 years on the guidance staff at Yeshiva University and recued scores of runaway teens from the streets of New York as documented in his previous book, *Times Square Rabbi*.

Today he is known as America's most streetwise family and teen expert. He regularly conducts seminars for public schools, private and alternative schools, parent groups, social service agencies, youth groups, hospitals, recovery centers and social workers. He is a popular guest on talk radio and TV nationwide, and a frequent contributor to scores of magazines and newspapers.

Currently, he resides in Florida and is the head of a new synagogue as well as teaching at a Hebrew high school. His dog Brooklyn is always by his side when he goes bass fishing. His citrus trees are his gardening joy. He never misses spring training for the New York Yankees and of course is a devoted Disneyophile.

For ongoing updates and additional free resources, please visit:
YehudaFine.com

Made in the USA
Middletown, DE
28 October 2016